Development and Its Discontents

Development and Its Discontents

Subhash Sharma

RAWAT PUBLICATIONS
Jaipur • New Delhi • Bangalore • Hyderabad • Guwahati • Kolkata

ISBN 978-81-316-0707-7

Published by
Prem Rawat for **Rawat Publications**
Satyam Apts, Sector 3, Jawahar Nagar, Jaipur 302 004 (India)
Phone: 0141 265 1748 / 7006 Fax: 0141 265 1748
E-mail: info@rawatbooks.com
Website: www.rawatbooks.com

New Delhi Office
4858/24, Ansari Road, Daryaganj, New Delhi 110 002
Phone: 011 2326 3290

Also at *Bangalore, Hyderabad, Guwahati* and *Kolkata*

Typeset by Rawat Computers, Jaipur
Printed at Chaman Enterprises, New Delhi

Dedicated to

Dr B.D. Sharma

who questioned

the one- sided and imposed mainstream development

and provided an alternative development paradigm

with vision and mission

for grass roots action.

Contents

Acknowledgement

While writing a book one is benefited directly or indirectly from numerous inspiring personalities, friends as well as colleagues working together, as knowledge comes out of formal, informal and non-formal learning from various experiences, experiments, exercises, actions and studies in different ways. Therefore, I express my sincere gratitude to my teachers at JNU like Professor Yogendra Singh, Professor R.K. Jain, Professor T.K. Oommen, Professor K.L. Sharma, Professor Partha Nath Mukherjee, Professor J.S. Gandhi, Professor Nirmal Singh, Professor C.N. Venugopal, Professor E. Haq and Professor Nandu Ram. In addition, I do acknowledge cooperation of my friends and well-wishers like Prof Hetukar Jha, Professor Avijit Pathak, Professor Anand Kumar, Professor Maitreyee Chaudhury and Professor E. Rodrigue. From time to time, I have been benefitted from my senior colleagues like Mr V.S. Dube, Mr K.B. Saxena, Mr S.K. Keshav, Mr Shankar Prasad, Mr K.K. Pandey, Mr R.J.M. Pillai, Mr V.K. Verma and Mr K.C. Saha, to name a few. I also remember my colleagues and friends like Mr Sunil Kumar Singh, Mr Rameshwar Singh. Professor Nawal K. Chaudhury, Dr Vijoy K. Choudhury, Mr R.S. Pandey, Dr M.P. Tripathi, Mr Anant Kumar Singh, Mr Jawahar Pandey – to cut the long list short. Acknowledging the contribution of my family members would be a formality indeed. Further, I also acknowledge the gratitude of various editors of reputed Indian journals like *Social Change* (Council for Social Development, New Delhi), *Indian Journal of Public Administration* (IIPA, New Delhi), *Management in Government* (Department of Administrative Reforms, Government of India) and others for inclusion of some of my articles published therein. Finally, I humbly confess that the interpretation, analysis and views expressed here are personal and I am solely responsible for errors, if any. I would be happy to receive any suggestion for further improvement of this book.

29 August 2014 **Subhash Sharma**
Patna

Preface

Development has been a contentious term from the very beginning. Unfortunately, some economists have reduced the development to merely 'economic growth' which is quantifiable, measureable, tradable in open market, visible, concrete, big in size and so on. These myths have been duly demystified here on the basis of both logic and fact. This is not correct because development is basically multi-dimensional, holistic and inclusive progress or planned change emancipation from any kind of bondage and subjugation, freedom from isolation, silence and exploitation, as well as cultural liberation. In fact, the dominant development discourse (DDD) has been one-dimensional, narrow, exclusive, rigid, hegemonic, top-down, casual and temporary. Therefore, an alternative development paradigm, namely Real Social Development (RSD), has been put forward here which is inclusive (both intra-generational and inter-generational), multi-dimensional, multi-faceted, flexible, socially equitable, economically viable, ecologically sustainable, politically participatory, organizationally transparent and culturally acceptable to the local people. Only when local people are actively involved in letter and spirit at all stages of planning, execution, monitoring and evaluation, development would take place in real sense. Earlier, India was rich with many voluntary agencies who worked selflessly with full sacrifice in public interest. However, over the years in recent past, there has been a flood of non-governmental organizations (NGOs) which are mostly donor-driven, with salary-based activists and hierarchy-maintained organizations. There is a need to identify genuine NGOs (by separating the chaff from the grains) and forge a critical partnership between policy-makers, executing agencies, civil society organizations and the local people through mutual trust and cooperation.

One major challenge before the Indian society is in the arena of natural resources like land, water, forest and mines. Unfortunately, most of the tribal areas like Jharkhand, Odisha, Madhya Pradesh, Chhattisgarh, etc. have been highly rich in forest, water, minerals land, etc. but these have remained undeveloped; hence, uneven development and regional imbalances have emerged. Since the inception of green revolution in India in late 1960s, there have emerged various problems like going down of groundwater table, salination of water and soil, plant diseases, ingredients of chemical fertilizers and insecticides found in agricultural produces like grains and vegetables, and crisis of water availability both for drinking and irrigation purposes, costly inputs rendering agriculture non-profitable and these have ultimately worsened the situation. Similarly, land, being a scarce resource, is not able to cope up with the increasing population, demands of industrialization (especially land acquisition for special economic zones/special export zones), urbanization and so on. Consequently, agriculture is contributing hardly 15 per cent to Gross Domestic Product (GDP) though more than two-thirds of India's population is still dependent on agriculture. Further, land is not merely a marketable commodity for the farmers for whom agriculture is also a mode of livelihood and a living culture – a way of life. But the land acquisition on a massive scale, in the name of 'public purpose', has abused the law, on the one hand, and does not give reasonable price to the landowners nor their adequate rehabilitation is done. Undoubtedly, displacement has been 'the last straw' for the farmers. It is expected that the new land acquisition law will protect the genuine interests of the farmers.

One may ask why development planning? Because our Constitution, especially its Preamble, Fundamental Rights and Directive Principles of State Policy, mentions various rights of citizens. Poverty has been a major problem in India for quite a long time, though various methods of measurement came out with different figures. For instance, Arjun Sengupta Commission on unorganized labour (National Commission for Enterprises in Unorganized Sectors) reported in 2008 that 77 per cent of people in India live on ₹ 20 daily – obviously they are poor. It recommended for National Minimum Social Security Package for all unorganized workers but Unorganized Social Security Act 2008 has not proved really useful as it does not provide for minimum entitlements to unorganized workers within a reasonable timeframe. The World Bank assesses that there are 40 crore poor people in India (living on $ 1.25 daily). B.N. Yugandhar (2014) rightly points out seven characteristics of the poor:

(a) Assetlessness;
(b) Illiteracy and absence of capabilities and poor skills;
(c) Deficit households with high priority for current consumption requirements;
(d) High labour participation rates – also high ratio of dependents to the able-bodied;
(e) Dependent households, especially during the lean season or emergencies;
(f) Vulnerable households with economic and social disabilities; and
(g) High degree of exclusion from the coverage of socio-economic sub-systems such as education, health, public distribution system, nutrition, credit, social protection and social security.

Earlier, most of the neo-liberal economists were of the view that free market economy will certainly create the wealth of the nation but the financial meltdown in 2008 in US and other developed countries disproved this myth because creating wealth, to a large extent, depends on distribution of wealth, One tends to agree with the view of Amit Bhaduri (2014: 80) that both central and state governments are not moderating 'the adverse impact of the market on the poor by providing them with the minimum essentials of life, high growth is being promoted by the government destroying many more livelihoods than creating employment'. He further observes that inequality and distress are growing because World Bank, IMF, WTO, etc. force the state to 'privatize expenditure in areas of social services like basic health, education and public distribution of food' (p. 81). Thus, it is clear that high growth rates are not sufficient and the economy of developing countries like India is very much influenced by the market and privatization-oriented policies of Bretten Woods institutions where liberalization, privatization and globalization are wrongly considered panacea of all evils. Further, the situation of health and education is quite unsatisfactory as due attention is not given on their quality and commercialization is ruling the roost in terms of flourishing of private schools/colleges and corporate hospitals in different towns of India. Therefore, there is a need to strengthen the public sector institutions. It should not be presumed that public sector per se is inefficient, corrupt and cost-ineffective because many Maharatnas, Navratnas and Mini ratnas have shown the positive outcome and have contributed to ensure economic independence and sovereignty of India (by not depending fully on foreign capital and aid that have many inherent conditionalities). Further many loss-making PSUs have turned around – e.g. Hindustan Shipyard Limited (Vishakhapatnam) has become profit-making unit due to its take over by the Government of India (Ministry of Defence) and thus by getting orders for ship-building it turned around.

Let us hope that this book will be useful to different sections of society because many burning questions have been dealt with here. Of course, views and opinions expressed here are my own and not concerned with my organization.

1

Development for What and Whom and at Whose Cost?

Reflections on Development of Tribes in India

Here, at first, an attempt has been made to demystify development that is associated with several myths. Second, we will discuss about the conception and categorization of tribes. Third, we will discuss development for what and for whom and at whose cost. Finally, we will suggest real social development for the people living at the margins of society.

Introduction

Whenever two or more persons, groups or organizations start discussing socio-economic problems, the word 'development' immediately creeps in as their fire-fighting solution. During elections, the voters, political parties and intellectuals start discussion on development and under-development. Those in power, realizing their poor performance, often argue that development is not an issue, while the opposition parties harp on development as the issue. The general public by and large remains almost silent and expresses its opinion in the form of casting votes. However, the general elections in 2014 was contested primarily on development agenda and it resulted into single party majority after decades of coalition politics.

However, there are several myths about development; therefore, it seems imperative to clarify what development is not, i.e. to 'demystify' development. The first and foremost myth is that development means economic growth, i.e. an increase in gross domestic product (GDP) and in per capita income. GDP is the total output of goods and services by both residents and non-residents but it does not include deductions for the depreciation of physical capital or the depletion of natural resources. When GDP is divided by the total population of a country, we get per capita GDP. This per capita GDP is considered to be a yardstick for the level of economic growth. Actually, however, it window-dresses the gaps between different individuals, groups and classes in a particular society. Table 1 provides a glimpse of per capita GDP in selected countries in 2001.

Table 1

Per Capita GDP in Selected Countries (2001)

S. No.	*Country*	*Per Capita GDP (in US$)*
1.	Nepal	1,310
2.	India	2,840
3.	China	4,020
4.	South Africa	11,290
5.	Saudi Arabia	13,330
6.	Japan	25,130
7.	Australia	25,370
8.	USA	34,320

Source: UNDP, Human Development Report 2003.

The above table provides a rough idea that Nepal, India and China are at the bottom of the growth ladder, South Africa and Saudi Arabia are in the middle, and Japan, Australia and the US are at the top. But this hides that the upper classes in India, Nepal and China have higher income than the lower classes. Similarly, the lower classes in Japan, Australia and the US have much lower income than the upper classes. In addition, the status of lower classes in Japan, Australia and the US is far better than that in India, Nepal and China. Further, four objections are raised from the viewpoint of environment[1] against this yardstick of development while the fifth is raised from the viewpoint of gender. These are:

(a) GDP includes only marketable goods and services, excluding unmarketable, unmarketed and non-marketable goods and services that contribute to human well-being; e.g. medicinal plants grown for medicine or fuel wood and fodder collected for own use, peace, freedom, and low crime rate, though non-marketed/marketable, contribute to human well-being.

(b) GDP does not take into account the nature of the goods and services produced; e.g. an investment made in cleaning polluted water shows an increase in GDP, whereas fresh and clean water is not accounted for in it, because it is considered as a free gift of nature.

(c) GDP does not consider traditional methods of conservation of nature (sacred groves of tribals) as these do not involve economic transactions.

(d) GDP may take into account the exploitation of natural resources if it yields money; e.g. having 50 per cent of land under forests may not feature in the GDP of a country but cutting down these forests for marketing will show an increase in it.

(e) GDP does not take into account the household work performed by the women, because it is not paid, quantifiable and marketable. Mother's milk and daily nurturing have no alternative and these contribute to the growth of persons as human resource for development.

That is why Anil Agrawal talked of Gross Nature Product (instead of Gross National Product) as a better measure of human and environmental well-being. Further, economists like W.W. Rostow talked of five stages of growth in a vertical way and equated the fourth stage of 'take off' as the growth stage. However, development is much more than quantifiable economic growth.

The second myth is that development means 'catching up' with the western model of capitalist industrialization – a model presumed to be universal and to transcend time and place. That is to say, developing countries, which are primarily agricultural economies, would have to follow the path of industrialization. This structural – functionalist modernization paradigm conceptualizes development as a transition from tradition to modernity 'to be brought about at the economic level by the operations of the market and foreign investment, at the social level by the adoption of appropriate western institutions, values and behaviour, and at the political level by the implementation of parliamentary democracy.'[2] In India, Jawaharlal Nehru adopted a mixed model of capitalism and socialism but his 'socialistic pattern' was more oriented towards modernization through capitalist industrialization. He had called industries and big dams 'modern temples'! We call this a myth because industry is only one of the three sectors of economy, and developing countries have sufficient agricultural resources (land, water, seeds, manure, etc.) but do not have adequate technology, capital and technical manpower required for industrialization. Besides, this theoretical myth suffers from over-simplification, over-optimism and Euroethnocentrism.

The third myth is that development is based on purely scientific parameters: rationality, quantifiability and measurability. That is, if something is not testable in a lab, it cannot be included in development. But various values of humanity like freedom, happiness, sacrifice, justice and equity are not quantifiable. Besides, various religious rituals performed may not be rational but they do contribute in the well-being of the people of a society, especially in communal harmony and peace.

The fourth myth is that development means a high level of consumerism – the greater the consumption, the more the development (more is considered better). In western countries, the expenditure on consumer items is increasing day by day. The principle in vogue is: 'I exist because I buy.' Hence, those who buy more and more, and that too costlier items, are considered of a high status. The irony is that spending on drinks or narcotics or luxuries does not lead to development.

The fifth myth is that development means big structures or things – 'size matters', propagating 'biggest is the best,' 'big is beautiful,' mass production (large quantity) and sophisticated technology. Thus big farm, big dam and big factory (with various shifts of production) are considered as signs of development. This is a sort of Nehruvian model of development. But because the truth is that a small earthen dam may be more useful and cheaper to the villages, micro hydro plants more useful to the local people (without causing displacement), and small land holding more equitable to local farmers.

The sixth myth is that more and faster development is the result of globalization, hence the latter is inevitable. It is assumed by scholars like Thomas Friedman (*The World is Flat*) and Jagdish Bhagwati that not only at the economic level but also at the level of culture, ideology and politics there has been interdependence, uniformity and integration among nations. The very concept of 'Third World development', argues Serge Latouche in his book *The Westernization of World* (1998), is rooted in the western ideas of technical progress and the accumulation of capital, and this leads to development policies that destroys the cultures of non-western peoples. Hence, Latouche maintains that the drive towards global uniformity in cultures, lifestyles and 'mentalities' has been responsible for the endemic civil wars, ecological disasters and national debts throughout the Third World.[3] Besides, this myth is limited to the one-sided globalization of capital and communication, ignoring the required globalization of labour.

The seventh myth is that development is changing the upper echelons of the society, who are economically better off, educationally more aware of the written knowledge, socially superior in the hierarchy and politically more conscious of their rights. Once they are more developed, the fruits of development would automatically 'trickle down' to the lower rungs of the society. In fact, neoclassical economists of the west (and several policy makers in developing countries, like Jawaharlal Nehru) presumed that this process would not require the intervention of the state to eliminate poverty from the lowest strata of the society. This, however, did not materialize in developing countries (including India) despite various kinds of 'trial and error' experimentation.

The eighth myth is that development means visible concrete structures like roads, buildings, power houses and water plants. Many persons (including intellectuals) identify development with the 'concrete jungles' proliferating in cities. But real development does not require skyscrapers, overbridges/flyovers and eight-lane national highways. Moreover, their mere existence does not guarantee that all the people residing in cities are developed.

The ninth myth is that development is, and can be, done only by government or semi-government machinery, and from government/semi-government fund, international development agencies, multinational corporations (MNCs) or national corporate capitalists. This myth reflects the dependency syndrome. In fact, small amounts of capital generated at local level by individuals, groups, communities, non-governmental organizations (NGOs), community-based organizations (CBOs) and civil society organizations (CSOs) may be utilized in a much better way by them. Any foreign aid may appear as a soft loan at one glance but in the long run its conditionalities prove to be the last straw on the camel's back.

The tenth myth is that the language of development needs to be 'external', usually English (foreign language). This presumes that the agency of preparation of a plan, programme, project or scheme is to be an expert (only he can envisage it), usually from outside the place of work, who prepares an estimate in English, just as an advocate drafts a petition in English for a Hindi-speaking petitioner, so that the community concerned may not understand the quantity and quality of the contents and the forms of the estimate. Thus, it ignores and de-recognizes the indigenous knowledge system and oral traditions of local communities. This myth excludes the local people from active participation at various stages, right from identifying the problem to formulation, execution, monitoring and evaluation. It often happens that the local people are not consulted (not to say of establishing an active dialogue with them) for the type of work, location, linkages and agency of the development schemes, resulting into non-utilization of check dams, culverts, houses, ponds, schools, and so on, by the local people for whom these are meant.

The eleventh myth is that development is 'immediate', that is, 'here and now', as phenomenologists, like Peter L. Berger, say. This presumes a short period and short cut, whereas, in reality, development is a long-term process (scattered ideas, systematic shape, sharing, planning, formulation, gestation, execution, adaptation, monitoring, evaluation and reshaping) which is usually defined and redefined in a particular context of time and place. There is no short cut to progress.

The twelfth myth is that the optimum utilization and exploitation of natural resources is necessary and inevitable for development. That is, it is presumed at first that the stock of natural resources is abundant and infinite, and, secondly, that its maximum exploitation would bring maximum development. But this is not true because the stock of natural resources is not infinite, but depleting, and, secondly, the over-exploitation of natural resources is leading to various negative consequences like high level of pollution of water, air, soil, climatic change, acid rain, hole in ozone layer as well as various diseases in humans, animals and plants – even extinction of many animal and plant species.

From the above discussion, it is amply clear that development is laden with several myths generated by the western world, especially Europe (hence Eurocentrism) and America, the capitalist corporate world, lobbies of development aids and financing agencies, and the culture of consumerism. Further, it depends to a large extent on the market forces, wherein the competition between individuals, groups or organizations, through demand and supply by rational choice for maximum utility and through the process of monetary exchange, would decide the prices of commodities and the amount and quality of wages and services. These myths do not take into account non-economic factors like social and moral values, gender aspects, environmental aspects, quality-of-life aspects, socio-cultural aspects, time and place contexts, and attitudes, perceptions and aspirations of the local community. Besides, unfortunately, they ignore and derecognize the indigenous knowledge systems of technology, medicine and education as well as the rich 'oral tradition' of the local people, whose contribution to history and civilization has been tremendous.

II
Tribes and Tribals: Conception and Categorization

An important nineteenth-century anthropologist Sir Henry Maine, in his classic book *Ancient Law*, identified tribalism with a pre-civilized stage of human society, and the derogatory use of the term to denote emotional, pre-scientific and irrational behaviour.[4] Various scholars, activists and organizations have given different nomenclatures to the tribes in India, the glimpse of which is given in Table 2.

Table 2

Different Nomenclatures of Tribes in India

Nomenclatures	*Scholars/activists/organizations*
Aborigines/Aboriginals	Risley, Elvin, Grigson, Lacey Sedewick, Martin, A.V. Thakkar, Shoobert, Tallents
Primitive Tribes	Hutton
'So-called aborigines', 'Backward Hindus'	G.S. Ghurye
'Submerged humanity'	Dr Das
'Vanvasi'	Rashtriya Swayam Sewak Sangh (RSS), Right-wing Hindu political parties.
Scheduled Tribes 'Anusuchit Janjati'	Indian Constitution (Articles 342, 366), Government of India (all departments/ministries and autonomous bodies like Planning Commission).
Subaltern	Subaltern historians (Ranjit Guha, G. Pandey and others)
'Adivasi' or indigenous people	Political and non-political activists, Jharkhand Mukti Morcha

If we analyse the nomenclatures given in Table 2, we may put them in the following categories:

The first category of 'aborigines', 'aboriginals' or 'primitive tribes' denotes a *'sympathetic identity for differentiation,'* wherein the scholars (especially the western ones) point out their distinct features and want to categorize them 'from above' for a separate identity, different from the dominant majority Hindus. It is an imposition from above by others.

The second category of 'so-called aborigines', 'backward Hindus', 'submerged humanity' and 'Vanvasis' denotes a 'sympathetic identity for acculturation' or 'assimilation', pointing out the features of tribals similar to majority Hindus. This, too, is an imposition from above by others.

The third category of 'ST' or 'Anusuchit Janjati' denotes a *'sympathetic identity for nationalism'*, with a view to modernizing or mainstreaming them as 'others' with measures of protective discrimination like reservation of seats for legislature for the tribals' political representation, reservation in jobs, economic upliftment through land re-distribution, welfare through scholarships, hostels, residential schools, books and stationery, and other incentives for contingencies like legal and medical aid, removing all kinds of discrimination at public places, and so on. This, too, is an imposition from above by others.

The fourth category of 'subaltern' puts the tribals along with lowest castes, women and minorities, denoting an *'empathic identity of sub-nationalism,'* carving out a separate autonomous space for them in the civil society without any kind of imposition from above. In contrast, this is a 'relatively shared identity' by some sections of tribals and non-tribals together.

The fifth category of 'adivasi' or indigenous people correctly and comprehensively denotes a fully autonomous self-determined and historically contextualized and hence a *'self-experienced identity of sub-nationalism'*. This very term signifies their originality in terms of indigeneity, historicity of tradition, relatively richer and more experiences, creativity, a permanent point of reference (comparing others with them, not vice versa) and cultural diversity. Therefore, to our minds, the term 'adivasi' should be accepted by one and all, including government and NGOs.

The Indian Constitution Order 1950 declared 212 tribes residing in 14 states of India as ST. But N.K. Bose assessed more than 400 tribes in the 1970s.

The next important issue of the tribals is that they are not in the same category and stage of development across the country. While the tribals in the North-Eastern region of India are quite well off and highly educated (literacy rate above 80%) those in Bihar, Maharashtra, Jharkhand, MP, Chhattisgarh, Uttarakhand and Andhra Pradesh lag far behind them. That is why V. Elvin categorizes tribals in four categories on the basis of their development. This may be seen in Table 3.

Table 3

Indian Tribes at Various Stages of Development

Stage/Class	*Main Features*
Class I	Purest of the pure tribal groups – they really live their religion, a life in unimpaired communal organization, no contacts with plains and other people, old practices of axe cultivation, hunting and gathering, simplest and most honest.
Class II	Contacts with plains, individualist life, not sharing things with fellow tribals, advanced ploughing, more complex life, less simple and less honest.
Class III	Largest population (four-fifths of all tribals), tribals in name but actually backward Hindus or Christians, adversely affected by British economic and political policies, uprooted from tribal mode of production, reduced to bonded labourers or semi-slaves, a section of them branded as 'criminal tribes' (as they could survive only by methods officially described as crimes because of loss of land/occupation and no accessibility to alternative occupation).
Class IV	A very small number consisting of 'old aristocracy' – great Bhils and Naga chieftains, Gond Rajas, a few Binghawar and Bhura landlords, Korki noblemen, wealthy Santhal and Oraon leaders and some Mundas – they retain tribal names, clans, totems and preserve elements of tribal religion, though they usually adopt the Hindu faith and have a modern lifestyle. They have won the battle of cultural contacts; they have acquired 'aristocratic traditions, economic stability, affluence, outside encouragement, a certain arrogance and self-confidence' – securing benefits of civilization without cultural injury.

Sources: Based on V. Elvin quoted in A.R. Desai (1978), *Rural Sociology in India.*

After this classification, Elvin is of the following view: 'The whole aboriginal problem is how to enable the tribesmen of the first and second classes to advance direct into the fourth class without having to suffer the despair and degradation of the third.'[5] On the other hand, famous sociologist G.S. Ghurye, in his book *The Scheduled Tribes*, has divided the so-called aboriginal tribes into three classes:[6]

(a) those (like Raj Gonds and others) who have succeeded in the social struggle and are recognized as members of a fairly high status within the Hindu society;

(b) the large mass that has been partially Hinduized and has come in closer contact with the Hindus; and

(c) those living on the hills with the greatest power of resistance to the alien cultures that have pressed upon their border.

Anthropologist N.K. Bose remarks perceptively: 'Altogether three or four different modes of production are current in India and practically all tribes, except the Jarwa and North Sentineles of the Andaman Islands, have adapted themselves in one way or another to one of these productive systems. Some have given up hunting and gathering and settled down as peasants using the plough or as lowly artisans. Others continue to rely on their ancient system of shifting cultivation and gathering in marginal areas where this is possible. A third section has been practically transformed into labourers working in plantations, mines and factories where they are usually employed in unskilled jobs.'[7]

When we look at the Tharus of Champaran (north Bihar), we find them well-settled in agriculture, though they have lost much of their original lands to the landlords or moneylenders. Secondly, they are now Hinduized to a large extent in terms of worship, social rituals at birth, marriage and death, lifestyles (women using vermilion in the parting of their hair), naming, etc. But their social status is at the bottom of the social hierarchy of the Hindus, though in certain ways better than that of SC (SC or Dalits). Only one out of three is literate among them. Though Tharus are the largest tribe in terms of number in Bihar (estimated to be about 1.75 to 2 lakhs; the district administration of West Champaran estimates them about 1.56 lakhs in West Champaran alone; however, since the Tharus were notified as a Scheduled Tribe only in 2003, they were not counted separately in the 2001 Census), their socio-economic position is not up to the mark. As far as the socio-economic stratification of the Tharus is concerned, it would not be just and viable to classify them into rich and poor, since only a very insignificant number could be said to be living comfortably. Rather, it would be useful to stratify them on the basis of the 'level of poverty' as:

(a) Ultra-poor or poorest of the poor (landless labourers)

(b) Poor (marginal farmers)

(c) Not-so-poor (the rising stratum of small farmers, petty shopkeepers, government or private servicemen)

How these three strata of Tharus inter-relate with 'others' (especially Hindus) and in what contexts may be seen in Table 4.

Table 4

Stratification of the Tharus and Their Relationship with Others in Various Contexts

Strata	*Relationship with Others*	*Contexts (Arena)*
Ultra-poor	Absolute dependence	Social, economic and political arena
Poor	Partial dependence	Economic and political arena
Not-so-poor	Interdependence	Economic arena

From Table 4, it is crystal clear that the position of the poorest of the poor (who are usually landless labourers) is pathetic because they are dependent on others in almost all arenas of life, hence they suffer from 'absolute dependence'.

Second, the 'poor' Tharus (marginal farmers), who also work under others, are dependent, only in the economic and political arenas, on others, while in the socio-cultural arena they are relatively free.

Third, the 'not-so-poor' Tharus are usually small farmers who have saved their lands, worked hard as shopkeepers, and got education and jobs. Their small size of family, less fragmentation of family holdings, restrained expenditure on social occasions, restrained drinking habits and better jobs outside the village (in private or public offices) are the major causes of their relatively better position. However, even they cannot be called rich, as they do not own sufficient means of production. Among them, those in government service enjoy a special status due to their better pay and allowances and better contacts with the outside world (especially the government machinery), facilitating their getting loans in the name of family members or co-villagers and getting priority from political parties as local representatives of the masses of illiterate and poor Tharus.

III
Development for What, Whom and at Whose Cost?

The fundamental questions that arise are: Development for what? Development for whom? And development at whose cost? While defining development, various scholars have included and emphasized one or the other elements/aspects of human flourishing. We first need to discuss the sociological theories of development and then the concepts of international agencies. In sociology, the two major theories of development are: modernization theory and dependency theory. Let us examine these in brief.

The notion of modernization denotes change in the pre-modern or traditional society to become 'advanced' technologically, prosperous economically, and liberal democracy politically. Neil Smelser[8] advocates that a developed economy and society is characterized as a highly differentiated structure whereas a traditional undeveloped society lacks such differentiation. His concept of differentiation (different from V.I. Lenin's concept of differentiation of peasantry in terms of classes) refers to a process by which more specialized and autonomous social units are established in the economy, family, polity and religious institutions. To him, economic development (meaning growth of output per head of population) takes place through four processes, occurring simultaneously or separately:

(a) modernization of agriculture – from simple techniques to application of scientific knowledge;

(b) commercialization of agriculture – 'from subsistence to cash-crops' production through use of wage labour;

(c) industrialization – from the use of human and animal power to machine power; and

(d) urbanization (change in ecology) – moving from farm and village to urban centres.

Because of these processes, most of the economic activities become separated from family, both physically and socially. Further, cash cropping leads to the separation of consumption and production activities, and wage labour comes in use in place of family labour. The authority of the elderly declines and joint family gives way to nuclear family. Thanks to the economic independence of women, personal choice becomes the main consideration in marriage. Further, in recruitment, ascription gives way to the achievement variable.

However, along with this process of differentiation, second process of integration also takes place. For instance, a traditional society, based on political integration bound by strong kinship, tribalism, control of economic resources and mystic sanctions, gives way to a modern society, integrated by political parties, pressure groups and bureaucracy. Similarly, in the economic arena, modern cooperative enterprises, trade unions and recruitment agencies are the integrating institutions. In the religious arena, churches, sects and religious bureaucracy play this role.

According to Smelser, a third aspect is the occurrence of movements and violence that reflects an uneven rate of change –

discontinuities occurring because of integration not keeping pace with the differentiation and, hence, leading to disorder. Thus, Smelser characterizes the process of changing the old as 'differentiation' and the new as 'integration'.

Similarly, Hoselitz, applying Talcott Parsons' pattern variables, argues that developed countries are characterized by universalism, achievement orientation and functional specificity, while developing countries have particularism, ascription and functional diffuseness.[9] Likewise, Eisenstadt, Dalton and Redfield redefined modernization theory in their own ways. For instance, Robert Redfield called rural societies as 'part societies' that become increasingly dependent upon the wider system as modernization is stepped up.

The modernization theory suffers from the following lacunae:

(a) It is Eurocentric: its development model is based on the historical, social economic and political experiences of Western Europe whereas the realities in developing countries are markedly different.

(b) It does not give due weight to the production relations in a society.

(c) It focuses more on the macro processes at the level of a nation but ignores the micro processes at the local level which are experienced in day-to-day life, thus remaining more of an ideal-type construct.[10]

On the other hand, the dependency theory was developed by Stavenhagen, Frank, Griffin, Samir Amin, Ranjit Sau, Cardoso and Feletto. As A.G. Frank wrote about the under-development of Chile, arguing that the structure of dependence 'extends from the micro metropolitan centre of the world capitalist system 'down' to the most supposedly isolated agricultural workers who, through this chain of interlinked metropolitan–satellite relationships, are tied to the central world metropolis and, thereby, incorporated into the world capitalist system as a whole. The nature and degree of these ties differ in time and place and these differences produce important differences in the economic and political consequences to which they give rise to rest on the exploitation of the satellite by the metropolis or on the tendency of the metropolis to expropriate and appropriate the economic surplus of the satellite.'[11]

The following points may be noted from the above argument.

First, the world capitalist system has the two poles of 'metropolis' (developed countries) and 'satellite' (developing countries) interlinked.

Second, this interlinking is very vast and complex and extends up to the agricultural workers in developing countries.

Third, the relationship is not of interdependence but that of dependency of the satellites, that is, the capitalist developed countries dominate over the satellites due to unequal exchange.

Fourth, the nature and degree of the dependency may differ in time and place but the essence remains the same.

Fifth, the metropolis expropriates and appropriates the economic surplus of the satellite; hence the latter is not able to accumulate its capital.

Sixth, there is a tendency of centralization in the capitalist system. Hence, the national metropolises, being satellites of the industrial countries, cannot achieve self-sustenance and autonomous development. However, the bourgeoisie of the two poles develop mutual interest in maintaining the system and, hence, some kind of interdependence takes place between them. But Frank also points out that when a weakening of relations of dependence occurs, the development takes an 'involuted' form – either 'passive capitalist involution' (in north and north-east Brazil in the late seventeenth century, sugar industry collapsed due to opening of plantations in West Indies) or 'active capitalist involution' allowing some degree of autonomous development but of a limited kind (industrialization in Brazil, Mexico, Argentina and India during the Great Depression and the Second World War, when the terms of trade for developing countries improved substantially but were short-lived and lasted only till the end of the War). Thus, to him, development of the satellites can never be long-term and independent.

Frank's theory of dependency, too, suffers from certain lacunae. First, it is very simplistic and assumes that the inroad of capitalism leads to dissolution of non-capitalist production mode; he rejects dual modes (feudal or other non-capitalist modes) along with the capitalist mode. But in many developing countries like India and Peru, the capitalist and non-capitalist modes of production co-exist, as empirically proved by economists like Amit Bhaduri (who talks of 'semi-feudalism') or Pradhan H. Prasad.

Second, Frank uses, in the context of the sixteenth century, the two terms *capital* and *capitalism* interchangeably, and deals with the problem from the viewpoint of commodity exchange rather than that of relations of production. Laclau (1971), however, expressed his doubts on whether the structural conditions of capitalism existed in sixteenth-century Europe: 'Could we consider free labour to be the rule then? By no means. Feudal dependence and urban handicrafts remained the basic forms of productive activity.'[12]

Third, Frank's concept of dependence is problematic. As Dos Santos points out, 'Dominant countries are endowed with technological, commercial, capital and socio-political dominance over dependent countries and can, therefore, exploit them, and extract part of the locally produced surplus. Dependence, then, is based upon an international division of labour.'[13]

Finally, in Frank's theory, the global dimension of trade and exchange overlooks the mode of production at the micro level in developing countries. As Meillassoux has argued rightly, exchange elements must be examined in relation to the part they play in reproducing the material conditions of existence.[14] In certain contexts, the capitalist mode of production can indirectly contribute to the persistence of the non-capitalist modes. For instance, in South Africa, the non-capitalist mode of agricultural production is a consequence of the requirement of the dominant capitalist sector that needs low wage labour for its mining, manufacturing and agro-industries. This is also true of India where dual modes co-exist – capitalist mode in industrial sector and feudal/semi-feudal mode in agricultural sector.

However, the dependency theory does provide an insight into the dialectics of development and it could be enriched by the mode-of-production approach on the one hand and ecological sustainability approach on the other.

The World Development Report prepared by the World Bank usually emphasizes on economic growth quantifiable and measurable in terms of increase in Gross Domestic Product and per capita income. Here the economic growth is to be achieved through an open competition in the free market and the state is not to intervene there. At the most, it would be a facilitator. But the United Nations Development Programme (UNDP), basing its paradigm primarily on the works of Pakistani economist Mahbub-ul-Haq and Indian economist Amartya Sen, talks of 'human development' wherein three elements are included:[15]

(a) Standard of living, measured by per capita income (through some kind of productive work) adjusted to purchasing power parity (PPP);

(b) Physical well-being measured by life expectancy (signifying nutrition and health); and

(c) Education measured by adult literacy rate and mean years of schooling.

Thus, UNDP has prepared a 'human development index' (HDI) on the basis of these three parameters and it has also come out with the concepts of 'human poverty index' (HPI) and 'gender development index' (GDI) in order to measure poverty and gender sensitivity, respectively. Thus, the proponents of human development broaden and give a human face to the neoclassic conception of socio-economic development. They add two aspects of health and education to the World Bank's paradigm of economic growth. However, they do not focus on the 'relations of production' prevailing in an economy and society at a particular time and place. Hence, we do find the human development approach lacking in encompassing the entire gamut of economic production, cultural pursuit, social processes of daily life and political participation. Hence, there is a need to look at 'social development', that is, 'real development,' and it may be called 'real social development'. The salient features of 'real social development' are the following:

First, the indigenous knowledge system (IKS) of the local tribals (or other subalterns) should be studied properly from their 'oral traditions' (old songs, plays, dances, proverbs, sayings, visuals, social/religious festivals, puzzles, folktales, technology, agricultural practices, etc.) and be used in different activities in different degrees, extent, range and depth contextually, though it may require certain modifications and refinement. It will actually 'enrich and sharpen' the 'written tradition' of 'packaged knowledge system' (PKS). D.R. Gadgil rightly suggests three ways of using indigenous knowledge system:[16]

(a) improvement of traditional technology (not copying and adopting as given);

(b) adjustment and adaptation – adapting advanced technology to suit local conditions depending on raw materials; and

(c) innovative experiential research, going beyond the adaptation and adjustment.

In Rajasthan, the local people have been using the engine of a pumping set machine and a trolley as a carrier of passengers and/or goods, like a mini tractor. This is called 'jugar' (managing). So is 'Chhakra' in vogue, with the engine of a motorcycle and a trolley, in Gujarat. In Bihar, the boatsmen use pumping set engine on their boats. Undoubtedly, such uses of indigenous technology are cheaper, simpler, easily repairable, team-oriented and confidence-building type, though the negative consequences of air and noise pollution are notable in some cases. This also erodes the hegemony of the so-called 'expert-driven', specialized, external-directed scientism on the one hand and creates a larger and creative space for the commoners in the civil society, essential for the true functioning of democracy, on the other. Therefore, the technology should be need-based, indigenous, self-reliant, transformative, cheap, cost-effective, simple-in-handling and ecologically sustainable.

Second, real social development also requires local initiative, and access to and use of local resources. That means that the new ideas for change should be backed by new initiatives and actions for change, just as conception should lead to safe delivery/birth, not to miscarriage or abortion! However, the local initiative may begin from within the local community or be inspired by an outsider individual or group as a catalyst agent. The issue of leadership in a process of social change is very crucial and it may have one or more of the following forms:

(a) Symbolic leader (as a patron of a group);

(b) Front leader or 'the' leader;

(c) Co-leader or associate leader (second-line leadership); and

(d) Leaders in making or activists (grassroots workers).

It needs to be emphasized here that a true leader does not create followers, rather creates 'leaders for the future'. Hence it is the duty of the civil society organizations (CSOs) to create future leaders amongst tribals in remote and sleepy villages. But, unfortunately, some rightist Hindu organizations in the name of bringing tribals in the mainstream or the Christian missionaries in the name of liberation and religious freedom indulge in selfish activities and hence their activities are against real social development.

Third, real social development is a collective empowerment, that is, development *with* the people, not *for* the people. This participation requires not merely delegation of power to the local community but also actual decentralization and devolution of power. Actual decentralization and devolution of power stimulates local initiative and people's genuine participation. Every individual or group should feel that he/she is a part of the decision-making process. Here we are tempted to quote James Y.C. Yen (from China), who rightly observed in the 1920s:[17]

'Go to the people
Live among the people
Learn from the people
Plan with the people
Work with the people ...'

Here two caveats are necessary: first, the term 'people' should mean the marginalized commoners; and second, all the views of the people should not be accepted uncritically, because due to various historical, social, economic and political reasons, they have followed and are still following certain social evils and obnoxious practices like 'sati', dowry, female foeticide, casteism, witchcraft, communalism, regionalism, etc. in various parts of India. Further, unfortunately, a substantial population has been socialized in corrupt ways of life and, hence, their views are to be verified critically.

Third, real social development encompasses the principle of 'think globally, act locally'. That is, at the level of ideas, theories, hypotheses and experience-sharing, one should be open and curious at the most in order to learn, but these should not be copied and adopted, rather these should be tested critically against the social facts given in a context of time and place. A few years back, during a massive cyclone in Hyderabad, various philanthropists and donor groups sent blankets to the victims, but these were of no use because Hyderabad has a comparatively hot temperature where blankets are not needed.

Fourth, real social development in a developing agrarian country like India (where two-thirds of the population are dependent on agriculture) means a comprehensive agricultural sustainability, not a superficial and neo-liberal type of 'sustainable development'. In a neoclassical manner, the Brundlandt Commission in its report 'Our Common Future' (1987) defined sustainable development as one 'that meets the needs of the present generation without compromising the ability of future generations to meet their own needs'. In the concept of sustainable development, sustainability (that is compatible with ecology) in itself is not the goal; rather, development (implying industrialization of mass production and consumerism) is the goal. On the other hand, agricultural sustainability presupposes the sustainability of an eco-system, integrated pest management, animal and bio-manures (instead of chemical fertilizers), bio insecticides (instead of chemical insecticides), biodiversity of seeds, conservation and prudent use of water, soil, mines and forests, nourishing of soil through eco-friendly indigenous methods, etc.

Fifth, real social development stands for inclusion, not exclusion. In India, various social forces like caste, class, religion, language and gender have been traditional forces of exclusion. But, of late, the new forces of exclusion are marketism, globalization, industrialization and urbanization. As Amitabh Kundu rightly remarks, 'Undoubtedly, the institution of market, be it that for goods or for services, happens to be the most effective factor which excludes people based on affordability. In case of labour market, too, it is productivity against wages demanded which determines who should be in and who should be out.'[18] Therefore, real social development includes all social strata, especially the downtrodden subalterns, so that a holistic development with equity and distributive justice is ensured in letter and spirit.

Sixth, real social development is ultimately collective self-reliance. It would be twofold: first, collective cooperation at all levels of economy (production, exchange, consumption and distribution), and, second, the elimination of 'dependency syndrome' (too much dependence on others, outsiders and government machinery). This self-reliance has to be operative from local to global levels and, therefore, the very notion of 'development aid' is to be questioned. Rather, the unequal exchange in the world system should be changed to equal and fair items of the world trade between developed and developing countries as well as between different developing countries or even sub-regions (like South Asia), because the processes and problems of development in developing countries cannot be comprehended without contextualizing them in the wider socio-economic, political and historical context of west European imperialism and industrial capitalism. To quote Griffin: 'Underdeveloped countries, as we observe *them* today, are a product of historical forces, especially those released by European expansion and world ascendancy – Europe did not 'discover' the underdeveloped countries; on the contrary, she created them.'[19] The existing adverse terms of world trade has been tilted further in favour of the developed countries and against the developing countries in the present era of globalization, especially after the World Trade Organization (WTO) Agreement on Agriculture. This very fact of 'unfair rules help rich countries grow' was aptly revealed by the Oxfam (an international NGO) at the World Social Forum in Mumbai on 17 January 2004: 'Farmers from poor countries pay 400 per cent higher tariffs when exporting to rich countries than the farmers from rich countries need to pay when they export!'

Seventh, real social development requires a change in the culture of consumerism and wasteful lifestyle of the upper classes, who 'afford to waste' as a result of mass production for profit and the widespread growth of market everywhere – from the kitchen to the drawing room, from the garden to the office or fields. In fact, the market has crept in even in our bedrooms as a 'hidden persuader' and has snatched our happiness and privacy at every moment of our life. Thus, the market and mass media promise us a 'consumer paradise'. Therefore, we need to curb our desires and wants that are often created by the market, not need-based. Over-consumption is also leading to various crimes against women and children. Here the words of Mahatma Gandhi are quite relevant: 'Our civilization, our culture, our Swaraj depend not upon multiplying our wants, self-indulgence, but upon restricting our wants, self-denial.'[20]

Eighth, real social development aspires for providing gainful employment (growth with jobs, not jobless growth as is the offshoot of liberalization, privatization and globalization), a decent livelihood with adequate nutrition for physical and mental health of the people at large so that a healthy human resource is created. Hence, the underprivileged are assured quality foodgrains through fair price shops without any hitch and unfair dealings.

Ninth, real social development aims at the education of all the people, not merely at literacy coverage with the simple ability of putting signature. To plan for education properly means to plan for a long period, for new generations and for the future citizens with required skills. Such an education will develop creative, critical and conducive skills among the youth so that they can start productive self-employment enterprises on their own. Thus, the goal of employment and self-reliance would be achieved simultaneously.

Fortunately, the Council for Social Development (New Delhi) has come out with a holistic report entitled 'India: Social Development Report', (2006) wherein it developed a comprehensive Social Development Index (SDI) comprising the following 21 indicators in six categories:[21]

(a) Demographic indicators: contraceptive prevalence rate, total fertility rate, and infant mortality rate.

(b) Health indicators: percentage of institutional delivery (in both private and public sectors), and percentage of undernourished children.

(c) Basic amenities indicators: percentage of households living in *pucca* houses, percentage of households with access to safe drinking water, percentage of households with toilet facility, and percentage of households with electricity.

(d) Educational attainment indicators: literacy rate, pupil–teacher ratio, and school attendance rate.

(e) Unemployment and poverty-related indicators: unemployment rate (current daily status), percentage of below poverty line, and Gini ratio for per capita consumption expenditure.

(f) Social deprivation – related indicators: the ratio of the literacy of SC population to the average literacy of the population; the ratio of the literacy of the ST (STs) population to the average literacy of the population; the ratio of the literacy of the female population to the average literacy of the total population; the ratio of female unemployment rates to total unemployment rates; and child sex ratio.

The following findings of the CSD (2006) are noteworthy from the viewpoint of real social development:

(i) In India, 26 per cent of the total population (26 crores) is living below the poverty line – 19.3 crores in rural areas and 6.7 crores in urban areas. Further, 43.8 per cent of the ST population, 36.2 per cent of the SC population and 21 per cent of the other backward classes (OBC) live below the poverty line.

(ii) During 1999–2000, the three poorest states were Odisha (47.15% poor), Bihar (42.6%) and Assam (36.09%), while the three least poor states were Punjab (6.16%), Haryana (8.74%) and Kerala (12.72%).

(iii) The three states with the highest infant mortality rate are Odisha (83 per 1,000 live births), MP (82) and UP (76), whereas those with the lowest infant mortality rate are Kerala (11), Mizoram (16) and Goa (16). Bihar, UP, MP and Rajasthan account for only 45 per cent of India's total population but for 67 per cent of total infant mortality (UP's share is 26 per cent of the total). The infant mortality rate among the SCs is 83, among the STs 85.2, among other deprived classes 76 and among the rest 61.8 per thousand.

(iv) Bihar, UP, MP and Rajasthan account for 67 per cent of the total maternal mortality in India.

(v) Children's immunization in Bihar, UP, MP and Rajasthan is less than 25 per cent.

(vi) In terms of social indicators, for rural areas, the five best states are Kerala, Himachal Pradesh, Punjab, Jammu and Kashmir, and Haryana, while the five worst states are Bihar, Jharkhand, UP, MP and Odisha. In urban areas, the five best states are Himachal Pradesh, Punjab, Kerala, Karnataka and Assam, while the five worst states are Bihar, UP, Jharkhand, Chhattisgarh and Odisha.

(vii) In terms of the least gender gap in literacy, Mizoram (4.56% points), Meghalaya (5.73) and Kerala (6.34) stand first, second and third, respectively. On the other hand, in terms of the highest gender gap in literacy, Rajasthan (32.12), Jharkhand (28.56) and UP (27.25) stand first, second and third, respectively.

(viii) The three best states in child sex ratio are Chhattisgarh (975 girls per 1,000 boys), Meghalaya (973) and Tripura (966), while the three states with the lowest child sex ratio are Punjab (798), Haryana (819) and Gujarat (883).

Subsequently, in 2008, CSD added seven more indicators in two categories of gender and social groups (SC/ST). Thus, it is crystal clear that the social development index has proved to be closer to socio-economic reality in most of the developing countries and more comprehensive than the human development index. Various states in India should come out with their own Social Development Reports so that a comprehensive picture of development emerges for different regions. Then it would help the policymakers and executing agencies positively.

Notes

1. Kalayani Kandula (2004) 'Environment and Development: The Links', in Kiran B. Chhokar et al. (eds), *Understanding Environment*, Sage Publications, New Delhi, p. 265 and pp. 263–78.
2. Gordon Marshall (1998) *Oxford Dictionary of Sociology*, Oxford University Press, Oxford, p. 155.
3. Ibid., p. 156.
4. Ibid., p. 674.
5. Cited in A.R. Desai (ed.) (1978) *Rural Sociology in India*, Popular Prakashan, Bombay, p. 226.
6. Ibid.

7. N.K. Bose (1982) *Some Indian Tribes*, National Book Trust, New Delhi, p. v.
8. N.S. Smelser (1963) 'Mechanism of Change and Adjustment to Change', in B.F. Hoselitz and W.E. Moore (eds), *Industrialization and Society*, Mouton, The Hague.
9. B.F. Hoselitz (1960) *Sociological Factors in Economic Development*, Free Press, Chicago.
10. Norman Long (1982) *Introduction to the Sociology of Rural Development*, Tavistock Publications Ltd, London.
11. A.G. Frank (1969) *Capitalism and Underdevelopment in Latin America*, Monthly Review Press, London, pp. 116–17.
12. Cited in Long, op. cit., p. 86.
13. Ibid., p. 88.
14. Ibid., p. 93.
15. UNDP (1990) *Human Development Report*, Oxford University Press, New Delhi.
16. Subhash Sharma (2010) *Why People Protest: An Analysis of Ecological Movements*, Publications Division, New Delhi.
17. Cited in Sharma, ibid., p. 257.
18. Amitabh Kundu (2006) 'Introduction', in Council for Social Development, *India: Social Development Report*, Oxford University Press, New Delhi, pp. xiii–xx.
19. K. Griffin (1968) *Underdevelopment in Spanish America*, George Allen and Unwin, London, p. 38.
20. Cited in Sharma, op. cit., p. 255.
21. CSD (2006) *India: Social Development Report*, Oxford University Press, New Delhi.

2

Population and Devel

Population
nation-sta
persons
However,
possessing
defines po
Demograph
three ever
social and
and diffe
consider
caste,
nutrition
such cha
time seri
tendenc
births, d
tious issu
relationsh
relationsh

Here
comprisi
dimension
world pop
between
between
and health
general

2

Population and Development

Critical Issues

Population is one of the main constituents of any group, community, nation-state or society. Population may be defined as the number of persons (human aggregates) residing at a particular time and place. However, a statistician may define population as all individuals possessing one or a few features at a given place and time. Genetics defines population in terms of genetic similarities and differences. Demographers see population in terms of trends and tendencies in three events: births, deaths and migration. Finally, sociologists and social anthropologists see population in terms of cultural similarities and differences (values, norms, customs, arts, etc.). They usually consider social, cultural and economic aspects like age structure, caste, class, gender, occupation, education, religion, health, nutrition, marriage etc of a population group. They often compare such characteristics of one population group with another or analyse time series of one group/society to point out emerging trends and tendencies. Population of an area changes due to major events like births, deaths or migration. Actually population has been a contentious issue in terms of its biological or cultural inheritance, its relationship with poverty, development and environment, its relationship with food production and technology and so on.

Here we will take a multi-dimensional critical perspective comprising demographic, economic environmental and sociological dimensions in order to analyse four critical issues: first, growth of world population in a historical perspective; second, the relationship between food production vis-à-vis population growth, as well as between population growth and social development (viz., education and health); third, consequences of population growth on society in general and on environment/ecology in particular; finally, what should be done to reduce the rate of population growth in India (in long and short terms).

History of Population Growth

Let us take first point first. World population has been increasing. At present, the world population is more than seven billions (700 crores), China (21.57% of world population), being the largest populous country, followed by India (17.5%), USA (4.77%), Indonesia (3.56%), Brazil (2.86%), Pakistan (2.35%), Bangladesh (2.30%), Japan (2.16%), Nigeria (1.89%), Mexico (1.65%) and Germany (1.4%). A brief history of world population growth may be seen in Table 1:

Table 1

History of World Population Growth (millions)

Year	*Estimated Population*	*Time Taken to Double the Population*	*Time Taken to Add 1,000 million*
10,000 BCE	0.10 – 10		
5,000 BCE	5 – 20		
0	200		
1,300 AD	400	1300 yrs	
1700	600		
1800	900	475 yrs	
1820	1,000		Thousands of yrs
1927	2,000	125 yrs	110 yrs
1960	3,040	62 yrs	33 yrs
1974	4,027		14 yrs
1987	5,000		13 yrs
1999	6,000	40 yrs	12 yrs
2013	7,000		14 yrs
2028	8,000	54 yrs	15 yrs
2054	9,000		26 yrs

Source: UNDP etc. cited in Majumdar (2010)

From the perusal of Table 1, it transpires that in 10,000 BCE, world population was one lakh (.10 million, liberal estimate puts it to 10 million) and reached to 5 million (liberal estimate puts it to 20 million). Second, in the beginning of the Common Era, world population was 200 million and it doubled in 1,300 to 400 million – that is, its 'doubling time' was 1,300 years. But subsequently world population's doubling time decreased consistently to 475 years in 1800 to 125 years in 1927 to 62 years in 1960 and to 40 years in 1999.

Thus, during two thousand years of Common Era, world population's doubling time got reduced by 1/32. However, it is projected that in 2028 its doubling time will increase to 44 years. Third, similarly the time taken to add 1,000 million persons in world population got drastically reduced from thousands of years in 1820 to 110 years in 1927 to 33 years in 1960, to 14 years in 1974 to 13 years in 1987 and to 12 years in 1999. Thus current time of such addition is 12 years only. However, it is expected that due to better and advanced family planning techniques and prevalence of small family norms, such time to add 1,000 million increased to 14 years in 2013, and will increase to 15 years in 2028 and 26 years in 2054. Fourth, in the last quarter of twentieth century (1974–1999) world population increased by 2,000 million – such increase in such small period was unprecedented. This is primarily because of a massive reduction in death rates but little reduction in crude birth rates in most of developing countries. This consistent increase in world population since the beginning of Common Era may be seen in Figure 1.

Figure 1

Rise in World Population

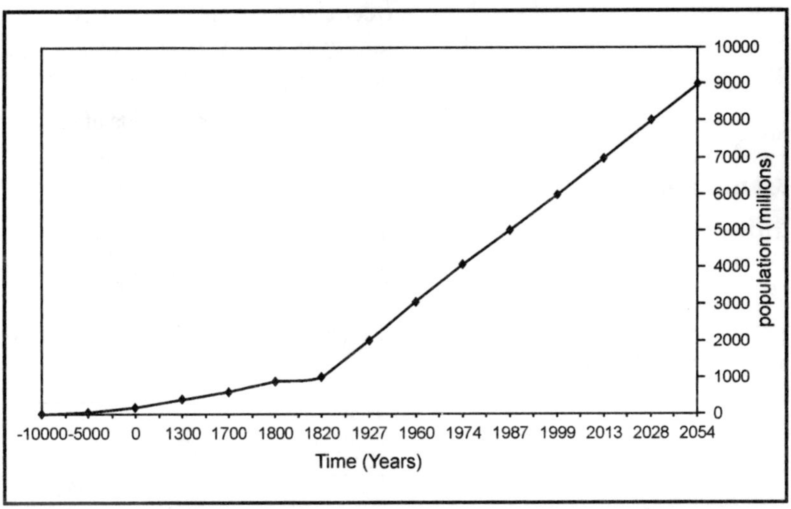

The latest data available for world population is 7,000 million (in 2013), out of which 5,600 million (80%) people live in developing countries. Further, average annual growth of world population has been 1.6 per cent during 1975–2005 but it was more than 2 per cent in most of developing countries and less than 1 per cent in developed countries. It is expected that average annual growth of world population during 2005–2015 would come down to 1.1 per cent. To put it simply, at present, every year world is gaining 78 million persons – equivalent to France, Greece and Sweden together. London was the world's largest city in 1800 with one million population but today 326 metropolitan cities have more than one million population and 16 cities have more than ten million people (India has four such metropolitan cities – Mumbai, Kolkata, Delhi and Chennai). It is expected that by 2025, 650 cities will have more than one million population each (Majumdar, 2010). In 2001, India had a total population of 1028 millions which reached to 1210 millions in March 2011. World population grew by 600 million during the entire nineteenth century while it grew by 4.4 billion in twentieth century due to technological and medical advancement to control mass deaths due to epidemics/deadly diseases like plague, malaria, small pox, TB, Cholera, etc. on the one hand, and 'baby boom' in the West, on the other – despite killing of millions of people in wars. World population continued to grow rapidly for decades despite lowering of fertility rates because of 'demographic momentum' – in the world there are one billion persons aged 15–24 years and about 2 billion persons aged below 15 years who will become parents soon. In 1901 India's decadal population growth rate was 1.1 per cent and 5.7 per cent in 1911 but declined to 0.3 per cent in 1921. Again in 1931, it was 11 per cent, 14.2 per cent in 1941, 13.3 per cent in 1951, 21.5 per cent in 1961, 24.8 per cent in 1971, 24.7 per cent in 1981, 23.8 per cent in 1991, 21.38 per cent in 2001 and 17.64 per cent in 2011.

Composition

However, different continents of the world have different shares in world population, while during 1950–2050 Africa, Asia and Latin America have a trend of increasing share, other continents (North America, Europe and Oceania) have a trend of decreasing share. This may be vividly seen in Table 2.

Table 2

Share of Continents in Total World Population (1950–2050)

Continents	*1950*	*1975*	*2003*	*2025*	*2050*
(a) Africa	8.75	9.98	13.49	16.46	20.22
(b) Asia	55.09	58.05	60.67	60.40	58.55
(c) Latin America	6.55	7.89	8.62	8.75	8.61

Cont'd ...

... Cont'd

(d) North America	6.55	5,82	5.17	5.02	5.02
(e) Europe	22.56	17.73	11.52	8.87	7.09
(f) Oceania	0.47	0.51	0.51	0.51	0.50
Total	100.00	100.00	100.00	100.00	100.00

Source: Majumdar (2010)

This may also be seen in pie chart (as in 2003) below:

Figure 2

Share of Continents in World Population

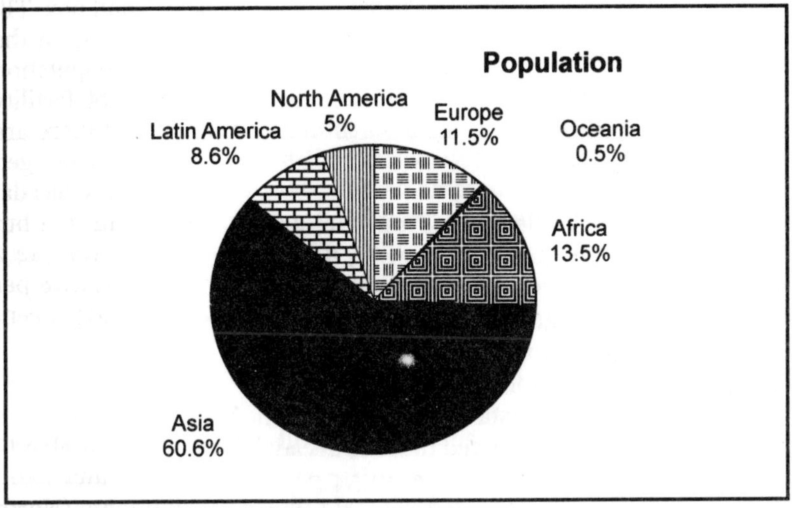

India's Population Growth

It is notable here that during 1950s, world population grew faster than what UN had estimated, especially Africa, Asia and Latin America grew at more than 2 per cent. Therefore, in 1974, the UN Conference on Population firmly resolved that 'development is the best contraceptive' (as Indian Prime Minister Mrs Indira Gandhi had coined the slogan). Similarly, though India's population was projected to be around 117 crores in 2011, yet 15th Census of India (provisional) in March 2011 put its total population at 121 crores (1.21 billion). The population growth in India during 1901–2011 may be seen in Table 3:

Table 3

India's Population Growth (1901–2011)

Year	*Population (cr)*
1901	23.84
1911	25.21
1921	25.13
1931	27.90
1941	31.87
1951	36.11
1961	43.92
1971	54.82
1981	68.33
1991	84.64
2001	102.87
2011	121.02

Source: Censuses of India

Thus, from Table 3, it is quite clear that during 1901–1965 India's population doubled from 23.84 cr to 47.68 cr and again doubled to 95 crores around 1996. Further, during 1901–2011, India's population grew five times (from 23.84 cr to 121.02 cr). In 2011, India's total population was 17.5 per cent of world population – its population is more than the combined population of US, Indonesia, Brazil, Pakistan, Bangladesh and Japan. However, one significant point has emerged that the decadal (2001–11) growth rate declined to 17.64 per cent from 21.54 per cent during 1991–2001. Further, it is also notable that six most populous states, UP (19.96 cr), Maharashtra (11.24 cr), Bihar (10.38 cr) West Bengal (9.13 cr), Andhra Pradesh (8.47 cr) and M.P. (7.26 cr), have all registered decline in decadal (2001–11) growth rate. Actually, 25 states and Union Territories have recorded annual population growth rate of 2 per cent or less during 2001–11 – with 15 states/UTs growing at less than 1.5 per cent annually (while in 2001 only 4 states/UTs had recorded growth rate of less than 1.5%). During 1975–80, world population growth rate declined slightly from 2 per cent in 1965–75 to 1.7 per cent, during 1985–2000 countries of high human development category showed an average of 0.7 per cent annual growth, medium human development category grew at 1.7 per cent annually, and low human development category grew at 2.7 per cent annually.

Actually average total fertility rate (TFR) was very high (2.8) in 2000 – 1.7 in high human development category, 2.6 for medium human development category, and 5.6 for low human development category. A comparative picture of annual population growth rate and total fertility rate may be seen in Table 4:

Table 4

Trends in Annual Population Growth Rate and Total Fertility Rate by Regions (1975–2015)

Country Categories	*Annual Population Growth Rate*		*Total Fertility Rate (TFR)*	
	1975–99	*1999–2015*	*1975–99*	*1999–2015*
(a) Developing countries	1.9	1.4	5.4	3.1
(b) High HDI	0.7	0.4	2.3	1.7
(c) Medium HDI	1.7	1.0	4.9	2.6
(d) Low HDI	2.7	2.5	6.7	5.6
(e) High income	0.7	0.4	2.1	1.7
(f) Medium income	1.5	0.9	4.6	2.2
(g) Low income	2.2	1.7	5.7	4.0
(h) World	1.6	1.2	4.5	2.8

Source: Adapted from UNDP, HDR 2001.

From Table 4, it transpires that human development index and income status have inverse relationship with annual population growth rate and total fertility rate. That is, higher the human development or income, lower the annual population growth rate and total fertility rate. Second, in 1975–99, annual population growth rate of low HDI countries (2.7%) was almost four times that of high HDI countries (0.7%). Similarly, TFR of low HDI countries (6.7) then was almost three times that of high HDI countries (2.3). Third, annual population growth rate and total fertility rate in 1975–99 was lowest in high income countries in comparison with medium income and low income countries. Fourth, during 1975–2015, a decreasing trend is projected in both annual population growth rate and total fertility rate across all country categories. However, while high HDI countries or high income countries will reach below the replacement level (1.7) in 2015, the low HDI countries will still have much higher TFR (5.6) and low income countries will have high TFR (4.0) in 2015 and then the TFR for the entire world would be 2.8 closer to medium HDI countries (2.6). It is also notable here that low HDI/low income countries like Ethiopia (6.8), Nigeria (5.9) and Pakistan (5.5) have very high TFR (1999) whereas developed countries like Russia (1.2), Italy (1.2), and Spain (1.2) have lowest TFR – much below the replacement level. From above it is crystal clear that human development (as popularized by UNDP) has positive effect on both annual population growth rate and total fertility rate. TFR in Goa (1.79), Andhra Pradesh (1.79), Tamil Nadu (1.8), Kerala (1.93), Karnataka (2.07), Sikkim (2.02), HP (1.94) and Punjab (1.99) is equal to or below the replacement level. Second, TFR is the highest in Bihar (4). Third, TFR in seven states is more than 3 but less than 4 – UP (3.82), Meghalaya (3.8), Nagaland (3.74), Jharkhand (3.3), MP (3.12), Arunachal Pradesh (3.03), and Rajasthan (3.21). Fourth, TFR in 13 states is more than 2 but less than 3 – Manipur (2.83), Mizoram (2.86), Assam (2.42), Tripura (2.22), West Bengal (2.27), Odisha (2.37), Chhattisgarh (2.62), Uttarakhand (2.55), J&K (2.38), Haryana (2.69), Delhi (2.13), Gujarat (2.42) and Maharashtra (2.11). Fifth, it is also found that the greatest difference in fertility rate is by education and family health – women in poorest families usually have two more children than women in richest households. Sixth, TFR is 3.1 for ST, 2.9 for SC and 2.8 for OBCs. Finally, TFR for Muslims (3.1) is higher than that of Hindus (2.7) – however, TFR for Muslims since 1998 is declining at faster rate than for Hindus. Still more fertility rate in India is because of preference for son – most men and women like to have one son and one daughter (NFHS3 – 2005–6). Different TFRs for different states may be seen in Table 5:

Table 5

TFR in Different States of India (2005–06)

	States	*TFR*
(a) Up to 2.0 (replacement level)	Goa	1.7
	Andhra Pradesh	1.79
	Tamil Nadu	1.80
	Kerala	1.93
	Himachal Pradesh	1.94
	Punjab	1.99
	Karnataka	2.07
	Sikkim	2.02

Cont'd ...

... Cont'd

(b) Above 2.0 but below 3.0	Maharashtra	2.11
	Delhi	2.13
	Tripura	2.22
	West Bengal	2.27
	Odisha	2.37
	J&K	2.38
	Assam	2.42
	Gujarat	2.42
	Chhattisgarh	2.62
	Haryana	2.69
	Manipur	2.83
	Mizoram	2.86
(c) Above 3.0 but below 4.0	Arunachal Pradesh	3.03
	Rajasthan	3.21
	MP	3.12
	Jharkhand	3.30
	Nagaland	3.74
	Meghalaya	3.80
	UP	3.82
(d) 4.0 or more	Bihar	4.0

Actually it was only after 1971 that Kerala's growth rate declined below that of India as a whole, and during 1991–2001 Tamil Nadu registered lowest growth rate. Similarly in Kerala, IMR declined from about 60 per thousand live births in 1971 to below 15 in mid 1990s and in Tamil Nadu IMR declined from about 110 in 1971 to 50 in mid 1990s and to about 45 in 2002. For such success in Kerala education played the most significant role – there, during the British period, Christian missionaries concentrated more on education and health than on proselytization and, interestingly, native rulers supported the cause of education by taking clue from indigenous tradition; migration from Kerala to gulf countries had also positive effect on status of women, especially Muslim women but Malappuram, with majority of Muslims, has higher TFR than replacement level (Zachariah and Rajan, 2011).

Two important aspects of population are: age composition and sex composition. Multiple age classification, better method than single age classification, gives disaggregates about young (dependent) age group below the age of 15 years, active age group (15–59 years or 15–64 years) and old age group (60+ or 65+, dependent senior citizens). The age composition of world and India's population may be seen in Table 6:

Table 6

Age Composition of Population (by regions) 1999–2015

Regions	*Below 15 yrs (1999)*	*Below 15 yrs (2015)*	*65+ (1999)*	*65+ (2015)*	*Active Population*	
					1999	*2015*
(a) World	30.2	25.8	6.9	8.3	62.9	65.9
(b) High income countries	18.6	15.8	14.5	18.3	66.9	65.9
(c) Middle income countries	27.8	22.2	6.5	8.5	65.7	69.3
(d) Low income countries	37.2	32.3	4.4	5.2	58.4	62.5
(e) Least developed countries	43.2	40.4	3.1	3.4	53.7	56.2
(f) India	33.9	26.9	4.9	6.4	61.2	66.7

Source: UNDP, Human Development Report 2001

From Table 6, following points emerge: first, a little less than 1/3 (30.2%) of world population (1999) is below 15 years and about 7 per cent is above 65 years (UNDP considers 65+ as old age) – in total 37.21 (30.2 + 6.9) per cent world population is dependent. Needless to say that a large share of young population implies more adults, more marriages/unions and birth of more children in near future (a challenge to support them) on the one hand and 'demographic dividend' on the other in that there would be more active adults in near future to work and earn livelihood (an opportunity due to rise in rate of economic growth due to rising share of working age people in total population). As famous demographer Ashish Bose rightly observes: 'The same teeming millions that once evoked images of hungry, wailing children in mid-seventies, have proved to be our biggest strength today in the form of vibrant workers and consumers. This was made possible because we were able to equip ourselves with scientific education and specialized skills' (Molekhi, 2011). However, this so-called 'demographic dividend' would be meaningful only when there is adequate priority to education, minimum level of learning, quality of education, and health and nutrition of such huge young population. Education (both school and higher) in India is not satisfactory in terms of both quantity and quality. As the Parliamentary Committee on Estimates observed that in India only 30 per cent of universities and 10 per cent of the colleges are of quality because UGC's financial support to state universities is extremely inadequate (*The Economic Times,* 2 August 2010). However, at global level not a single Indian University (including IIT) ranks in top 100 universities of the world whereas US has 45 universities in top 100, UK has 12, Japan has 5, Australia (4), Germany (4), Canada (4) and the Netherlands (4) based on a survey of 13,388 academics from 131 countries in the world, as per Times Higher Education. Harvard University ranks 1, MIT 2, Cambridge University (UK) 3, University of California, Berkeley 4, Oxford University 6, Tokyo University 8 (*The Times of India,* 12 March 2011). Second, in high income (developed) countries, 18.6 per cent population is below 15 years and 14.5 per cent above 65 years – in total 33.1 (18.6 + 14.5) population is dependent. Third, in middle income countries, 27.8 per cent population is below 15 years and 6.5 per cent is above 65 years – in total 34.3 per cent (27.8 + 6.5) is dependent. Fourth, in low income countries, 37.2 per cent population is below 15 years and 4.4 per cent of population is above 65 years – in total 41.6 per cent (37.2 + 4.4) population is dependent. Fifth, in least developed countries, 43.2 per cent population is below 15 years and 3.1 per cent is above 65 years – in total 46.3 per cent (43.2 + 3.1) population is dependent. Sixth, in India, 33.9 per cent population is below 15 years and 4.9 per cent is above 65 years – in total 38.8 per cent population is dependent. Seventh, it is expected that in 2015 world's young-age population will decrease from 30.2 per cent to 25.8 per cent but old age population will increase from almost 7 per cent to 8.3 per cent – the percentage of total dependents will decrease from 37 per cent to 34 per cent – that is, active population percentage will increase by 3 percentage points. Eighth, in 2015, young-age population in high income countries will decrease from 18.6 per cent to 15.8 per cent but old age population will increase from 14.5 per cent to 18.3 per cent – in total the percentage of dependents will increase by one percentage point from 33 per cent to 34 per cent. This is mainly because of increase in older people and that is because the total fertility rate (TFR) in developed countries is below the replacement level as well as due to high increase in longevity. However, it will have negative implications as there would be far less active working people. For instance, in Japan, 22.5 per cent population is 65+ and is expected to be 40 per cent in 2055. Japanese population will decrease from 128 million to 96 million in 2050 and to 64 million in 2100. During 2006–7 Japan's population decreased by 29,000. Nineth, in middle income, low income and least developed countries young population will decrease substantially but old-age population will increase, though marginally. Finally, across all the regions young-age population will decrease substantially by 2015. However, in case of percentage of older population, except high income countries (where there will be substantial increase from 14.5% to 18.3%), other regions will have only a marginal increase in 2015. Obviously, except high income countries (whose active working population will decrease from 66.9% to 65.9%) during 1999–2015, active working population will increase across all regions – at world level by 3 percentage points, in middle income countries by almost 4 percentage points, in low income countries by 4 percentage points, in least developed countries by 2.5 percentage points and in India substantially by 6.5 percentage points (maximum % gain).

Dependency Ratio

Now the question arises about dependency ratio. There are young age (youth) dependency ratio, old age or aged dependency ratio, and total dependency ratio. Young dependency ratio means: size of young population (0–14) at a particular point of time, divided by the size of actively working population (15–64 years) at the same time and multiplied by 100. Old age dependency ratio means: size of old age population (65+), divided by the size of actively working population (15–64 years), and multiplied by 100. Total dependency ratio means young age dependency ratio plus old age dependency ratio. Table 7 shows dependency ratio by regions:

From Table 7, following points emerge: First, at the world level young dependency ratio is high at 48 but old age dependency ratio is low (11) and total dependency ratio is 59. It is expected that young dependency ratio will decrease (to 39), old age dependency ratio will increase (to 13) and total dependency ratio will come down to 52 in 2015. Second, young dependency ratio in high income countries is lowest (28) among all regions but its old age dependency ratio is highest (22) among all regions, and total dependency ratio is lowest (50) among all regions. It is expected that there, in 2015, young age dependency ratio will decrease to 24 but old age dependency ratio and total dependency ratio will increase (28 and 52, respectively).

Third, across all the regions, as the income category decreases, young age dependency ratio increases but old age dependency ratio decreases and total dependency ratio increases. Fourth, it is expected that in 2015 young dependency ratio will decrease in all regions – from 42 to 32 in middle income countries, from 64 to 52 in low income countries, from 80 to 72 in least developed countries, and from 55 to 40 in India. Fifth, in 2015, old dependency ratio will increase across all regions: from 10 to 12 in middle income countries, from 6 to 8 in low income countries, from 8 to 10 in India but it will be stable in least developed countries at 6. Finally, except high income countries, total dependency ratio will decrease in all the regions – from 52 to 44 in middle income countries, from 70 to 60 in low income countries, from 86 to 78 in least developed countries, and from 63 to 50 in India. However, in 2015 the total dependency ratio in middle income countries will be lower (44) than all other regions in developing countries (including India), developed countries as well as the world average.

Table 7

Dependency Ratio by Region (1999–2015)

Regions	*1999*			*2015 (Projected)*		
	Young	*Old*	*Total*	*Young*	*Old*	*Total*
(a) World	48	11	59	39	13	52
(b) High income countries	28	22	49	24	28	52
(c) Middle income countries	42	10	52	32	12	44
(d) Low income countries	64	6	70	52	8	60
(e) Least developed countries	80	6	86	72	6	78
(f) India	55	8	63	40	10	50

Source: UNDP, HDR 2001

Sex Ratio

Further, the sex ratio (females for 1,000 males) is not favourable in India – 940 (2011) at national level but many states, like Haryana, Punjab, Delhi, Gujarat, Bihar, UP, Chhattisgarh, MP, Uttarakhand and Jharkhand, have lower sex ratio than the national average. Further it is also notable that sex ratio in India has consistently declined from 972 in 1901, to 964 in 1911, to 955 in 1921, to 950 in 1931, to 945 in 1941, then remained almost constant in 1951 at 946 but again declined to 941 in 1961, to 930 in 1971; then slightly increased to 934 in 1981 but again declined to 927 in 1991 and later in 2001 slightly increased to 933 in 2001 and again slightly increased to 940 in 2011. This increase in overall sex ratio at national level is primarily because of increase in the life expectancy of women – more older women now than 10 years ago or better care to survived women by families, and better performance in education and jobs by women in different regions. The overall sex ratio was highest in Kerala State in 2011 (1,084), followed by Puducherry (1,038) and Tamil Nadu (995). Among the districts, Mahe (Puducherry) has the highest sex ratio (1,176) followed by Almora (1,142) in Uttarakhand. Among the states/UTs, Daman & Diu has the lowest sex ratio of 618, followed by Dadra and Nagar Haveli (775). Among the districts, Daman has lowest sex ratio (533), followed by Leh (583) in J&K. Sex ratio of 10 most populous countries is shown in Table 8:

Table 8

Sex Ratio of Ten Most Populous Countries

Countries	*2001*	*2011*
China	944	926
India	933	940
US	1029	1025
Indonesia	1004	988
Brazil	1025	1042
Pakistan	938	943
Russian Federation	1140	1167
Bangladesh	958	978
Japan	1041	1055
Nigeria	1016	987
World	986	984

From Table 8, it is clear that US, Brazil, Russia and Japan have more females than males.

Again, in the age group of 0–6, child sex ratio in India declined from 945 in 1991 to 927 in 2001 and further down to 914 in 2011 – a matter of great concern. In this age group, child sex ratio (2001) in developed states like Punjab (793), Haryana (820), Chandigarh (845), Delhi (865), Gujarat (878) and Himachal Pradesh (897) was a matter of concern as therein the practice of foeticide/infanticide has been more prevalent than in other states, and new technology (sex-determination test) has been anti-women, especially in these parts of India. In 2011 Census (provisional) in 27 states/UTs, child sex ratio has declined over 2001 Census – this is a matter of grave concern. However, Punjab and Haryana have improved child sex ratio in 2011 – 846 and 830, respectively but Haryana (in 2011) has lowest child sex ratio in India. Himachal Pradesh, Gujarat, Tamil Nadu, Mizoram (971) and Andaman and Nicobar Islands are the only other states/UTs that have shown an increase in child sex ratio. Besides Punjab and Haryana, UP (decline from 916 to 899), Maharashtra (decline from 913 to 883), Chandigarh (867), Delhi (decline from 868 to 866) and J&K (decline from 937 to 859) have worrisome child sex ratio. Though southern states of India namely Kerala (959), Andhra Pradesh (943), Karnataka (943) and Tamil Nadu (946) have better child sex ratio than the national average (914 in 2011), yet they are worse off compared to 2001. Decline in child sex ratio is mainly because of sex discrimination (less food, less health care, less education and less affection to girls) and female foeticide/infanticide (due to preference for sons). To some demographers, like P.M. Kulkarni the sex ratio at birth should ideally be 950 girls per 1000 boys. Child sex ratio is highest in Mizoram (971). At the district level Lahaul and Spiti in Himachal Pradesh has the highest child sex ratio of 1,013, followed by Tawang district (Arunachal Pradesh) with 1,005. It is lowest in Jhajjar (774) and Mahendragarh (778) in Haryana. Child sex ratio in different states of India may be seen in Table 9:

Table 9

State-wise Child Sex Ratio (2001–2011)

State/UT	*2001*	*2011*
Andaman and Nicobar Islands	965	966
Andhra Pradesh	964	943
Arunachal Pradesh	961	960
Assam	964	957
Bihar	938	933
Chandigarh	845	867
Chhattisgarh	975	964
Dadra and Nagar Haveli	973	924

Cont'd ...

... Cont'd

Daman and Diu	925	909
Delhi	868	866
Goa	933	920
Gujarat	878	886
Haryana	820	830
Himachal Pradesh	897	906
Jammu and Kashmir	937	859
Jharkhand	966	943
Karnataka	949	943
Kerala	963	959
Lakshadweep	974	908
Madhya Pradesh	929	912
Maharashtra	917	883
Manipur	961	934
Meghalaya	975	970
Mizoram	971	971
Nagaland	975	944
Odisha	950	934
Puducherry	958	965
Punjab	793	846
Rajasthan	909	883
Sikkim	974	944
Tamil Nadu	939	946
Tripura	975	953
Uttar Pradesh	916	899
Uttarakhand	906	886
West Bengal	963	950
India	927	914

Life Expectancy

Needless to say that on an average, due to better facilities (accessibility to health, nutrition, low fertility as well as more purchasing power), longevity has increased across all regions (80 yrs in developed countries and 59 years in low income countries), hence number of old-aged persons has increased. Among all advanced countries, France has the longest life expectancy of 83.5 years (2000) but by 2050 Japan will have the longest life expectancy of 90 years. This may be seen in Table 10:

Table 10

Life Expectancy in Selected Developed Countries (2000–2050)

Developed Countries	*Life Expectancy in Years (2000)*	*Projected Life Expectancy in 2050*
(a) France	83.5	87.0
(b) Japan	82.9	90.0
(c) Italy	82.5	86.2
(d) Canada	81.6	85.2
(e) UK	82.5	83.7
(f) Germany	81.5	83.1
(g) USA	80.4	82.9

Source: Mountain View Research, Los Altos, California (*The Times of India,* 17 June 2000)

On the other hand, many African countries like Sierra Leon have very low life expectancy at birth 37.3 (1995–2000) with very high infant mortality rate of 182 (1999). In India, life expectancy is above 65 years and number of its old-aged people increased from 12 million in 1901 to 20 million in 1951 to 73 million in 2001. It is estimated that India's older population will be 175 million in 2025. Further, in India 90 per cent of older people are from unorganized sector (mostly in rural areas) with hardly any social security though 30 per cent of them live below poverty line. Again about 73 per cent of them are illiterate and 55 per cent of women over 60 years are widows because usually their life expectancy is higher than men. About 2 lakh older persons in India have crossed the age of 100 years (Majumdar, 2010). As indicated earlier, the share of older population has been increasing across all regions during the last three decades and it will increase further due to better medical facilities, nutrition, purchasing power, sanitation, health consciousness, fitness facilities, social security (pension) from different agencies like family, civil society, NGOs, state and market. The UN declared 1999 as the International Year of Older Persons. A glimpse of a trend of increasing share of older people by regions over time is shown below in Table 11:

Table 11

Percentage Share of Older Population by Regions (1980–2025)

Year	*World*	*More Developed Regions*	*Less Developed Regions*
1980	8.6	15.5	6.4
1985	8.9	16.4	6.6
1990	9.2	17.6	6.9
1995	9.5	18.4	7.2
2000	10.0	19.4	7.7
2025	15.0	25.0	12.0

Source: UN Demographic Yearbook 2003 and others, cited in E. Haq (2007)

Needless to say that increasing trend of ageing process has several consequences for the society at large. First, in developing countries like India, there used to be proper care of old-aged persons in joint families due to religious and moral duty as well as need of the elders to talk to, play with and engage the young ones. But due to disintegration of joint family system, on the one hand and lack of sufficient old age care homes on the other, there is a 'social care vacuum' in family and society and even market has not entered this area because of high risk and less gain. Second, the number, quality and concerns of philanthropists, volunteers and voluntary agencies to do social service have been on fast decline. Third, though government of India has made a law, namely, Maintenance and Welfare of Parents and Senior Citizens Act 2007, where the legal successors like sons and daughters, grand sons and grand daughters or close relatives have been made responsible for care of the parents and senior citizens, but due to lack of mass awareness, complexity in the legal process of court case, disinclination to file court cases against near and dear ones, physical inability to pursue the court case, threats from relatives, etc. this legal provision to get care and facility is hardly availed of by the needy in different parts of India. Finally, the substantial 'authority of elders' in the families has absolutely eroded and they have been reduced to only nominal/titular heads of families for merely traditional and ritual purposes because of a new trend of selfishness, individualism, nuclear family, consumerism and shrinking of resources (like small house in urban areas).

II
Population Growth and Food Production

Now we will discuss the relationship between population growth and food production in the world in general and in India in particular. In this regard, the father of modern demography, Thomas Robert Malthus (1766–1834), wrote a book *An Essay on the Principle of Population* (1798) wherein he formulated a hypothesis that food is necessary for the existence of man but his ability to reproduce is greater than his ability to produce the necessities of life. Further, the capacity of land to produce the subsistence for any number of populations is limited despite the scientific and technological innovations. According to him, the food production grows arithmetically (1, 2, 3, 4, 5, 6) because of limited capacity of earth due to the 'law of diminishing return' in practice, while the human population grows geometrically (1, 2, 4, 8, 16, 32) because of unlimited capacity of humans to reproduce. Thus, population tends to double every 25 years (e.g. in USA then). This is the immutable law of nature. Second, to Malthus, social evils like poverty, inequality, exploitation of labour, misery of working class and suffering of masses exist not because of institutions, rules, greedy employees, merchants and landlords but because of internal factor – man's very nature and unlimited passion between the two sexes to reproduce more. Third, to him, the antagonism between geometrical progression of population and arithmetical progression of food production has various implications:

(i) higher population growth causes poverty and misery that affects mortality (especially infant mortality), hence more children are reproduced – poverty is both cause and effect of population;

(ii) it encourages lower age of marriage and subsequently early pregnancies and more child births, hence higher dependency ratio leads to poverty;

(iii) broader lower age structure (as child labour) pushes active working age group in unemployed labour force, resulting into misery;

(iv) poor laws create dependency and parasitism;

(v) population pressure compels lower classes to divert resources, otherwise to be spent on education, health care, etc. to spend on food; hence early marriage and fertility rate increase;

(vi) ultimately it increases political instability.

Finally, Malthus thinks in order to keep the potentials of population and food production equal, two types of checks are needed. Positive checks on diseases, epidemics, famine, natural calamities, infanticide, wars, hunger, vicious customs and traditions, occupational hazards, etc. – these checks increase mortality. To quote Malthus, 'The race of plants and the race of animals shrink under this restrictive law. And the race of man cannot, by efforts of reason, escape from it. Among plants and animals its effects are waste of feed, sickness, and premature death, among mankind, misery and vice' (Majumdar, 2010: 84). Prudential or preventive checks of voluntary moral restraint (celibacy, delay in marriage, abstinence after marriage, and extra-marital relations) are also to be practiced. Malthus did not approve of artificial methods of family planning like contraceptives (that were prevalent then in France and Scandinavian countries) due to his orthodox religious (Catholic) belief.

Let us examine whether such Malthusian apprehensions are empirically correct or not. Actually Malthus wrote that book as a critique of Marquis de Condorcet (French Philosopher) and William Godwin who had blamed the church and the imperialist regime for corruption, bad laws, misery, poverty and inequality between individuals, between classes and between nations. To them, existing oppressive system does not allow people to bring the best out of them, hence an ideal system will remove unhealthy competition between people and also between nations and will also eliminate wars. Karl Marx criticized Malthusian theory of population on following counts:

(i) surplus population is not the cause but the consequence of capitalist mode of production wherein wages of labour are kept minimum and the profit of capitalist class is maximum;

(ii) labour-displacing machines are used, so there is more unemployment leading to poverty;

(iii) land distribution is unequal, hence low productivity;

(iv) there cannot be a universal theory of population because production process keeps on changing in a particular society;

(v) after eliminating capitalism, collective socialist mode of production will provide adequate employment and well-being for all.

The history of food production and productivity in the world has shown that it is faster than population growth rate due to better scientific and technological innovations in food production, more cultivable land, multiple cropping pattern, human capital, social capital (informal networks) and so on. At international level surplus food is available (though no accessibility and security in some developing countries). During 1965–95 world population increased by 70 per cent (from 3,337 million to 5,666 million) but world's total cereal consumption doubled (from 942 million tons to 1811 million tons) during the same period. During 1965–95, annual growth of population was 1.8 per cent while annual growth of total cereal consumption was 2.2 per cent. Similarly, during the same period world's per capita calorie supply from cereal and other products increased by 16 per cent – from 2,356 Kcal to 2,733 Kcal. In India, Green Revolution began in mid-1960s and food production and productivity increased manifold. India is now a food surplus nation and is exporting rice, wheat and other agricultural produces on a large scale. Amartya Sen analysed various famines and concluded that the purchasing power and entitlement for food is more significant than the physical availability/supply of foodgrains. Sometimes food scarcity may not be directly due to less supply of foodgrains but because of prosperity leading to eating more or better diets. As the former RBI Governor, D. Subbarao (2011) observed: 'Since rural incomes are going up, people are eating better by shifting from cereal to protein (rich diet) and it is leading to food scarcity.' However, food and nutrition security is a contentious issue. We are of the view that so long as people in a society shift towards food/diet diversification, it is appreciable if it increases nutritional intake (including micronutrients). Further, there is prevalence of corruption at various levels in public distribution system – 30 per cent foodgrains as transmission loss, theft of foodgrains of ₹ 20,000 crores, as admitted by the former Union Minister of State for Food Mr K.V. Thomas (NDTV, 2 March 2011). However, there is difference in the purpose of cereals production in developed and developing countries – while in developing countries the primary purpose is food (62%) rather than feed (25.6%) or industrial and other purposes (12.4%), in developed countries it is produced mainly for animal feed (60%) rather than food (22%) or industrial and other purposes (18%). This may be seen in Table 12:

Table 12

Purposes of Cereal Production by Regions

Region	*Food (%)*	*Feed (%)*	*Industrial and Others (%)*
(a) Developed countries	22	60	18
(b) Developing countries	62	25.6	12.4
(c) World	50	36	14

Another aspect notable is that despite population growth, due to intervention of the state as well as due to more trade and better market mechanisms, different regions of the world have experienced decline in income poverty (at one dollar daily) during 1981–2001 (Table 13):

Table 13

Decline in Income Poverty (1981–2001)

Regions	*1981 (%)*	*2001 (%)*
(a) East Asia Pacific	56.7	14.3
(b) Europe and Central Asia	0.8	3.5
(c) Latin America and Caribbean	10.1	9.9
(d) Middle East and North Africa	5.1	2.4
(e) South Asia	51.5	31.9
(f) Sub Saharan Africa	40.4	20.7

Source: UNDP, HDR 2005

On the other hand, it is a bitter truth that different regions' share in world population and world Gross Domestic Product (GDP) is asymmetrical. For instance, developed countries share only 10 per cent of world population but take a lion's share in world GDP (80%), whereas developing countries, with 79 per cent of world population, have only 20 per cent share in world GDP and the least developed countries with 11 per cent population have merely 0.6 per cent share in world GDP (Table 14):

Table 14

Share in World Population and GDP by Regions

Regions	*Share in World Population (%)*	*Share in world GDP (%)*
(a) Developed countries	10	79.4
(b) Developing countries	79	20
(c) Least developed countries	11	0.6
Total	100	100

Source: UNDP, HDR 2005

This asymmetry of income distribution is more glaring if we compare US and India at per capita level. An average US citizen lives on $27,648 annually (PPP – $37,562) while an average Indian citizen lives on mere $564 annually (PPP $2,892). An average American consumes

150 kg meat (as protein) in a year, while an Indian eats only 5 kg meat in a year. If we compare the income of the 20 per cent poorest and the 20 per cent richest in the world, we find that the gap has increased from 30 times to 103 times during 1960–2003 (Table 15):

Table 15

Share in World Income by Classes (1960–2003)

Period	*World's richest 20 per cent income*	*World's poorest 20 per cent income*
1960	30 X	X
1990	60Y	Y
2003	103 Z	Z

Source: UNDP, HDR 2005

Similarly, the richest 20 per cent of world population consume more than 80 per cent of world GDP (84%), energy (82%), fuel oil (90%) and forest produce (85%) whereas all the poorest of world consume these only 16 per cent, 18 per cent, 10 per cent and 15 per cent, respectively (Table 16):

Table 16

Profile of Consumption by the Rich and Poor in the World

Consumption	*By richest 20 per cent of world population (%)*	*By all the poorest of world population (%)*
(a) World GDP	84	16
(b) Energy	82	18
(c) Fuel oil	90	10
(d) Forest produce	85	15

Source: UNDP, HDR 2005

A glimpse of inegalitarian world order is also seen in the fact that in 2000, low and medium income countries received $53.6 billion loan from global multilateral banks (World Bank, International Monetary Fund) and bilateral aid agencies but unfortunately in the same year, these low and medium income countries paid to those lenders $77.6 billion as interest on earlier loans – thus net outflow from low and medium income countries was then $24 billion! But unfortunately, Malthus did not see these unequal relationships which are not because of population growth but because of unequal exchange and unfair terms of international trade.

Population and Education

Malthus could also not foresee the mass communication revolution that helped in fast spreading of the new agricultural technology, generated mass awareness among eligible couples for family planning, provided new means of entertainment (in lieu of sexual activity) and widened the 'shared spaces'. Transport communication facilitated the supply of various food products from world's one corner to another through trade or aid within less time, especially during natural calamities. He also could not understand the onset of process of industrialization and urbanization that have helped in the popularizing of small family norm. Further Malthus could not visualise the popular use of contraceptives, due to his Orthodox Catholic beliefs that prevented millions of births all around the world. His conception of greater passion to reproduce has also been falsified because of new trends of pre-marital sex, dissociation between marriage and sex, dissociation between sex and child-bearing, dissociation between marriage and child-bearing, live-in relationship, adoption of children and so on. In most of the world, population growth is due to decline in death rates due to medical facilities but Malthus emphasized only on the rising birth rate. In all the countries, developed and developing, literacy/education in general and that of women in particular has massively contributed to the decline of TFR both in rural and urban areas due to ensuing attitudinal change, use of family planning techniques (abstinence, pill, contraceptives, spacing), information sharing, health consciousness, better care of infants (including their immunization) and so on. Educated women and men duly understand the available family resource kit, cost of upbringing of an additional child and distribution of resources (spending thinly/extensively on many children or intensively on one or two only). A glimpse of an inverse relationships pattern between literacy rate and fertility rate may be seen in Table 17:

Table 17

Relationship Pattern between Literacy Rates and Fertility Rates in India (1901–2001)

Year	*Literacy Rate (%)*	*Fertility Rate (%)*
1901	5.4	49.2
1911	9.9	48.1
1921	7.2	46.4
1931	9.5	45.2

Cont'd ...

... Cont'd

1941	16.1	39.9
1951	18.3	41.7
1961	28.3	41.3
1971	34.5	36.9
1981	43.6	33.9
1991	52.2	29.5
2001	65.2	25.4
2011	73.0	17.5

Source: Censuses of India

From Table 17, it is crystal clear that in 1901 literacy rate in India was very low at 5.4 per cent (due to neglect by the British government) and then fertility rate was very high (49.2%). But it started declining due to more literacy, especially as the literacy rate increased to more than 1/3rd (34.5%) in 1971, there was a perceptive change – decline in fertility rate (36.9%) and in 2001, when literacy rate increased to 65.2 per cent, the fertility rate substantially declined to 25.4 per cent. During 2001–11 literacy rate further increased to 73 per cent, while fertility rate declined to 17.5 per cent; however, there has been a wide disparity by sex, caste, class and region – on national level women (55% in 15–49 years) lagged almost 23 percentage points behind men (78%) in literacy rate (NFHS3, 2005–06) and state of Kerala had the highest literacy rate (90%) in 2005–06 and the lowest fertility rate, while Rajasthan, Bihar, UP, MP, Chhattisgarh, Odisha, Uttarakhand, Jharkhand and Assam have lower literacy rates and higher fertility rates. As per 2011 Census, overall national literacy rate was 73 per cent but while male literacy rate increased from 75.26 per cent in 2001 to 82.14 per cent, female literacy rate increased (at faster rate) from 53.67 per cent to 65.46 per cent, thus showing a gender gap of 16.6 percentage points. Kerala had again the highest literacy rate of 93.91 per cent (2011) among states, followed by Lakshadweep (92.28%) while Mizoram's Serchhip district (98.76%) and Aizal (98.5%) recorded the highest literacy rate among districts. On the other hand, Bihar ranks lowest in literacy rate at 63.82 per cent, followed by Arunachal Pradesh (66.95%). Among the districts, Alirajpur (MP) has the lowest literacy rate (37.22%) followed by Bijapur (41.58%) in Chhattisgarh. Ten states/UTs, including Kerala, Lakshadweep, Mizoram, Tripura, Goa, Daman & Diu, Puducherry, Chandigarh, Delhi, and Andaman and Nicobar Islands, achieved a literacy rate of above 85 per cent in 2011 – Planning Commission had set such a target by 2011–12. Another significant point is that the gap between male-female literacy rate has been reduced to 16.6 per cent points (as against 21.59% points in 2001 Census). State-wise literacy rates may be seen in Table 18:

Table 18

State Literacy Rates in India

State/UT	*2001*	*2011*
Andaman and Nicobar Islands	81.18	86.27
Andhra Pradesh	61.11	67.66
Arunachal Pradesh	54.74	66.95
Assam	64.28	73.18
Bihar	47.53	63.82
Chandigarh	81.76	86.43
Chhattisgarh	65.18	71.04
Dadra and Nagar Haveli	60.03	77.65
Daman and Diu	81.09	87.07
Delhi	81.82	86.34
Goa	82.32	87.40
Gujarat	69.97	79.31
Haryana	68.59	76.64
Himachal Pradesh	77.13	83.78
Jammu and Kashmir	54.46	68.74
Jharkhand	54.13	67.63
Karnataka	67.04	75.6
Kerala	90.92	93.91
Lakshadweep	87.52	92.28
Madhya Pradesh	64.11	70.63
Maharashtra	77.27	82.91
Manipur	68.87	79.85
Meghalaya	63.31	75.48
Mizoram	88.49	91.58
Nagaland	67.11	80.11

Cont'd ...

... Cont'd

Odisha	63.61	73.45
Puducherry	81.49	86.55
Punjab	69.98	76.68
Rajasthan	61.03	67.06
Sikkim	69.68	82.20
Tamil Nadu	73.47	80.33
Tripura	73.66	87.75
Uttar Pradesh	57.36	69.72
Uttarakhand	77.28.	79.63
West Bengal	69.22	77.08
India	65.38	73.0

Source: Censuses of India

Planning Commission targetted to reduce the gender gap in literacy to 10 percentage points only by 2011–12. Further there is fall in the number of illiterate persons by 3.119 crores and during 2001–11 the literates added were 2.177 crore (1.10 cr females and 1.076 cr males). Actually, scheduled castes/tribes have lower literacy rates and higher fertility rates. Moreover, it is also seen that most of poor families, especially in rural areas, have high infant mortality rate, hence they reproduce more children. Further, being assetless/resourceless they see children as economic assets (more hands to work), hence they reproduce more children – which results into a vicious cycle of poverty → large family → poverty.

Population and Health

Similarly, health has a good effect on fertility behaviour. If there is high infant mortality rate (IMR), child mortality rate (CMR) and maternal mortality rate (MMR), there will also be high birth rate correspondingly. In India, MMR is 230 (2008), that is 230 women at every one lakh live births die during delivery due to various causes like anaemia, non-immunization, bleeding, handling of delivery by untrained 'dais' at homes, lack of medical facilities, etc. In developed countries, MMR is as low as 9 (2005). Unfortunately, 70 per cent of pregnant women in India suffer from anaemia – in backward states like Bihar, UP, Assam, Uttarakhand, Chhattisgarh, MP, Jharkhand, Rajasthan, etc. this percentage is higher. Further, as per National Family Health Survey 3 (2005–06), 80 per cent children, 70 per cent pregnant women and 24 per cent adult men suffer from anaemia. Anaemia in children (6–59 months) is highest in Bihar (78%), MP (74.1%), UP (73.9%), Haryana (72.3%), Chhattisgarh (71.2%) and Jharkhand (70.3%). A report of UNICEF (2011) states that 47 per cent of girls in the age group of 11–19 years are underweight in India. Further, 56 per cent of girls (15–19 years) are anaemic (in backward states like Assam it is more – 68%). Second, as per UNICEF report, 40 per cent of India's 243 million adolescents (11–19 yrs) are out of school, 43 per cent girls get married before 18 years (2007–08) – though it decreased from 54 per cent in 1992–93, it remains the eighth highest in the world. As per NFHS3 (2005–06), incidence of malnutrition (underweight) among children under three years declined from 52 per cent in 1992–93 to 46 per cent in 2005–06. But there was wide variation among different states: 27 per cent in Punjab, 29 per cent in Kerala, and J&K, but as high as 60 per cent in MP, 58 per cent in Bihar and 52 per cent in Chhattisgarh. Further, it is also notable that nutritional status of children in middle-income states like Kerala and Tamil Nadu is better than that of higher income states like Maharashtra (40%) and Gujarat (47%). Thus, the government's priority is more significant for reducing malnutrition than the state GDP. Further, North-Eastern states (except Assam) have better nutritional status (despite low per capita GDP) due to access to forest produces, better gender equity and social consciousness. Moreover, it has been confirmed that probability of a child's malnutrition decreases with the improvement of mother's nutritional stocks, her education, age and ante-natal visits but increases if the mother in a poor family is working or if the family is large (Balakrishna and Ravi, 2004). Due to malnutrition, lack of medical facilities and lack of affordability by the parents, IMR in India is as high as 50 per thousand live births (2009) – that is, 13 lakh infants (below one year) die every year – whereas IMR in developed countries like Japan, Sweden, Finland, etc. is, on an average, 3 per thousand.

Further, classical economist Adam Smith (1776), in his book, *An Inquiry into the Nature and Causes of the Wealth of Nations* had rightly asked why some countries are richer than others. He found his answer in the division of labour due to which workers became more productive by honing their skills in more specialized works.

MDGs

It is a well-known fact that in 2000 following 8 Millennium Development Goals (MDGs) were jointly declared by 189 countries under the aegis of UN, to be realized by 2015:

1. Eradicate extreme hunger and poverty – halving the proportion of people living on less than $1 daily and halving malnutrition.
2. Achieve universal primary education – ensuring that all children are able to complete primary education.
3. Promote gender equality and empower women eliminating gender disparity in primary and secondary schooling, preferably by 2005 and not later than 2015.
4. Reduce child mortality – cutting under five death rate by two-thirds.
5. Improve maternal health – reducing the maternal mortality rate by three quarters.
6. Combat HIV/AIDS, malaria and other diseases – halting and beginning to reverse HIV/AIDS and other killer diseases.
7. Ensure environmental stability – cutting by half the proportion of people without sustainable access to safe drinking water and sanitation.
8. Develop a global partnership for development – reforming aid and trade with special treatment for the poorest countries.

While goal numbers 4, 5 and 6 are directly related to plan population growth, other goals are indirectly related to it. However, both at world level and at national level we have not achieved these goals proportionally so far and most likely by 2015 these will not be achieved. As per HDR 2005, less than 20 per cent of the developing countries' population are expected to achieve the goals of reducing child mortality by 2/3. India and China are not in this category. With the present trend, Sub-Saharan Africa would achieve this goal only in 2115 – one hundred years lagging behind! At world level more than 45 per cent of child death occur in 52 countries including India with little progress and most of child deaths occur in poorer sections. That is, there would be 4.4 million additional child deaths – above UN's MDG projection – and there would be a cumulative additional 41 million child deaths between 2005 and 2015. Second, 210 million people would not have access to safe drinking water and 2 billion people will lack access to improved sanitation by 2015. In India, only 21 per cent of rural population have access to improved sanitation facilities and 69 per cent people resort to open defecation (2008) open defecation is 50 per cent even in 2014. Further 84 per cent people in rural India are reported to have access to safe drinking water (WHO and UNICEF, 2010). Third, global poverty would decline from 21 per cent to 14 per cent in 2015 but poverty in Sub-Saharan Africa would increase from 24 per cent to 41 per cent in

2015. As per HDR 2005, 57 countries are in high human development category, 88 in medium human development category and 32 in low human development category. Income inequality varies widely across regions (Gini coefficient 0 value indicates perfect equality, value exceeding 50 shows high degree of inequality and 100 shows perfect inequality): South Asia (33.4), high income OECD (36.8), Central East Europe & CIS (42.8), East Asia & Pacific (52), Latin America & the Caribbean (57.1), World (67) and Sub-Saharan Africa (72.2). Fourth, there would be 670 million people suffering from malnutrition in 2015, 230 million more than if the target were achieved. More than 150 million children up to 5 years of age are under-weight and over 10 million children dying annually. Fifth, with present trend, 46 developing countries would not achieve universal primary education before 2040 and by 2015, there would be 47 million children out of schools. Further, gender disparity in primary education cannot be achieved before 2040. Sixth, globally only 15 per cent of legislative seats are held by women – in countries like Saudi Arabia and UAE women have no representation. But a Muslim country like Malaysia has higher Gender Empowerment Measure (GEM) than Korean Republic, Hungary and Greece. Actually, high income is not a prerequisite to creating opportunities for women. For instance, Rwanda, Costa Rica, South Africa, Mozambique and some other countries with less income have more gender equality than Japan, Italy, France, UK and USA. Seventh, HIV/AIDS has taken an epidemic form in most of Sub-Saharan Africa and affected life expectancy as well as productivity.

In India, Council for Social Development's Social Development Report 2010 has improved its social development index (SDI) – broader than HDI – comprising eight types of indicators to assess multiple deprivation: demographic, economic, education, health, social, basic amenities, social group and gender. Due to such a holistic index, it is not necessary that a country or region with high per capita income will rank high in SDI, e.g. Kerala ranks first among all states of India though it has less per capita income than Punjab (2), Haryana (8), Gujarat (7), Maharashtra (4) and Tamil Nadu (3).

The relationship between socio-economic development, technology and demographic process has been explained by a 'theory of demographic transition'. It states three stages of demographic changes. In the first stage (primitive), death rate is very high due to epidemics, frequent wars, lack of medical facilities, etc. and, therefore, fertility rate is also very high. Thus, high death rate and high birth rate counter balance each other and consequently net population growth rate is very low. Most of Sub-Saharan Africa is still in this stage. In the second stage (intermediate) due to advancement in medical science/technology and better socio-economic development the death sharply declines. However, fertility rate does not decline due to socio-cultural factors (early marriage, preference for son, children as assets, children as social security in old age, etc). Hence, there is high population growth rate. Latin America, South Asia and West Asia are in this stage. In the third stage (modern), both the birth rate and death rate at very low rate get stabilized at the replacement level. Europe and North America are in this stage. In India, Southern states (Kerala, TN, AP and Karnataka) and Goa, Punjab, Himachal Pradesh and Sikkim are now in third stage, and other states of India are in second stage.

III
Consequences of Population Growth

Now we will discuss about the consequences of population growth in future, especially on economic, human resource, health, education, migration and environmental fronts. On the positive side, human population growth is considered as an asset because of new human resource to contribute to economy, culture, politics and society. Julian Lincoln Simon (1981) wrote a famous book *The Ultimate Resource* in which he challenged the apprehension that due to high population growth rate natural resources are running out. Rather, according to him, as a particular resource becomes more scarce, its price rises that creates an incentive for people to discover more of the resource, ration it and eventually develop substitutes. This conception of 'ultimate resource' is not a particular physical object but the capacity for humans to invent and adapt. In its revised edition of 1996, Simon showed that since prices for most raw materials (e.g. copper) fell between 1800 and 1990 (adjusting for wages and inflation), such materials have become less scarce (as low price indicates abundance). He further distinguishes between 'engineering' and 'economic' forecasting – the former estimates the amount of known physical resources and extrapolates the rate of use from current use and subtracts one from the other. However, such focus on proven resources may be useful in only business context but there exists undiscovered sources, sources not yet economically feasible to extract, sources not yet technologically feasible to extract, and unconceived resources that could prove useful but are not yet worthy trying to discover. Hence, he talks of 'economic forecasting' because:

(a) Known reserves are of uncertain amounts;

(b) New resources may become available, either through discovery or via the development of new extraction techniques;

(c) Recycling;
(d) More efficient utilization of existing reserves – now less copper required to pass a given message than a hundred years ago;
(e) Development of economic equivalents, e.g. optic fibre in case of copper for telecommunications.

Thus, in his view, people usually add to a civilization more than they take away. However, if we critically analyse the global and national scenario we find that despite technological innovations in agriculture and availability of foodgrains at aggregate level, individually a large number of persons are not able to purchase bare minimum foodgrains (1.20 billions in world and about 350–450 millions in India) because of lack of purchasing power. Even a substantial number of skilled or semi-skilled labour is unemployed. Further due to limited and highly subdivided land, for redistribution hardly any land is available (with exception in some districts in states like Bihar). Further, there is prevalence of 'law of diminishing return' – growth rate decreasing after the optimal point – pressure of population does have ultimately a negative impact on land – fragmentation. Again there are environmental consequences – due to over-exploitation, underground water table is going further down in Punjab, Haryana, Western UP and other parts of India. Needless to say that green revolution came with high dependence on chemical fertilisers, pesticides, insecticides and weedicides; most of indigenous varieties of seeds have disappeared, and soil has been salinised and desertified. There have also been health hazards (chemicals in food grains/vegetables passing to human bodies). Again, India and other developing countries are losing huge chunks of lands due to soil erosion. About 53 per cent of total land in India is susceptible to environmental degradation.

Further, developed countries use 44 per cent of primary water supply (PWS) for industrial use compared to only 9 per cent in developing countries; developing countries use 85 per cent of PWS for irrigation compared to only 42 per cent in developed countries. Moreover, fresh water (only 0.03% of total world water) is becoming scarce due to dumping of wastes/filths in water bodies or salinity in water of sea/ocean. It has been assessed that due to climate change and 'black carbon' many glaciers in the Himalayas are melting – Himalayan Glaciers provide water to 1.5 billion people in South Asia. By 2025, about two-thirds of countries in the world will face water scarcity due to demand of more water or due to bad quality of available water. India may face water scarcity even earlier than 2020 itself. The optimists are also realizing now that the assumption of fully taking care of additional population by the industrialization is being falsified because of less jobs with high growth rate of industrialization (jobless growth), sacrifice of fertile land for industries, construction of houses, roads, bridges, bus/rail/air terminals and other infrastructures as well as high pollution level due to emission of CFC gases. Industrialization, power houses, automobile emissions and fossil fuel processing/distribution together contribute about 63 per cent of total greenhouse gas emissions. Further, as per NASA, 14 per cent of Arctic Ice (of the size of Turkey/Pakistan) disappeared between 2004 and 2006 due to global warming and the thickness of Arctic Ice reduced from 8–10 metres to 2 metres. In addition, British scientists have found that global temperature could rise by 2–11°C by 2050 (Majumdar, 2010). This will have negative consequences for growing of food crops. Pollution necessarily increases social costs. Needless to say that pure water should have biological oxygen demand (BOD) value of less than 5 PPM (or 3 mg per litre) but Damodar river near Asansol (West Bengal) has BOD of 270 mg per litre and suspended particles are above one lakh mg per litre. Further E coli bacteria accompany total solids (TS), dissolved solids (DS) and suspended solids (SS). The most probable number (MPN) value for potable water ideally is zero per 100 ml of water but Japan recommends less than 50 per 100 ml for class one water while Indian standard for inland surface water recommends up to 5,000 MPN for 100 ml of water. Before Yamuna river enters Delhi, 100 ml of water contains about 7,500 coliform organisms and after receiving wastage discharge from Delhi, MPN reaches to 2.4 crore per 100 ml (Majumdar, 2010). Needless to say, in India, 80 per cent of diseases are water-borne. Further, fossil fuel stocks are depleting and their world prices are regularly going up. India has only 22–23 per cent forest cover against 33 per cent globally. National Committee on Environment Planning estimates that only 12 per cent of India's total land surface is under adequate forest cover. As per IUCN, India lost 2.5 mha of mangrove forests in first 80 years of twentieth century. Hence, problems of fuel wood, water-logging, salinity, infertility or desertification of soil, high winds, less rain, soil erosion, etc. are increasing. High population growth would compound these problems. Hence, India is facing environmental problems in different parts due to five factors:

(a) lack of socio-economic development – poor people have no substitute for firewood in rural areas or no access to safe drinking water and sanitation;

(b) lack of environmental safeguards – no adequate safeguards for air, water, noise, and soil pollution as well as unsafe disposal of wastes;

(c) development-induced displacement, eg, big dams, big airports/ports, expressways, industries, SEZ, power plants etc;

(d) mismatch between natural resources and development – mineral-rich areas like Jharkhand, Odisha and Chattisgarh produce 80 per cent of minerals like iron ores, bauxite and aluminium but are most backward areas;

(e) global environmental crisis (ozone depletion, marine pollution, global warming, nuclear radiation and its impact on imported food items, dumping of wastes from abroad (obsolete machines, equipment, tools and ships for dismantling at ports like Alang), CFC gas emissions (especially due to automobile technology, deforestation due to mining and exports of minerals etc.).

Undoubtedly, the annual per capita consumption of electricity in US (in 2002) was 10,458 kwh, compared to 1484 kwh in China and 569 kwh in India then – an average person in developed countries uses 200 times more energy than a person in developing countries. On per capita basis, US emits 20 times more CO_2 than India, yet it was emphasized in the UN Conference on Climate Change at Copenhagen (2009) and at Cancun (2010) that on cumulative basis, the emission of carbon gases in China and India (the two largest countries in the world) is substantial and, therefore, they were convinced to cut down their emissions: China committed to cut down by 45–50 per cent and India by 20–25 per cent. Furthermore, there may also be drinking water problem due to population pressure in different parts of the world because of 'draw down effect' of the water tables, resulting into arsenic oxides and arsensus acid (soluble in water), as prevailing in parts of West Bengal (Majumdar, 2010). It is apprehended that third world war would be fought on water issue. Needless to add that historically the greatest advances in longevity and mortality reduction have come from better public health facilities like modern drainage and sewerage systems, improved drinking water system and sanitation facilities (not from treatment of individual disease) (Virmani, 2007).

Further, it is notable that many developed countries are dumping industrial, radioactive and electronic wastes in developing countries which import these wastes due to less stock of plastic, lead, zinc, etc. as well as to provide jobs through recycling. Since 69-member Organisation of African Unity (OAU) resolved not to import such wastes, Indian sub-continent is the preferred dumping ground for such wastes. Alang in Gujarat is the biggest ship-breaking yard where old ships (with thousands of tons of asbestos and other carcinogenic toxic substances) are dumped by developed countries (that do not allow such pollution in their own countries) due to demand for employment of a large number of persons, though with huge costs in terms of health hazards and environmental pollution. That is why Brundtlandt Commission Report 'Our Common Future' (1987) rightly talked of sustainable development as 'the development that meets the needs of the present generation without compromising the ability of future generations to meet their own needs'. It focused on population, food security, ecosystems, energy, industry, and urban settlements. Later, Rio Declaration (1992) talked of 'developmental and environmental policies' though Stockholm Conference in 1972 had focused on 'environmental policies' only (more appropriate). In Kyoto Protocol (1997), several nations agreed for Clean Development Mechanism (CDM) and asked for reduction in emissions of carbon dioxide, methane, nitrous oxide and other Green House Gases to 1990 level by 2000 – a target of 5 per cent reduction from 1990 level by 2012. But the US did not sign it. Later, Inter-Governmental Panel on Climate Change (IPCC) also held people responsible for climate change and recommended for 'polluter pays' principle.

Another significant consequence of high population growth is mass migration from rural areas to urban areas in search of employment because Indian agriculture with 'disguised employment' (Gunnar Myrdal) cannot sustain more people. Thus, there occurs rural-urban migration due to 'push factors' more than due to 'pull factors'. Urban population in India is expected to increase from 28 per cent to 40 per cent in 2015. But metropolitan cities are unable to sustain more people. Two-thirds of Mumbai and Kolkata and half of Delhi and ¼th of entire urban population in India are already living in slums. In the whole world one billion people live in slums and this figure will increase to two billion in 2030. In India, NSSO (in 2002) identified 51,688 urban slums, of these 50 per cent are notified slums and in 84 per cent of such notified slums main source of water supply is tap. But in Bihar no slum gets tap water supply; in UP, Gujarat and Chhattisgarh, less than 35 per cent of slums get water supply. Further, 44 per cent of non-notified slums do not have a drainage system and only 15 per cent of notified slums have a drainage system. Again half of the non-notified slums do not have a latrine and 17 per cent of the notified slums do not have a latrine. In 2001, 75 million people lived in urban slums in India and this number increased to 93 million in 2011. Further, more migration to urban areas has negative effect on transport, roads, railways, water supply, foods, sanitation, health, education, housing and so on. Further, due to mass migration demographic composition of a city changes and there are several consequences. Politically, the local and insider 'sons (and daughters) of soil' raise vociferously the issue of creation of overcrowding, dirt, crime, unemployment etc against the outsiders/immigrants – 'us' versus 'them', e.g. in Mumbai, Shiv Sena and Maharashtra Navnirman Sena (MNS) have been succeeding in elections on this plank for a few decades. Thus insider-outsider conflicts take different forms (mostly violent) to protest against the large scale immigration. While women migrate primarily for marriage and secondarily for jobs, men migrate primarily for jobs. In India, 41 per cent of people migrate for jobs. At present, maximum migrants to cities come from Bihar where 42 per cent people live below poverty line and there was hardly any worthwhile investment in agriculture till 2005. As per a report by Mckinsey Global Institute, India requires capital investment of $1,200 billion in her cities for massive migration over the next two decades (Singh, 2011).

Further more population has a serious bearing on public health system. At present, India has just one doctor for every 1700 persons whereas globally doctor-population ratio is 1.5:1000. Even developing countries like Thailand, Brazil, Singapore, South Korea, China and Egypt have much better ratio than India in this regard. This may be seen in Table 19.

Table 19

Doctor-Population Ratio in Selected Countries

S. No.	*Countries*	*Doctor-Population Ratio*
1.	Germany	1:296
2	US	1:350
3	UK	1:469
4	Thailand	1:500
5	Japan	1:606
6	Singapore	1:714
7	Brazil	1:844
8	South Korea	1:951
9	China	1:1063
10	Egypt	1:1484
11	India	1:1700
12	Pakistan	1:1923
13	Somalia	1:10,000
14	World	1:606

Source: Medical Council of India, Undergraduate Education Working Group Note, *The Times of India*, 7 March 2011.

Table 20

Pros and Cons of Population Growth

Dimensions	*Positive Effects*	*Negative Effects*
(a) Human	(i) 'ultimate resource' – human capital (ii) new ideas from more persons	(i) more numbers create conflicts (ii) privacy is disturbed
(b) Economic	(i) necessity is the mother of invention (ii) more hands for work (iii) division of labour leads to specialization – skills (iv) more demand gives better prices to producers	(i) more mouths to feed – more poverty (ii) increase in costs of nourishment, education, health, sanitation (iii) more demand leads to scarcity/overuse of resources (iv) mass migration as a pressure on city's infrastructures (v) wages decline & unemployment rises
(c) Social	(i) 'shared space' increases (ii) unity in diversity – organic solidarity leads to impartiality (iii) quantity changes into quality – more justice to deprived sections (iv) more social capital (networking)	(i) homogeneity disappears – mechanical solidarity is disturbed (ii) struggle for survival of the fittest increases (iii) authority of elders is eroded (iv) joint family gives way to nuclear family – social security to widows, old, disabled and ill persons disappears

Cont'd ...

... Cont'd

(d)	Environmental	(i) impetus to use new/different resources – plastic, rubber (ii) tendency to recycle, reuse (iii) new technology leads to less use of natural resources – wireless, satellite phone/TV/radio (iv) experiences from new movements and new resources lead to prudent use of resources — sprinkler irrigation method in place of flood irrigation — bucket-mug method of bath in place of shower	(i) limited 'carrying capacity' of earth – productivity of land, water, oil, minerals, metals decreases (ii) more use of water leads to falling down of water table, salinity – and desertification of soil, poison in water due to over-pumping (iii) third world war looms large on water issue-damming of rivers for irrigation & water supply to cities leads to displacement (iv) more people, more pollution/waste (v) land cannot be stretched, so new food habits have negative consequences (vi) more demand for fuel wood leads to deforestation that leads to soil erosion and less rain
(e)	Political	(i) pressure groups for making democracy work (ii) diversified representation has a sense of belongingness	(i) political instability (ii) more ethnic, caste, communal conflicts, often with political motive

Further, as per Planning Commission, India is short of six lakh doctors, 10 lakh nurses and two lakh dental surgeons. On the other hand, about 60,000 Indian physicians are working in countries like US, UK, Canada and Australia alone. Medical Council of India (MCI), has assessed that, with 330 medical colleges in India at present with an intake of about 35,000 students, by 2031 there would be the short fall of 9.54 lakh doctors in India in order to have one doctor for 1000 persons. Further, as per MCI, there is a shortage of 6340 teachers in existing medical colleges. Needless to say that medical facility (especially doctors and nurses) cannot be placed as and when required – it takes minimum six years of gestation period (including internship) for starting medical practice by a new doctor. The pros and cons of population growth may be seen in Table 20.

IV
Family Planning

As early as 1939 (at Tripuri Congress), Subhash Chanda Bose had expressed his concern: 'With regard to the long term programme of a free India, the first problem to tackle is that of our increasing population' (Molekhi, 2011). In the following year, a population panel linked population stabilization to socio-economic development. However, in free India, Jawaharlal Nehru was not much worried on this issue: 'a large population is the greatest source of power for any nation,' he once told JRD Tata. In 1952, however, India became the first country to launch national programme on family planning as a part of First Five Year Plan. National Family Planning Commission observed that, being a sensitive issue, family planning should not be imposed on people but recommended for awareness generation and health care of mothers and children by the state. In first two Five Year Plans (1951–61) India practiced a 'Clinical Approach' with the establishment of clinics (4165 clinics by the end of second plan) in order to provide birth control measures for 'reducing its birth rate to levels commensurate with its developmental aspirations'. But this approach could not succeed due to lack of mass awareness. Hence, in 1962–69, 'Extension Approach' was adopted with extension workers as facilitators or catalysts. It was a health-based, incentive-driven, time-bound, target-oriented camp-approach. Later in 1969, in view of the advice of UN Evaluation Mission, India adopted 'Cafeteria Approach' by providing assistance on a wide range of choices for birth control methods. Then mass sterilization camps were organized. In 1971, Medical Termination of Pregnancy Act was passed where, with certain conditions, abortion was legalized. In 1972–73, a total of 31,22,000 sterilizations were performed but in 1973–74 it declined to 7 lakhs due to criticism (Majumdar, 2010).

Now we will discuss about the long-term and short-term measures to reduce population growth. On 16 April 1976, National Population Policy placed (but not discussed) in Lok Sabha, talked of:

(a) reducing the rate of population growth will have to be treated as top national priority and commitment;

(b) to wait for education and economic development to bring about a drop in fertility is not a practical solution; and

(c) population control must play a crucial role in the movement towards economic independence and social transformation.

During the second half of emergency (1976) in just nine months through coercive 'target approach', eight million sterilizations (6 million vasectomies) were done – half of that in the whole world. Then, under the leadership of Sanjay Gandhi, family planning and afforestation (for environment protection) were given topmost priority by the central and state governments as well as district administrations. Though he had a foresight, wrong strategies (by force) and communication techniques were adopted. Subsequently, during Janata Party government at the centre, family planning was fully ignored though during that period China adopted one-child policy (1979) by which it reduced fertility rate from 6 to 2. In 1992, family planning was transferred to Panchayati Raj system and in 1996 government abolished method-specific contraceptive targets and replaced it with target-free approach. After a long interval, National Population Policy 2000 talked of 'voluntary and informed choice' of citizens, target-free approach, improved family welfare services, incentives to individuals, rewarding panchayats for universalizing small family norms, Balika Samriddhi Yojana (₹ 500 incentive) to promote care of girl child, maternity benefit scheme (₹ 500 to a mother of first child after 19 years of age), family welfare linked health insurance (₹ 5,000), better choice of contraceptives, safe abortion, freezing the number of Parliamentarians at 1971 census till 2026, strict enforcement of Child Marriage Restraint Act (1929) and Pre-Natal Diagnostic Techniques Act (1994), etc. It focused on improved family welfare services in high fertility rate in states like Bihar, UP, MP, Rajasthan, Odisha, Jharkhand, Chhattisgarh and Uttarakhand. It also talked of addressing wider issues like reproductive and child health (RCH) and partnership between government, industry and NGOs. During 1981–2001, MTP cases doubled from 3.88 lakh to 7.23 lakh and about a quarter of such cases were followed by sterilization and additional 15 per cent were given IUD – thus, legalizing abortion has been successful and emancipatory. However, the bitter truth remains that there is no adequate focus on awareness generation, motivation, and providing better services of family welfare by Union, state and local governments and administrative machinery since 1978. Hardly any wall writing for publicity is seen in the last 30 years or so; no ads on TV, radio, cinema, internet, etc.; no public debates and no priority in educational institutions. As a result, couple protection rate is not more than half. Like China, we should have planned birth programme as a part of Indian way of life. Not only first child should be ensured to be born at a matured age of about 25 to 32 years but also there should be sufficient spacing between two births because 33 per cent of births in India occur at the interval of 24 months only.

Second, education (especially women's education) plays a major role in adapting small family norm in following ways:

(i) late marriages, especially of girls;

(ii) late employment leading to late marriage;

(iii) higher aspirations for social mobility;

(iv) attitudinal changes towards small family;

(v) tendency to migrate for new employment or to change present job or to have spouse from wider options;

(vi) questioning of derogatory customs of early marriage, preference for son, children as assets, children as gift of god, girl as 'parayadhan' (other's wealth), etc.

However, there is a very high rate of dropouts by 10th standard, especially of girls, though various studies, including one by World Bank, have confirmed that ten years' schooling of girls has a positive effect for small family norm. Needless to say that girls' performance in school/college education is better in recent years in India. Right to free and compulsory education (Act of 2009) till elementary level is significant achievement since 1 April 2010 but minimum level of learning is not satisfactory, as even those studying in standard 6th are not able to read, write and do simple arithmetic in different parts of country, as Pratham has found. Further, Gross Enrolment Ratio in higher education is only 13 per cent, whereas it is 50 per cent in developed countries as a whole. Further, we have not been able to fully check early marriages, especially in northern and western India. This has to be restrained more through social consciousness – generation than just by enforcing the law as, unlike China, India is a democratic nation. Due to lack of awareness only 56 per cent of currently married women use contraceptives and the highest adoption rate of female sterilization (67%) is among women with three children having two sons – that is, the custom of son preference is prevalent. Again, usually the wife gets sterilized, not the husband – some sort of gender-bias exists in family planning too. Further, it is an established fact that autonomous status of women, as in south India, east India and south-east Asia, due to rice cultivation with higher women's work participation rate, has a positive role in reducing fertility rate (Balakrishnan, 2011). Therefore, as Kothari Commission (1964–66) had recommended, public spending on education should be 6 per cent of GDP in India – at present it is 3–4 per cent only in India. However, the quality of education at all levels is also to be ensured and it should be more productive and job-oriented in order to have a better planned family. As Economic Survey (2010–11: 331) perceptively remarks: 'While a skilled and trained and healthy young population with the right type of education is an asset, an uneducated or ill-educated, unskilled, unhealthy and unemployed population could lead to a demographic disaster. Reaping the demographic dividend needs a vision, a long-term plan, and bold decisions. While the National Skill Development Mission is a step in the right direction, much more is required both in terms of achievements and speed.'

Third, reproductive health is to be improved on priority. Despite National Rural Health Mission (with ASHA activist), which was started on 12 April 2005 in the entire country, the pregnant women's anaemia is to be tackled drastically by fortifying milk and flour, facility of mobile health care in rural areas, awareness –generation, better wages in rural areas under MNREGA to have better purchasing power, etc. China, Sri Lanka and Cuba have done wonderful in rural public health, hygiene and sanitation. We may adapt their best practices. Like China, spending on health should be more than 5 per cent of GDP; at present India spends hardly 2 per cent of GDP on health. National Health Policy 1983 had talked of 'health for all' by 2000 but it could not be realized even after passing of one decade and five years from the target year. There should be synergy between National Health Policy (2002), National Rural Health Mission (2005) and National Population Policy (2000).

Fourth, some kind of consensus should emerge among all political parties for two-child norm. Rhetoric of caste/religious identity politics should be rationally discarded in national interest. More incentives should be given to parents of only one child. China has been able to implement one child norm but India needs to be made a more functioning democracy like Scandinavian countries to reach replacement level, as southern states of India have achieved it. Every political party, therefore, should mandatorily keep family welfare in its manifesto in clear terms – 'putting the small family first'.

Fifth, since poverty has a very close association with large family, hence all the poor segments (irrespective of caste, religion, region) should be given top priority in development policy for self-employment. Sustainable credit and subsidy should be transparently disbursed without any cumbersome process. Status of all workers employed in unorganized sector should be improved in a targeted and time-bound manner because development is the best contraceptive. Food security is also to be ensured in rural and urban areas by revamping public distribution system (PDS) for all sections of population but there is no consensus so far between government and other stakeholders on two counts: how much food grains should be given per month; second, to cover below poverty line families only or also above poverty line families. It should take into account minimum required calorie per head per month for all strata.

Sixth, private sector should be encouraged for 'corporate social responsibility' for 100 per cent coverage of its employees under family welfare services and motivation for single child norm. Such enterprises should take care of health and nutrition of their employees' spouses and children too. They should spend about 1 per cent of their profit on family welfare. However, it is a bitter fact that public private partnership (PPP) model is less successful in rural areas/agriculture sector than in industrial sector/urban area.

Seventh, recruitment policy in public sector should provide incentives like extra increments, priority for housing, more maternity/paternity leave, more tuition fee for the child if the employee actually ensured not more than one child till retirement.

Eighth, Population Stabilization Fund in India is practically defunct but it has rightly suggested to have a scheme of one lakh rupees as social security at old age to benefit couples opting for sterilization just after one child. If properly implemented, it will address the problems of financial insecurity among old age poor, lead to a stable population and be economical to the nation on opportunity cost principle. If one lakh couples every year in each of UP, Bihar, MP and Rajasthan (with high fertility rates) are sterilized (on the basis of incentive of ₹ 1 lakh) the nation will save ₹ 15 lakh per couple (cost of upbringing till 20 years) or ₹ 60,000 crore over the next 20 years in these four states.

Ninth, there has been a linkage between segments of population and job reservation, especially job reservation for other backward classes. There was also a strong demand for conducting OBC census which was conducted after the general census. Such political consideration often leads to impetus for higher fertility rate and no concern for planned births and parenthood in rural areas and it also decelerates development (because number finally matters in job reservation policy). It would be just and appropriate (in view of many sociologists) if such tension is avoided and other parameters are evolved for recruitment – like some weightage (say five marks) for OBC candidates so that its negative effect on population growth may be avoided.

Finally, it is imperative now to realize that various natural resources are not unlimited. As per 2011 Census (provisional), population density in India has increased from 325 to 382 persons per sq km. Delhi, with 11,297 persons per sq km, tops the list among states/UTs and among districts, north-east district of Delhi has the highest density of 37,346 persons per sq km. Due to overuse of groundwater for irrigation, especially in Punjab, Haryana, and Western UP, water table is falling down rapidly. As a recent study of three villages in Amritsar district of Punjab shows disturbing trends (Sarkar, 2011):

(i) direct control over water resource enhances the output; water buyers have lower yield for both wheat and rice crops;

(ii) water is exchanged with farm labour and buyer of water is expected to do all kinds of labour as and when required by the water sellers;

(iii) bilateral bargaining is subjected to personal affinities and kinship ties, thus degree of exploitation varies from buyer to buyer;

(iv) water has become more significant input in agriculture than the land; if there is no functioning tubewell, bargaining power of landowner and the value of land declines;

(v) since cost of deepening of tubewell is very high, small and medium farmers are unable to do so and so they lease out their land to big landowners;

(vi) water buyers provide all inputs like seeds, fertilisers, insecticides (except water) in full and the water seller takes half of the produce – adverse terms of production.

Therefore, there is need to develop such varieties of seeds of different crops which consume less water and mature earlier (short term), especially sowing of oilseeds, pulses and maize should be promoted. Further, due to increasing population density in northern states, most of the traditional natural resources like ponds, forests, grazing grounds, etc. have been encroached upon by different social strata for purposes like housing, agriculture, etc. thus, 'shared public spaces' have been converted into 'exclusive private spaces' for selfish gains depriving the masses of use of the common property resources (CPRs). Now there should be more focus on sustainable agriculture than on industrialization through more public investment in various agricultural infrastructure/inputs like irrigation, seeds, electricity, roads, cold storage, market linkage, pest management, extension, etc. Actually, strategies for 'green development' are called for, especially developing short-term high yielding varieties suitable to agro-climatic regions of India, green manures, bio-fertilizers, indigenous natural pesticides/insecticides (neem leaves, cakes, oil), etc. There should be better and holistic coordination and interdependence between eight national missions, namely Jawaharlal Nehru National Solar Mission, National Mission on Energy Conservation and Efficiency, National Mission on Strategic Knowledge for Climate Change, National Mission for Sustainable Himalayan Ecosystem, National Water Mission, Green India Mission, National Mission on Sustainable Habitat & National Mission for Sustainable Agriculture.

Thus, we may conclude that poverty is both cause and effect of high population growth. However, it would be unreasonable to wait for socio-economic development, education, sanitation, health, etc. to be in perfect state. Rather a genuine drive for planned birth and parenthood (not population control with force) is to be launched without any loss of time because a lower population growth rate would be conducive for better socio-economic development, both in the short term and long term. Regarding population growth, neither an extremist critical view nor an extremist optimist view is helpful. Rather, a pragmatic and neutralist view, based on experience and scientific knowledge, needs to be taken considering the long term limits of natural resources, social equity, sustainability of eco-friendly development, restraining the culture of consumerism, creating the skilled and culturally conscious human resource, and optimum well-being of the people. Actually the capitalist mode of production has inherent contradictions, hence it needs to be changed suitably. Only then northern states, with higher fertility rates, would be able to catch up with the southern states of India, especially Kerala and Tamil Nadu. It is necessary, therefore, that the Union, state and local governments, civil society, NGOs, individual activists, corporate sector and society at large should join hands together to accept the challenge of both poverty and high population growth rate at the same time in a dynamic, critical and interdependent manner.

References

Balakrishna, R. and C. Ravi (2004) 'Malnutrition in India', *Economic and Political Weekly*, 39 (7), pp. 671–76.

Balakrishnan, Rajiv (ed.) (2011) *Demographic Transition: An Asian Perspective*, Konark Publishers, New Delhi.

GOI (2007) *National Family Health Survey 3–2005–6*, Vol. I, International Institute for Population Sciences, Mumbai.

— (2011) *Economic Survey 2010–11*, Ministry of Finance, Department of Economic Affairs, New Delhi.

Haq, E. (2007) *Sociology of Population in India*, Macmillan India Ltd, New Delhi.

Majumdar, P.K. (2010) *Fundamentals of Demography*, Rawat Publications, Jaipur.

MCI (2011) 'Undergraduate Education Working Group Note', *The Times of India*, 7 March.

Molekhi, Pankaj (2011) 'Population Explosion or Celebration?', *The Economic Times*, 30 January.

Sarkar, Anindita (2011) 'Socio-Economic Implications of Depleting Ground-water Resource in Punjab', *Economic and Political Weekly*, 12–18 February, pp. 59–66.

Simon, Julian L. (1981) *The Ultimate Resource*, Princeton University Press, Princeton, NJ (2nd ed. 1996).

Singh, Pallavi (2011) 'More Population Means More Migration', *The Economic Times*, 30 January.

Smith, Adam (1776) *An Inquiry into the Nature and Causes of the Wealth of Nations*, W. Strahan and T. Cadell, London.

Subbarao, D. (2011) 'Rural Prosperity is Fuelling Food Inflation', *The Economic Times*, 28 February.

UNDP (2001) *Human Development Report 2001*, Palgrave Macmillan, New York.

— (2005) *Human Development Report 2005*, Palgrave Macmillan, New York.

UNICEF (2011) *State of the World's Children*, Geneva.

Virmani, Arvind (2007) 'The Sudoku of Growth, Poverty and Malnutrition: Policy Implications for Lagging States', Working Paper No. 2/2007, Planning Commission of India, New Delhi.

WHO and UNICEF (2010) *Progress on Sanitation and Water – 2010 Update*, Geneva.

Zachariah, K.C. and S. Irudaya Rajan (2011) 'Demographic Transition in Kerala and Tamil Nadu', in Rajiv Balakrishnan (ed.), *Demographic Transition: An Asian Perspective*, Konark Publishers, New Delhi.

3

Food Security

Critical Issues and Perspectives

When the food prices have been spiralling in India and the world, the issue of food security has become more topical. Food security is not merely for physical survival but for the complete well-being of all human beings. Second, while a massive food production at the national/state level or full buffer stock in godowns even at the district level may be a necessary condition, it is not a sufficient one for food security that requires purchasing power of a household, on the one hand, and just distribution within the household, on the other. Here we will discuss the global scenario, national scenario, causes and consequences of food crisis, and policy implications in the five sections given below.

Introduction

The National Commission on Farmers, in its first report (2004), points out five basic factors for the agrarian crisis: unfinished agenda in land reform, quantity and quality of water, technology fatigue, access, adequacy and timeliness of institutional credit, and opportunities for assured and remunerative marketing. The worst affected in the agrarian crisis are small and marginal farmers, landless labourers and women. That is why, long back in 1946 at Noakhali, Mahatma Gandhi had remarked perceptively: 'To the hungry, God is bread.' After the Second World War, US President Roosevelt talked of four types of freedom: freedom of expression, freedom of worship, freedom from fear, and freedom from hunger. Even Jawaharlal Nehru had announced in 1947: 'Everything else can wait, but not agriculture.' However, India did not accord the priority to agriculture (in terms of investment) which it deserved. Needless to say that hunger and starvation are violations of fundamental human rights in the Universal Declaration of Human Rights (1948). Right to food is a birthright of every individual, group, family or community. The Supreme Court of India has deliberated in several judicial decisions that right to food is an integral part of right to life enshrined in Article 21 of the Indian Constitution.

Wheat, rice and maize are three major cereals in the world. Rice is preferred in Asia, maize in America and Africa, and wheat in Europe and Australia. In India, maize, rice and wheat are eaten at present with difference in regional/cultural preferences – rice in south and east, and wheat and maize in north and west. Robert Zeigler (D.G., International Rice Research Institute, Manila) once said: 'In Asia, rice has cultural, social and, in many places, even a religious role, so it carries much more psychological weight.' In 2008, 423 million tonnes of world rice production was estimated. Asia produced 91 per cent of world's rice in 2007 but a 4 per cent decrease in global rice trade was projected in 2008. Unfortunately, the prices of both rice and wheat spiralled in 2006–07 and 2007–08. The Indians, like most of the Asians, spend almost half of their weekly budget on food – double that in the West.

In fact, massive food production at the macro level is a necessary but not sufficient condition for ensuring actual food security at the micro level. Food security connotes adequate food entitlement of every person at any given time and place, from local to global levels, not only for his or her mere physical survival but complete well-being, intra-household just distribution of food with minimum nutrition, and absorption by the body for a healthy life. The World Bank has defined food security as 'access by all people at all times to sufficient food for active and healthy life' (Guha-Khasnobis et al., 2008) but we require a 'sustainable food security'.

> According to M.S. Swaminathan (2008), 'Sustainable food security involves physical, economic and social access to a balanced diet and clean drinking water to every child, woman and man in the country. For achieving physical access, production and productivity of major crops should go up, so that there is a proper match between demand and supply. For economic access, there is a need for adequate purchasing power, which, in turn, can be achieved through work and income security. Social access involves attention to the gender, class and caste dimensions of food security.'

However, the experience of the Green Revolution in agriculture shows that India's focus only on major crops like wheat and paddy led to the neglect of common people's food crops (considered minor crops) like *jowar, bajra, ragi, mandua, sawan, kodo,* maize and barley that require less irrigation but mature faster than wheat and paddy. Further these foodgrains are more nutritious. Needless to emphasize that the food security paradigm has changed on four scores since the World Food Conference (1974): first, from the availability of food at the global level to the national, sub-national, household and finally to the individual level; second, a change from 'food first' perspective to 'livelihood' perspective; third, a change from physical access to economic and social access as well; fourth, a change from objective indicators (rising income leading to increase in purchasing power, lower prices of foodgrains leading to better consumption of foodgrains) to subjective perceptions (changing attitudes, food habits, gender and age equity in the household, etc.). In fact, the question of food security, in totality, involves various aspects at various levels of a human society with corresponding necessary conditions at a given time: viz., individual, intra-household, household, sub-national and national levels. It has been shown in Table 1.

However, in the present globalized or globalizing era, the problem of food security crosses the national boundaries because of world trade of food-grains due to WTO's Agreement on Agriculture. Sometimes, domestic compulsions affect the global food situation, and at other times, the global food situation affects the domestic food situation.

II
Global Scenario

If we look at the global scenario of food security, the following facts are notable (Guha-Khasnobis et al., 2008; Streitfeld and Bradsher, 2008; Brown, 2008; Sachs, 2008; Varma, 2008):

(a) A large number of people in the world are food-insecure, especially in Sub-Saharan Africa and South Asia – 840 million people worldwide are malnourished or chronically food-insecure (about 30 per cent of world population).

(b) About 2.8 million children and 3 lakh women die annually in developing countries, especially in Sub-Saharan Africa and South Asia.

(c) The World Food Summit and the Millennium Development Goals of halving the number/share of the undernourished people by 2015 are nowhere close to being achieved as the

Table 1

Aspects, Levels of Availability and Necessary Conditions of Food Security

Aspect	*Level of Availability*	*Necessary Conditions*
Food production and productivity (general physical access)	National, State and District levels	Right to agri-inputs – Inputs' availability like seeds, fertilizers, pesticides, electricity for irrigation, institutional credit, minimum support price, delivery and storage agencies, pucca road and adequate transport, and market linkage
Food availability (specific physical access)	Block or Panchayat level	Availability of foodgrains in local market or public distribution system shops or cooperatives or panchayat stores (grain banks)
Food accessibility (economic access – purchasing power)	Household level	Right to work and income – Minimum wages for increasing purchasing power of the labourers, better remunerative prices for agricultural produce to farmers, foodgrains at cheaper rates
Food consumption for well-being (social access)	Intra-household (age, gender, sickness, disability) level	Right to food to all – gender-consciousness, sound health care for growing children, working adults, lactating/pregnant women, aged, infirm and ill persons – just distribution of food
Food absorption (healthy life/well-being)	Individual level (physiological)	Safe drinking water, hygiene, clean environment, primary health care

number of thc undernourished has been reduced only by a million by now.

(d) Though food production increased to 2.3 billion tonnes in 2007 and world cereal output has tripled since 1961, grain stocks are at the lowest levels in three decades (due to the hoarding of foodgrains by some governments in countries like the US, the Philippines, India, Japan or more consumption due to population growth and better purchasing power) and price rise has continuously been high, leading to global food crisis.

(e) American corn and soybean farmers suffered from too much rain while Australian wheat farmers have suffered from drought for three years. In America, due to late sowing of corn, germination was less and later damage was also caused due to heat; in Australia, due to no rain many farmers could not sow wheat in time.

(f) Climate change is showing negative consequences for food security; e.g. droughts and floods recur in some countries; if the Antarctica ice melts, the sea level will rise by 7 metres and Bangladesh would lose 40 per cent of its rice land; two-thirds of the Chinese glaciers will disappear by 2060; Gangotri glacier in India is also melting; Bangladesh and West Bengal would lose Sunderbans and marine biodiversity.

(g) Rapid exploitation of natural resources and a six-fold rise in population during 1830–2005 (6.5 billion) have also negative consequences for food security – further increase in per capita income from 2,000 dollars in 1950 to 6,000 dollars in 2000, in some way or the other, led to more food consumption due to better purchasing power and more demand for food.

(h) Trans-National Companies (TNCs) are doing a highly profitable business. Monsanto (US) and Syngenta (Europe) have pushed in their genetically modified (GM) seeds, which usually have crop failures and pest attacks in developing countries like India. Syngenta earned a net profit of 1.1 billion dollars in 2007. Similarly, fertilizer TNCs like Potash Corp (of Canada) and Yara (of Norway) made a huge profit of one billion dollars each in 2007. Other fertilizer TNCs like Mosaic and Agrium (of US) and TCL (of Israel) made a profit of half a billion dollars in 2007.

(i) In 2005, according to the FAO, due to food shortage at domestic level, 207 out of 216 countries in the world had to import wheat and 170 had to import rice from international markets; at the global level, FAO estimates, 'each year hunger robs 46 million years of productive disability-free life from people valued at over 16 billion dollars.'

(j) On 3 June 2008, at the FAO Summit in Rome, UN Secretary General Ban Ki-Moon highlighted that the world food production needs to be increased by 50 per cent by 2030 to meet the rising food demand. He called for a support of 1.7 billion dollars to low-income countries with seeds and other agricultural support but also warned against food export restrictions imposed by some countries leading to distortion of market prices.

III
National Scenario

Though a huge population in India is dependent on agriculture, its contribution to Gross Domestic Product has been declining over the years because of less public investment and under-employment. As per FAO, the population depending on agriculture in India will touch around 57.84 crores in 2010 and then start declining slowly to reach 57.47 crores in 2020 (from around 55.74 crores in 2000). Further, the employment in agriculture, being 60 per cent of the economically active population in 2000, will decline to 55 per cent in 2010 and further to 50 per cent in 2020. Thus, FAO projects India's population to 115.22 crores in 2010 and 127.22 crores in 2020 (Chakrabarti and Dutta, 2000). As per Census of 2011, India's population is 121 crores. Naturally, it will have implications on food security in India.

Various studies have pointed out that in India, even if the total food production of a small/marginal farmer is not sufficient for family consumption for a year, he has to sell a part of it in the market due to the monetized economy in order to meet his various needs like purchase of utensils, clothes, social obligations, health and education – that is, there exists a 'compulsive involvement', to use Krishna Bhardwaj's term (1974), with the market. Thus, almost all the landholders, while sowing their crops, take into account this very factor. Second, they also grow cash crops like mustard, rapeseed, sugarcane, spices, peas and potato which are more remunerative than the foodgrains. Third, while sowing crops they also consider that they have to pay wages to the labourers on time. Earlier, for the purpose of wage payment, coarse grains used to be sown, but nowadays the trend has changed as the labourers are not willing to accept coarse grains; rather, cash is paid after selling foodgrains or cash crops. Further, food habits of the farmers themselves have also changed substantially and, therefore, they do not like to grow coarse grains like barley, maize, *madua, sawan, kodo* and *ragi* (though these are nutritious). Fourth, most of the farmers also take into account expected social obligations like festivals, religious ceremonies, marriage and birth ceremonies and debt repayment schedule while planning their cropping pattern.

The difference in the attitude of the 'net sellers' and that of the petty farmers at the time of sale of foodgrains is that while the former keep most of their produce in store after the harvest and sell 90 per cent of the marketable surplus later in lean season (Paush–Magh, i.e. December–January) when the prices rise due to more demand and less supply, the latter have to sell most of the surplus or, out of necessity, even the annual stock just after the harvest, in order to meet their non-food requirements like medicine, education, clothing, house repair and social functions, at cheaper rates due to more supply of foodgrains than the demand in *Chaitra* (April–May). During the lean season, there is no adequate employment opportunity in agriculture and the petty farmers purchase foodgrains at a higher rate – i.e. they become 'net buyers'. Then even the public distribution system shops do not cope up with the demand more because of corruption and malfunctioning than because of non-availability of foodgrains in the government stock.

Consequently, either the area under food crops ('acreage response') or the yield of food crops per acre ('yield response') is to be increased to cope up with the demand of the high population growth. In order to ensure adequate food production, the necessary condition is ensuring adequate inputs in time. It transpires from discussions with many villagers in UP and Bihar that subsidy in seeds, fertilizers, pesticides, irrigation and credit contributes to about 50 per cent of the increase in production (but partly siphoned off) and, on the other hand, better remunerative prices contribute to 30 per cent of the increase, while an increase in the wages of the labour will affect the production about 20 per cent. Most farmers cannot afford costly inputs and high wages; hence, agriculture has become a loss-making activity of production. India has been providing subsidies on seeds, fertilizers, irrigation (electricity charges), crop loans, etc. But the Government has, under pressure from the World Trade Organization's Agreement on Agriculture, reduced the subsidy on fertilizers, though in comparison with the developed countries the subsidy on Indian agriculture is very low. Though the western nations pressurize developing countries like India to reduce such subsidy, they provide huge agricultural subsidies to their own farmers. For instance, total subsidy provided to Indian agricultural sector by the government is only ₹ 4,500 crores or about one billion dollars while the same in the Organisation of Economic Cooperation and Development (OECD) countries is 362 billion dollars (Sharma, 2002). A comparison of India and some developed countries regarding such subsidy per hectare is shown in Table 2.

Table 2

A Comparison of Agricultural Subsidy in Different Countries

Country	*Amount of Subsidy (per ha) ($)*
European Union	1,016
Japan	6,915
New Zealand	317
US	184
Canada	167
India	17.8

Source: S. Sharma (2002)

However, due to subsidized fertilizers, many farmers use more chemical fertilizers and this trend has to be curtailed by awareness generation among the farmers about the health hazards these fertilizers cause and soil degradation. Rather, organic manures and green bio-fertilizers for ecological sustainability should be popularized.

In order to encourage farmers to increase production, on the other hand, the Government of India fixes minimum support prices (MSP) of various foodgrains, pulses, oilseeds and cash crops. Minimum support/procurement price works as a safety valve, or rather 'security mechanism', for the farmers. Though the output of foodgrains declined by 6.3 per cent in 2000–01, the procurement of wheat and rice rose to 35.6 million tonnes (15.1 million tonnes of rice and 20.5 million tonnes of wheat). Punjab and Haryana states bought 96 per cent of the total wheat to the market and crowded out private traders (Jha, 2001). In 2008, the wheat procurement was at an all-time high – 22 million tonnes – and this indicates adequate general physical access at national level.

One may adjudge the performance of Indian agriculture in foodgrains in three ways: (a) comparing India's average yield per hectare with the world's average yield per hectare, (b) India's percentage share in world production, and (c) comparing India's per capita annual average availability of foodgrains with the world's per capita annual average availability of foodgrains.

Regarding yield, India lags far behind the world average. First, against the world average yield of wheat being 2,624 kg per ha, India produces only 2,578 kg per ha, whereas France's yield is 7,603 kg per ha (1998). Second, against the world average of yield of rice being 3,747 kg per ha, India produces only 2,890 kg per ha, while Egypt produces 8,527 kg per ha (1998). Third, against the world average of yield of maize being 4,395 kg per ha, India produces only 1,613 kg per ha while Italy produces 9,322 kg per ha (1998). Further, in wheat, India shares 11.1 per cent of total world wheat production, and ranks third, while in rice, it shares 21.6 per cent of total world rice production and ranks second, but in maize it shares just 1.7 per cent of total world maize production and ranks seventh (with Romania). Thus, it is not satisfactory in view of its huge population being 17 per cent of that of the world. Finally, in per capita availability, India has only 176.3 kg of food-grains per year (an average for 1999–2001) against the world average of 358.4 kg a year, though the minimum requirement in India, as per the National Institute of Nutrition (Hyderabad), is 182.5 kg per head per year (i.e. about half a kg per day). Thus, the yield lags behind the population growth in India.

However, the moot point is that the availability of foodgrains at the national level is only a necessary condition for ensuring food availability at the local level, not a sufficient one. Until and unless foodgrains are made available at the local village/panchayat stores, local market, public distribution system (PDS) shops or cooperative stores, the farmers and labourers will not be able to have even a specific physical access because of hoarding or black-marketing, and thus an artificial shortage is created. The PDS in most of the rural areas (except in Kerala and Tamil Nadu) is in a deplorable condition characterized by non-lifting by state government, non-lifting by PDS dealers, unreasonable distance, prevalence of ghost ration cards, black-marketing by dealers, taking extra charges and giving less than due quantity, and lack of awareness among people. Further, the dealers are also compelled to pay bribes to the officials concerned. In fact, during 1996–97 to 2002–03, there was a massive increase in food subsidy from ₹ 6,066 crores to ₹ 2,400 crores. N.C. Saxena (2004) rightly remarks: 'The centre is spending more on food subsidy than what it spends on Agriculture, Rural Development, and Irrigation and Flood Control taken together, but benefits to the poor are hardly satisfying.' A public hearing at Shankargarh (Allahabad) revealed that a bribe of ₹ 38 per quintal is given by the PDS dealer to many officials ranging from the godown in-charge to the SDM.

The third important aspect of food security is food accessibility at the household level. The purchasing power of the agricultural labourers and farmers reflects the economic access to food. Though India had 30 per cent of its grain production in public stock (over 60 million tonnes) by 2000, about 25 per cent Indians were under-nourished and food-insecure. The farmers have a feeling that the minimum support prices for paddy and wheat remain more theoretical than practical, being meagre in comparison to the rising costs of production. Besides, there are not sufficient purchase centres. Further, the government employees posted at the block purchase centre indulge in all sorts of corrupt practices by dilly-dallying and wrongly declaring more than the permissible level of moisture in the paddy and hence offer the farmers lower prices than due. They do not pay in cash and the bank cheques issued are delayed by the banks in their encashment. Again, due to the long distance between the village and the block, most farmers cannot take their paddy to the block purchase centre. The farmers are, therefore, compelled to sell paddy to local traders or local 'net buyers' of villages at less than remunerative rates. In addition, labourers do not get adequate wages.

Therefore, as far as economic accessibility is concerned, people living below the income poverty line (26 per cent as per the Planning Commission) cannot afford to buy food. In rural areas, despite the Mahatma Gandhi National Rural Employment Guarantee (MNREG) scheme of giving 100 days' work to all needy adults, in practice, people do not get work. They do not get unemployment allowance either and often get less than the minimum wages, as pointed out by the CAG in sample checking. However, it is also a fact that the MNREG schemes have contributed to checking starvation and the huge migration from the poor pockets of Andhra Pradesh, Bihar, Odisha, UP, MP, Chhattisgarh, Uttarakhand and Jharkhand to the urban areas and creating ecologically sustainable development, thus in some way strengthening the grassroots democracy. To be more specific, in 2005, three lakh families had migrated from Mahabubnagar district (AP) to Mumbai, Pune, Surat, etc. as unskilled labour, but in 2008, the number of such migrants reduced to 53,000 due to the Mahatma Gandhi National Rural Employment Guarantee schemes (*Jansatta,* 25 June 2008).

The fourth aspect of food security is the food consumption pattern for the well-being at intra-household level. There is often a visible discrimination against the females, children, the aged, the disabled, widows, and the wife and children of unemployed male adults either because of scarcity of food in the family or because of discriminatory social practices or individual biases of the head of the family. Hence, even a large annual family income is not always sufficient for food security.

Finally, food absorption is another aspect of food security at the individual level. Medically, it has been proved that holistic nourishment and a sound health also require safe drinking water, hygiene and clean environment as much as the staple diet. Unfortunately, about 19 per cent of the Indians do not have access to safe drinking water and 69 per cent don't have access to sanitation services. Since some family members often do not get nutritious food in terms of required calories, there is an increase in the number of underweight children, children with stunted growth, and those infected with diseases due to malnourishment; infirmity as well as weakness results into early mortality. In India, 47 per cent of children below five years are undernourished; 80 per cent of children in India suffer from water-borne diseases; and over 7 lakh of these children die every year. In 1996, 65,000 villages in India became waterless (Pant, 2003).

IV
Causes and Consequences of Food Crisis

Though food production has been increasing, its prices have been spiralling for the following reasons :

(a) Rising long-term demand in developing countries like China and India, where rising prosperity has led to eating more. The US Department of Agriculture estimates that the worldwide rice consumption increased 0.9 per cent in 2007 (about 424 million tonnes) but the production increased less than 0.7 per cent.

(b) Short-term supply shocks due to unusually cold weather (due to climate change) and pest infestation in Vietnam, the second largest rice supplier in the world. The aggregate production of maize, rice and soybean stagnated in 2006 and 2007 due to drought, while the drought in Australia led to a decrease in wheat production.

(c) Diversion of a huge chunk of America's corn crop to ethanol production boosting demand for other staples like rice (Wolf, 2008; Ritter, 2008).

However, Peter Ritter also points out that though the trade of foodgrains had been liberalized since the 1990s at the global level, in recent years there has been a ban on the export of wheat/rice by many developing countries. This has worsened the global food crisis. The Philippines imports only 15 per cent of its rice requirement but it is facing the most acute rice shortage in Asia. Consequently, Vietnamese rice is going to the Philippines, thus depriving Africa. We can imagine what is happening in many Sub-Saharan African countries that import up to 40 per cent.

There seems to be a grand linkage between the prices of energy, industrial raw materials and foodstuffs. The social consequence of such food price spikes is tremendous – food riots have taken place in the Philippines, Bangladesh, Egypt, Haiti and even in Murshidabad in West Bengal. Second, one of the ecological consequences is, in terms of more pressure, on water and soil. Third, the price hike has led to hoarding locally and nationally. For instance, India, China, Cambodia and Vietnam have banned rice exports in order to ease domestic pressure, ultimately depriving the poor in food-deficit countries like Sub-Saharan Africa. This has an inflationary effect at the global level. On the other hand, the world food crisis is also giving us an opportunity to rethink about the development paradigm, especially to question the WTO Agreement on Agriculture and the so-called Green Revolution ('How green is the Green Revolution?' is the moot question), to adjust to climate change and to practise 'ever-green revolution' (sustainable agriculture through bio-fertilizers, efficient use of water through drip irrigation, short-term varieties of seeds, dry land farming, integrated pest management and improving indigenous seeds).

V
Policy Implications: What is to be done?

Peter Mandelson (2008), European Union Trade Commissioner, suggests two ways to overcome world food crisis: First, 'greater production capacity' through better land use and crop practices – e.g. better/more fertilizers, improved technology and better infra-structure. For this, the developed world should provide development aid to the developing countries. Second, a dynamic farm market to encourage farmers to improve productivity in order 'to feed a growing world market'. To quote him, 'One country's temporary food security can be another's food scarcity.' In order to turn this crisis into a political opportunity, both developed and developing worlds should invest more in agriculture and reform global farm trade. This line of thought has been shared by many western and Indian scholars of neo-liberal perspective. Sunil Kewalramani (2008), a consultant with multinational companies, is of a similar view that the US in the 1970s changed its policy to encourage output rather than to support prices by limiting production and imposing export curbs. Boosting research on improving farm yields, investing more in irrigation and rural transportation and powering farms with solar and wind energy seem necessary to him to tackle the impending food crisis. He thinks even GM food is essential for the developing countries.

On the other side, two views have emerged, mostly in developing countries, with an eco-sustainability and social equity perspective. First, the diversion of agricultural lands from foodgrains' production to bio-fuel (ethanol) should be reversed immediately, especially in United States of America. This practice is taking deep roots and even in some developing countries like Brazil and India, the cultivation of *jatropha* (bio-fuel) is slowly picking up. As a report by Oxfam (2008) points out, rich countries' demand for more bio-fuels in their transport is causing food price inflation. Grain reserves are now at an all-time low: Rich countries spent up to 15 billion dollars in 2007 supporting bio-fuels while blocking cheaper Brazilian ethanol, which is far less damaging for global food security. Consequently, bio-fuels are responsible for 30 per cent of increase in global food prices, pushing 30 million people worldwide into poverty. Hence, developed countries should scrap bio-fuels targets, including the EU plan to get 10 per cent of its transport fuel from renewable sources like bio-fuels by 2020. Global bio-fuel production is projected to rise from 1.3 million barrels per day in 2010 to 2.7 million barrels per day in 2030 with the US accounting for almost half that growth.

Further, in a study by US scientists led by Jennifer Burney (University of California) analysed 30 years of data in India and found that air pollution caused wheat yields in densely populated states to be 50 per cent lower than what could have been in 2010 – up to 90 per cent of the decrease in potential food production is linked to smog (mix of black carbon and other pollutants) and the rest 10 per cent decrease is linked to global warming and precipitation level. Obviously tackling global warming requires international action while the problem of smog can be tackled at national level (*Hindustan Times*, 5 November 2014).

Second, in many developed countries, animals are fed food-grains for more meat though animals are very inefficient converters of food-grains to meat – a cow eats 16 kg of foodgrains to develop only one kg of beef! But unfortunately, as Arun Firodia rightly points out, over 70 per cent of foodgrains produced in the US are consumed by cows and pigs for producing more meat. An average American eats 125 kg of meat annually (against Indian average of just 3 kg) and all Americans eat 35 million tonnes of meat every year (against just 3 million tonnes in India). In China, annual per capita meat consumption is 70 kg (total 100 million tonnes in a year). World meat consumption increased five-fold in the last five decades, leading to diversion of foodgrains to animal feed. So, for countries like the US and China, meat is the actual food and not foodgrains, hence they don't bother much for the price rise of foodgrains. Again, Arun Firodia rightly points out that for producing just one kg of beef, 10,000 litres of water are needed. But an animal generates 100 times more waste than a human being – so how to dispose off such a huge waste of 50,000 million such animals? And the processing and storage of meat require a huge amount of energy. Hence, if humans consume grains directly rather than cycle them through animals, to eat their meat, there would be enough food to feed the world.

M.S. Swaminathan (2004) has rightly suggested the following nine-point State Action Plan for food security:

(a) To identify who are hungry – about 10–15 per cent of villagers (as found in Tamil Nadu).

(b) People should be made aware of all the development and welfare programmes/schemes of central and state governments through 'entitlement cards' (disaggregated by gender, age, caste and class, giving details of each family, its entitlement and how to access it).

(c) To eliminate energy deprivation and under-nutrition – to have a lifecycle approach of horizontal linkages among vertically structured programmes.

(d) Integrated food-based approach to hidden hunger through chemical and bio-fortification.

(e) To ensure safe drinking water – Jal Swaraj is doing good work for water security.

(f) To provide opportunities for sustainable livelihood – microfinance–led self-help group should be organized with market linkages, otherwise it would remain a 'numbers' game; further, a paradigm shift from unskilled to skilled work is needed to overcome poverty.

(g) Special attention to pregnant mothers and infants (as low-weight baby at birth – 2.2 kg or below – is prevalent) is necessary and also to the adverse female–male sex ratio in many states in India. So, maternal and foetal under-nutrition is to be accorded priority, as malnutrition is reducing national GDP by more than 3 per cent.

(h) Capacity-building programmes should be organized in such a way that all able-bodied persons are ultimately able to earn their livelihood. While the deprived people may be helped under state support, training and empowerment should be combined so that even after the discontinuing of the state support, this lateral learning may provide food with freedom and human dignity, and not make people 'beneficiaries' of a 'patronage' approach. Actually, according to Swaminathan, people are not the beneficiaries; rather government officers are the 'real beneficiaries' as 85 per cent of the public money in the form of taxes goes to their salary!

(i) The formation of a Consultative Group for Freedom from Hunger at state level under the Chairmanship of Chief Minister is imperative in order to coordinate civil society organizations, women's groups, government departments, academic experts, media, and international agencies like FAO, WFP, UNICEF, UNESCO and UNDP.

Swaminathan also suggests employment guarantee schemes with a paradigm shift at national level from "jobless" to "job-led" growth, from green to evergreen revolution, and an Employment Impact Audit in all government programmes and mobilization of one million elected women members of panchayats. To quote him, 'We must establish community Food, Feed and Fodder Banks in every state .... We may consider developing a Job for Indians Act in order to provide guidelines for achieving the goal of work for all. "Work for all" is the only means of ensuring "food for all" in an economically sustainable manner.'

On the other hand, assuming that there are only 261 million poor people in India, N.C. Saxena (Commissioner deputed by

Supreme Court) assesses that only 10 million tonnes of foodgrains are required to wipe out hunger and food-based poverty in India. Hence, the following steps are suggested in this regard:

(a) Improve the implementation of food-based schemes like Targeted PDS, Sampoorna Gramin Rozgar Yojana, Mid-day Meals Scheme and Annapurna.

(b) Correct the price distortions by lowering the MSP (it should be reduced to a level comparable with international prices).

(c) Improve the policy framework of procurement of foodgrains (controls have suppressed private foodgrain marketing, undercutting its potential for long-term food security).

(d) Push the non-farm economy to increase the purchasing power of the poor.

(e) Improve agricultural production in poorer regions (through watershed and wasteland development in a participatory way).

(f) Improve governance to achieve the above – to conduct 'social audit' of all such schemes by genuine bodies.

In fact, we have to give the highest priority to the basic needs of all human beings – food, water, primary health, education, shelter and clothing – in an integrated manner, not merely as a risk management or relief measure. Not only 'development with dignity' (Amit Bhaduri) but also 'food with dignity' is the need of the hour as right to food is an integral part of our fundamental right to life as enshrined in Article 21 of the Indian Constitution as well as in the Universal Declaration of Human Rights (1948). That is, in most of the development programmes/schemes like Mahatma Gandhi National Rural Employment Guarantee Scheme, Mid-day Meals, Integrated Child Development Scheme, Total Sanitation Campaign and Hygiene, the component of nutritious food and safe drinking water should be included through entitlement card so that it may become inclusive social development. However, to avoid the sole dependency and patronage syndrome, it is imperative that most of the youth working in employment schemes are trained adequately for new or complementary skills. In addition, awareness about requirement of nutrition at the various stages of lifecycle is to be generated, especially about micronutrients, absorption capacity of body and inadequacy of calories. Hence, nutrition-based, food-based and knowledge-based approaches should be adopted simultaneously.

But, for that, there should also be genuine land reforms in states like Bihar, AP, Rajasthan and MP. Again, special attention should be given to vulnerable groups, 'hunger pockets', etc.

Second, to realize such a lofty ideal, we have to adapt the decentralization of implementation through Panchayats for more transparency, accountability and benefit by practising the concept of 'think globally, act locally.' No doubt, in some cases of Panchayat works, there is corruption, but it may be eliminated through checks and balances by both the local supervisory/monitoring authorities and the civil society organizations (CSOs) and NGOs. Panchayats, CSOs and NGOs can easily manage food banks locally.

Third, since adequate quantity of foodgrains is always available in government godowns with increasing costs of storage, it would be appropriate to allow minimum foodgrains even to the so-called 'Above Poverty Line' (APL) families. National Advisory Council rightly recommended (14 July 2010) to go in for a universalization of grain entitlement across the country in a phased manner: one-fourth of the poorest blocks (about 2000 blocks) to be brought under the ambit of National Food Security Act in the first phase and in the remaining 6000 blocks special food distribution scheme to be strengthened with a focus on infants, children, the aged, pregnant women, homeless, primitive tribes and seriously ill persons. But now, under the National Food Security Act 2013, only two-third population (67%) will get 35 kg of foodgrains (rice at the rate of ₹ 3 and wheat at rate of ₹ 2). Further, the allocation and lifting of food grains by PDS dealers should be publicized.

Fourth, there should be more public investment in agriculture, because still about two-thirds of the Indians are engaged in agriculture (though there is 'disguised unemployment' because more family members being employed for agricultural tasks requires less number of labourers). This has to ensure both bringing wastelands under cultivation and increasing yield per acre – production and productivity. Undoubtedly, various case studies (including the one in Sultanpur, UP by this author) have clearly found that public investment in agricultural infrastructure induces private investment in various agricultural activities. Further, agriculture is not merely a means of livelihood but also a social and cultural way of life; hence, attention should be given to sensitivity, preferences and experiential knowledge of the local people while adapting new technologies for ecological sustainability.

Fifth, the policy makers have to ensure that agriculture should continue to get various subsidies in fertilizers, seeds, irrigation, pesticides, etc. However, it should be changed from chemical fertilizers to green and bio-fertilizers, from chemical pesticide/insecticide/weedicide to integrated bio pest management, from GM seeds to improved indigenous seeds, from flood irrigation to drip irrigation through sprinklers because Green Revolution in Punjab, Haryana and Western UP has also proved detrimental in terms of water table going down fast, salinity in soil, high quantity of residues of pesticides/insecticides/weedicides found in foodgrains, and pulses, fruits and vegetables grown there. The high potential of traditional indigenous knowledge system should be tapped fully. Thus, a paradigm shift from green revolution to 'Evergreen Revolution', to use M.S. Swaminathan's term, is earnestly called for.

These measures are realizable for 'real social development' with genuine political and administrative will – for this, we have to wake up 'here and now' because the food question cannot wait any more in the present context of severe mass poverty and partial hunger in many parts of India like Bihar, Odisha, Eastern UP, Rajasthan, Uttarakhand, Chhattisgarh, West Bengal, Assam, Jharkhand and Andhra Pradesh. We have to ensure food sufficiency, social equity and ecological sustainability of agriculture in an integrated way so that there is an intra-generational and inter-generational equity for our better future.

References

Bhardwaj, Krishna (1974) *Production Conditions in Indian Agriculture*, Cambridge University Press, Cambridge.

Brown, Lester R. (2008) 'Business as Usual is No Longer a Viable Option', *The Indian Express*, 13 June.

Chakrabarti, M. and S.K. Datta (2000) 'Agriculture', in *Alternative Economic Survey 1998–2000*, Rainbow Publishers Ltd, Delhi.

Firodia, Arun (2008) 'Rising Food Prices: The Blame Game', *The Economic Times*, 9 June.

Government of India (2004) *Serving Farmers and Saving Farming*, National Commission on Farmers, Ministry of Agriculture, New Delhi.

Guha-Khasnobis, Basudeb, S.S. Acharya and B. Davis (eds) (2008) *Food Security*, Oxford University Press, Oxford.

Jha, P.S. (2001) 'Political Economy of Crisis Management', *The Hindu*, 2 October.

Kewalramani, S. (2008) 'Green Revolution II Needed, and Not Export Curbs', *The Hindu, Business Line*, 7 June.

Oxfam (2008) 'Bio-fuels Pushing Thirty Million into Poverty', *The Times of India*, 26 June.

Pant, Ruchi (2003) 'From Communities' Hands to MNCs' BOOTS: A Case Study from India on Right to Water', Paper submitted to Rights and Humanity, UK.

Ritter, Peter (2008) 'No Grain, Big Pain', *Time*, 21 April.

Sachs, J. (2008) *Common Wealth*, Penguin, Allen Lane, London.

Saxena, N.C. (2004) 'Synergising Government Efforts for Food Security', in M.S. Swaminathan and Pedro Medrano (eds), *Towards Hunger Free India*, East West Books Pvt Ltd, Chennai.

Sharma, Subhash (2002) *Dialectics of Agrarian Development: A Sociological Study in North India*, Yash Publications, New Delhi.

Streitfeld, D. and K. Bradsher (2008) 'Weather Adds to Challenge of Food Shortages', *The Hindu*, 11 June.

Swaminathan, M.S. (2004) 'Vision for a Hunger Free India', in M.S. Swaminathan and Pedro Medrano (eds), *Towards Hunger Free India: From Vision to Action*, East West Books Pvt Ltd, Chennai.

— (2008) 'Food for Thought', *Yojana*, 52, June.

Varma, Subodh (2008) 'As Food Crisis Worsens, Firms Push GM Seeds', *The Times of India*, 4 June.

Wolf, Martin (2008) 'The Food Crisis is a Chance to Reform Global Agriculture', *Financial Times* (London), 30 May.

4

Dynamics of Use of Water

Here we p
depict the
analyse the
water avail
the comm
remarks f
water as a

Global S

Water is
resource
non-human
The World
shortage is
urbaniza
the global
is decreas
countries
the period
for Life,
declared t
water-relat
mentation
awarenes
water avai
is availabl

natural res
for irrigati

4

Dynamics of Use and Abuse of Water

A Critical Appraisal

Here we point out the various aspects of the water issue. First, we depict the general global and Indian water scenarios. Second, we analyse the status of groundwater in India. Third, we analyse the water availability and pollution of rivers in India. Fourth, we discuss the commodification of water. Finally, we make some concluding remarks for policy implications from eco-humanistic viewpoint of water as a social need.

Global Scenario

Water is not merely a natural resource but also a life-supporting resource only next to air as any living organisms (human or non-human) cannot survive without water for more than a few days. The World Water Commission (2000) expressed its concern for water shortage by 2020 due to growing water pollution, population growth, urbanization and inappropriate water use/management practices. At the global level, too, water demand is increasing though water supply is decreasing. As per UN estimates, 7,000 million people in 60 countries would face water scarcity by 2050. The UN rightly declared the period of 2005–15 as the International Decade for Action 'Water for Life', and 22 March as World Water Day. Government of India declared the year 2007 as Water Year 'with a view to address the water-related issues in a focused manner, ensure successful implementation of policies and programmes, and to launch a massive awareness programme all over the country.'[1] The total amount of water available on earth is 1,400 million km^3 but only 2.7 per cent of it is available as fresh water, but even most of this 2.7 per cent is frozen or is in deep aquifers and cannot be used easily. Thus, it is a finite natural resource. Out of this available water, about 70 per cent is used for irrigation in agriculture globally.

In addition, it is also notable that there is unequal/uneven distribution of water between various regions. For instance, Asia has 60 per cent of the world's population but only 36 per cent of the global run-off, while South America, with 6 per cent of the world's population, has 26 per cent of the global run-off – Amazon alone contributes 20 per cent of the global run-off.[2] The uneven distribution of water is also reflected in the context of India that has 16 per cent of world's population but only 4 per cent of the world's fresh water supply with 2 per cent of the world's area. This unevenness was duly recognized at the Stockholm Water Symposium (2000):

> One-third of world's population lives in countries with some level of water stress, a number that could increase to two-thirds by the year 2025. Twenty per cent of the world's population in 30 countries face water shortage, a figure that could rise to 30 per cent of world's population in 50 countries by 2025. One thousand fresh water fish species – and 1000 bird species – have been pushed to the edge of extinction by contamination of water. An unacceptably large portion of world population – one person in five – does not have access to safe and affordable drinking water. Every second person does not have access to safe and sufficient sanitation. Each year at least 3–4 million people die of water-borne diseases, including more than 2 million children.[3]

One of the Millennium Development Goals is to reduce the proportion of people without access to safe drinking water by half by 2015 and to stop unsustainable exploitation of water. But though we are nearing 2015, we have not succeeded in achieving such an important goal so far.

Indian Scenario

The following facts give a glimpse of the alarming water situation in India:[4]

(i) Many areas in India have been declared 'grey' – i.e. non-availability of groundwater; e.g. in UP, out of 97,134 villages, 6,000 have no groundwater; almost similar is the situation in parts of Punjab, Haryana, Rajasthan, Andhra Pradesh, Karnataka, Chhattisgarh and Bihar.

(ii) In 10 towns of Rajasthan, water is supplied only once in three days! Similarly, about 1 crore people in 35 cities in India are supplied 38 per cent less water than the usual supply earlier.

(iii) In Delhi, about 80 crore litres of water leaks from its water pipes of 8,300 km length.

(iv) In north Gujarat and Saurashtra–Kutch region, in six out of 10 tubewells dug, water is not available even at a depth of 1,200 feet.

(v) In the four metros (Delhi, Chennai, Kolkata and Mumbai), 90 crore litres of dirty water is thrown out, of which only 30 per cent is treated daily.

Further, in the Indian context, the rainfall is highly erratic, uneven and inadequate. For instance, 75 per cent of the total annual rainfall (1,150 mm on an average) occurs within four-five months of the rainy season. Hence, there is a shortage of water for irrigation, electricity generation, and industries in the remaining seven-eight months of the year. As per an estimate by Falkenmark, 100 litres of water a day is the minimum requirement per capita for basic human needs.[5] According to Tony Allen (2004), total water requirement per person per year will be: one cubic metre for drinking, 100 cubic metre for cleaning and 1,000 cubic metre for production of eatables.[6] Unfortunately, the annual per capita availability of renewable fresh water in India fell from about 5,277 cubic metres in 1955 to 2,245 cubic metre in 2001. Further, in 2001, 15,000 villages in India were without any source of potable water, 2 lakh villages were partially covered by drinking water schemes, 2.17 lakh villages had problems of quality of water – though it is claimed that in 2001, about 81 per cent of India's total population had access to safe drinking water.[7] The water budget in India has been shown in Table 1.

Table 1

Water Budget in India (2001)

Item		*Water Resource (million cu m)*	*Percentage of Total*
a	Total quantity of water in river system	1,64,500	35.04
b	Economically exploitable groundwater	2,10,000	44.73
c	Groundwater already being used	95,000	20.23
	Total	4,69,500	100.00

Source: M.M. Jana (2005), p. 43.

India has many river basins consisting of 12 major (catchment area of more than 20,000 km^2), 44 medium (above 2,000 km^2 but below 20,000 km^2) and 55 minor (2,000 km^2 or less) river basins.

These river basins share 83 per cent of the drainage basins, accounting for 85 per cent of the surface flow and housing 85 per cent of the total population of India. Needless to say that rivers in north and north-eastern parts of India have high water potential due to more rainfall (rain-fed) while those in south have low water potential due to less rainfall (non-rain-fed). The annual precipitation, including snowfall, is 4,000 billion cubic metre (BCM), of which 3,000 BCM precipitates during the monsoon season (June–September). As per Government of India estimates, the average availability of water in India is 1,869 BCM, of which utilizable water resource is 1,123 BCM (690 BCM of surface water and 433 BCM of replenishable groundwater). The total storage capacity of 212.78 BCM has been created in India through major and medium projects, and projects under construction will add 76.26 BCM. The total availability of water in 76 major reservoirs was 109.77 BCM at the end of the monsoons of 2005.[8]

Now, the next question arises about the use and abuse of water. In India, water is used for irrigation, electricity generation, industries, drinking and other domestic purposes – often, the repetitive use of water leads to deterioration of water quality. This is vividly shown in Table 2.

Table 2

Use of Water for Different Purposes

Item	*Percentage Use*	*Water Used (000 million cu m)*	*Water Consumed (000 million cu m)*	*Water Reused (000 million cu m)*
1. Agriculture	78	–	–	–
(a) Irrigation	77	860	774	86
(b) Livestock	01	09	09	–
2. Electricity generation	13	150	05	145
3. Industries	03	85	10	25
4. Domestic uses	06	62	31	31
Total	100	1,116	829	287

Source: M.M. Jana (2005), p. 46.

Thus, it transpires from Table 2 that maximum water is used for irrigation (77%), followed by electricity generation (13%).

Status of Groundwater in India

It is an established fact that due to high rate of deforestation and soil erosion, percolation of groundwater is decreasing. In fact, groundwater plays a vital role in the development process as a whole due to the following factors:[9]

(a) Its good quality ensures substantial savings in treatment costs compared to surface water sources.

(b) Security as a source of supply during extended dry periods compared to most surface water sources.

(c) Suitability for independent public supply and private use.

(d) Attractiveness in terms of capital investment as exploitation can progress in stages with rising water demands.

(e) Availability wherever needed, without being confined to streams and river beds.

At present, groundwater in India is about 3,700 million hectare metres (mham) – about 10 times more than the annual rainfall here. Usable groundwater potential, however, is very uneven in different parts of the country (Table 3).

Table 3

Useable Groundwater Potential in India

Useable Potential in mham	*Category*	*No. of States*	*Name of States*
< 1.0	Very low	8	Arunachal Pradesh, Goa, Haryana, Himachal Pradesh, J&K, Manipur, Meghalaya, Tripura
1.0–2.0	Low	3	Assam, Karnataka, Punjab
2.0–3.0	Moderate	4	Bihar, Gujarat, Odisha, TN
3.0–4.0	High	2	Andhra Pradesh, Maharashtra
>4.0	Very high	1	MP

Source: M.M. Jana (2005), p. 49.

It has been found that only 30 per cent of actual groundwater potential has been harnessed in India due to lack of infrastructure for irrigation (as 85 per cent of currently exploited groundwater is used for irrigation). Though India has the largest irrigation infrastructure in the world, its irrigation efficiency is only 35 per cent. About 10 per cent increase in irrigation efficiency may lead to an additional potential of 14 mham. Due to advanced agriculture in Haryana and Punjab, most of the groundwater is used, 98 per cent and 80 per cent, respectively (Table 4)

Table 4

Use of Groundwater in Various States of India

Use of Water per cent	*Category*	*No. of States*	*Name of States*
Below 20	Low	9	Arunachal Pradesh, Assam, J&K, Karnataka, M.P; Maharashtra, Meghalaya, Odisha, Tripura
20–50	Moderate	5	Andhra Pradesh, Bihar, Gujarat, Himachal Pradesh, TN
>50	High	2	Haryana, Punjab

Source: M.M. Jana (2005), p. 49.

Due to the excessive use of groundwater in many parts of the country, the water table has gone down (especially in Punjab, Haryana, UP, Maharashtra, Karnataka and TN). In India, 90 per cent of the total extracted groundwater is used for irrigation purpose, while the world average is 69 per cent – in developed countries, drip irrigation, sprinkles, reuse of rain water and short-duration crops require less water.

Second, there has been an increase of arsenic in water, causing human diseases, especially in West Bengal and Tripura, like in Bangladesh and Cambodia. In fact, in 17 states of India, various poisonous chemicals/metals are found in groundwater like fluoride, sulphide, iron, manganese, arsenic, nitrate, chloride, zinc and chromium. Groundwater pollution may lead to the worst kind of disaster – it is a time bomb ticking for humans and animals!

Third, there is an increase of salinity in groundwater in many states, especially Punjab, Haryana and Western UP.

Fourth, even for domestic consumption, groundwater is used excessively and wasted, especially in taking bath, cleansing of clothes and utensils, flushing of toilet, etc. As per an FAO study, 6,800 gallons of water is utilized to produce just one day's meal for a four-member family![10]

Fifth, many industries are, on the one hand, exploiting groundwater excessively and, on the other, throwing the industrial toxic wastes/refuse (effluents) in the nearby rivers – resulting into the colouring of river water and passing of chemicals into the groundwater. Developed countries use about 23 per cent of the total extracted groundwater for industries; whereas developing countries like India do so to the extent of only 6 per cent. India's daily discharge of domestic sewage of 3.6 million cubic metre (Delhi alone discharges 20 crore litres of domestic sewage daily) causes various health hazards.

Finally, due to the lowering of groundwater table and increasing salinity or poisonous chemicals/metals, many small and marginal farmers have to abandon farming and migrate to urban areas for new livelihoods. This has several negative consequences on the urban areas' work, transport, food, water, sanitation and health systems. Unfortunately, groundwater is changing from an 'invisible resource' to a highly visible resource due to abuse, overdraft and pollution, affecting the present and future generations.

Needless to emphasize that water availability per capita in India in 1947 was 6,000 cubic metre, which was reduced to 2266 cubic metre in 1997, and is expected to be 1,000 cubic metre in 2047 AD. Usually, a person needs 1,700 cubic metre of water in a year, and if it is reduced to less than 1,000 cubic metre per head in a year, it amounts to water crisis in that region. In fact, groundwater is like a bank account from where we constantly withdraw water but hardly deposit any. Though we celebrate World Water Day on 22 March every year, we are hardly sensitized to the range and depth of the problem.

Water Availability and Pollution in Rivers in India

Unfortunately, problems of both quantity and quality exist side by side in Indian rivers. It is interesting to note that water utilization from major river basins varies from 85 per cent to 30 per cent (due to insufficient storage in areas of low rainfall). Though the Brahmaputra river basin has a high water potential, yet some of its parts like Cherrapunji (in Meghalaya) face an acute scarcity of drinking water during dry season. The highest per capita water availability (16,589 cm) is in the Brahmaputra basin while the lowest (360 cm) is in the Sabarmati basin. Water availability of less than 1000 cm per capita is considered (internationally) as a scarcity condition.[11] Table 5 shows the growing water scarcity in major river basins in India.

Table 5

Growing Water Scarcity in Major River Basins in India

Year	*No. of River Basins*	*Name of River Basins*
2001	4	Sabarmati, east-flowing rivers between Pennar and Kanya Kumari, and west-flowing rivers of Kutch and Saurashtra
2010	7	Cauvery, east-flowing rivers between Mahanadi and Pennar, Tapti, Mahi, Krishna, Suvarnarekha and Ganga
2025	6	Indus, Godavari, Mahanadi, Brahmani-Baitarani, Narmada, and west-flowing rivers from Tapti to Tadri
2050	2	Barak and Brahmputra

Source: M.M. Jana (2005), p. 48.

Various rivers in India are highly polluted due to the various pollutants thrown there. The Central Pollution Control Board listed 191 highly polluting industries in UP, six in Bihar, and 67 in West Bengal. A glimpse of this is shown in Table 6.

Table 6

Pollution of Rivers in India

River	*Sources of Pollution*
1. Kali (Meerut)	Sugar mills, distilleries, paint, soap, rayon, silk yarn, tin and glycerine industries
2. Yamuna (Delhi)	DD factory, sewage, Indraprastha power station
3. Ganga (Kanpur)	Jute, chemical, metal and surgical industries, tanneries, textile mills, sewage
4. Gomati (Lucknow)	Paper and pulp mills, sewage
5. Dajora (Bareilly)	Synthetic rubber factories
6. Damodar (Bokaro and Panchet)	Fertilizers, fly ash from steel factory, suspended coal particles from coal washeries and thermal power station
7. Hoogly (Kolkata)	Power station, paper and pulp mills, textiles, chemical factories, paints, varnishes, metal steel, hydrogenated vegetable oils, rayon, soap, metal shellac and polythene industries, sewage
8. Bhadra (Karnataka)	Paper, pulp and steel factories

Cont'd...

... Cont'd

9.	Cooum, Adyara Buckingham canal (Chennai)	Domestic sewage, automobile workshops
10.	Kaveri (TN)	Sewage, tanneries, distilleries, paper and rayon mills
11.	Godavari (TN)	Paper mills
12.	Kulu (Mumbai and Kalyan)	Chemical factories, rayon mills and tanneries
13.	Suwao (Balrampur)	Sugar industries

Source: P.S. Varma and V.K. Agrawal (1996), *Environmental Biology*, S. Chand and Co., New Delhi.

Needless to reiterate that due to pollution, 70 per cent of India's inland water is unfit for human consumption. For instance, in the Hoogly river in Kolkata, untreated water of about 160 industries is discharged. Between Gangotri and Kolkata, thousands of rivulets fall in the Ganga with sewage, untreated effluents and industrial wastes. Water pollution also occurs due to toxic and radioactive materials, which have pathological effects on the humans (Table 7).

Table 7

Pathological Effects of Heavy Metal Pollutants on Humans

	Metal Pollutants	*Pathological Effects*
1.	Mercury	Abdominal pain, headache, diarrhoea, chest pain
2.	Lead	Anaemia, vomiting, loss of appetite, convulsions, damage of brain, liver and kidney
3.	Arsenic	Disturbed peripheral circulation, mental disturbance, liver cirrhosis, hyperkerotosis, lung cancer, ulcer in gastro-intestinal tract, kidney damage
4.	Cadmium	Diarrhoea, growth retardation, bone reformation, kidney damage, testicular atrophy, anaemia, injury of central nervous system and liver, hypertension.
5.	Copper	Hypertension, uremia, coma, sporadic fever
6.	Barium	Excessive salivation, vomiting, diarrhoea, paralysis, colic pain, renal damage, cramps
7.	Zinc	Vomiting, renal damage, cramps

Cont'd...

... Cont'd

8.	Selenium	Damage of liver, kidney and spleen, fever, nervousness, vomiting, low blood pressure, blindness, even death
9.	Hexavalent	Nephritis, gastro-intestinal ulceration, disease in central nervous system, cancer
10.	Chromium	Diarrhoea, low blood pressure, lung irritation, bone deformities, paralysis

Source: P.S. Verma and V.K. Agrawal (1996).

Needless to say that as per WHO, 80 per cent of diseases are water-borne e.g. diarrhoea, typhoid, jaundice, cholera and dysentery.

One major contradiction in the Indians' way of life is that, on the one hand, we worship and give highest regards to rivers (especially the Ganga) as 'pure', 'salvation-giver', 'mother', 'goddess', 'liberator', and so on, but, on the other, we pollute these rivers callously. Brahmandpurana prohibits 13 activities in Ganga water: defecation, ablution, urination, throwing of used floral offerings, rubbing of filth, body shampooing, frolicking, acceptance of donations, obscenity, offering of inappropriate praises, discharge of garments, beating, and swimming across the river. There is a need for awareness generation among the masses about these as the Biochemical Oxygen Demand (BOD) level in the Ganga exceeded the permissible limits (three) at 10 out of 27 sampling stations in 1999. Similarly, the BOD level in the Yamuna exceeded the permissible limits at 14 out of 25 sampling stations in 1999.[12]

Pure and safe drinking water should meet the following physical and chemical standards (Table 8):

Table 8

Properties of Safe Drinking Water

Features	*Properties*
Colour	Transparent
Odour	Odourless
Taste	Tasteless
pH	7– 8.5
Total hardness	200–600 (mg per litre)
Calcium	75–200 (mg per litre)
Magnesium	30–150 (mg per litre)

Cont'd...

... Cont'd

Fluoride	1–1.5 (mg per litre)
Chloride	200–1000 (mg per litre)
Sulphate	200–400 (mg per litre)
Arsenic	< 0.05 (mg per litre)
Cadmium	< 0.01 (mg per litre)

Commodification of Water

In an era of globalization, water has been reduced to a saleable commodity in the market. There is privatization of rivers in India, though these have been common property resources and symbols of faith since time immemorial. The following facts reveal the alarming situation of privatization of water sources in India:[13]

(a) In 2004, the World Bank gave a loan of ₹ 1,868 crores for water projects to be operated by private/multinational companies.

(b) In India, the demand for bottled water has been increasing manifold and its rate is the highest (25 per cent per year) in the world – 8.2 per cent in US, 8.8 per cent in Mexico, 20 per cent in China, 15.4 per cent in Brazil, 3.6 per cent in Italy, 4.4 per cent in Germany, 4.2 per cent in France, 6.2 per cent in Spain, and 16.5 per cent in Indonesia. Hence, private companies are monopolizing the bottled water trade.

(c) In India, privatization of water is operating in 19 towns with legal permission and in 40 towns illegally.

(d) The Bhawani river in Tamil Nadu and Shivnath river in Chhattisgarh have been privatized by the state governments. While Coca Cola has purchased the Bhawani river in Tamil Nadu at ₹ 5 lakhs annually, Radius Water Ltd (Kailash Soni) has purchased the Shivnath river for a paltry sum of ₹ 1.50 lakhs annually. Similarly, the Maharashtra government sold the Neera river with the Deogarh dam to a private enterprise.

Unfortunately, the neo-liberal economists and policy makers of the World Bank consider water more as an economic good than a social need. They are of the view that 'public water and sanitation services are often plagued by inefficiency.'[14] Hence, privatization is inevitable to them.

The following justifications are given for the privatization of water sources and services:

(a) Private utilities are likely to work under greater scrutiny than public systems because of the controversy surrounding privatization.

(b) Government itself is more likely to criticize and act against a private operator than a Government Corporation.

(c) A private utility has a greater incentive to reduce losses because lost water means lost profits.

(d) Private operators are more likely to draw upon international experience and know-how (technology) than are government utilities.

In fact, the concept of water, simply as an economic good (not a social need), leads to its 'commodification'. In Bolivia, the privatization of water led to doubling or more of the water rates. Surprisingly, even the World Bank recognizes that 'the privatization process itself can create corrupt incentives. A firm may pay ... to be favoured in the selection process (and) to obtain ... subsidies, monopoly benefits and regulatory laxness in the future.'[15]

In Indonesia also, the government itself violated the law granting water concessions to private entities without subjecting them to competitive tender.[16] Even in a developed country like France, in Grenoble, in 1996, a government minister and an executive of Svez Lyonnaise were imprisoned for taking and giving bribes to award a water contract to a subsidiary of Svez Lyonnaise des Eaux.[17] Usually, the experience is that the big companies or multinational corporations succeed in getting water projects at the highest bids but they do not pay attention to the issues of ecological sustainability and social need of the people.

There are contrasting perceptions of water (as a natural resource, a commodity and social need) which have broader ramifications for the humans, animals and the entire planet. A glimpse of these perceptions may be vividly seen in Table 9 in which we may easily see that, at one extreme, the eco-centric view of water considers it as a natural resource with an intrinsic value (value in itself, not simply for humans/animals) to be managed by both the civil society and the state without any role of the market – the state playing a partial role of preserver of nature, with partial equity and full sustainability. At the other extreme lies the utilitarian–neo-liberal economic view (anthropocentric), which considers nature simply as a commodity (to be bought and sold) with an instrumental value, to be managed by private users/owners as individual consumers, where the market plays a full and free role, but the state plays a role of facilitator to private consumers, without any care for equity and sustainability. Finally, the eco-humanistic view considers water as a common property resource, a social need or common good, where community and voluntary agencies (civil society) manage the water with the local people's participation with a restrained role of market, and the state playing a role of facilitator to the community/society with full equity and sustainability. Thus, to our minds, the eco-humanistic view should be taken in the Indian situation.

Table 9

Contrasting Perceptions of Water

Dimensions	*Eco-centric View*	*Utilitarian–neo-liberal Economic View (anthropocentric)*	*Eco-humanistic View*
(a) Water	A natural resource with intrinsic value	A commodity with instrumental value (economic good)	A social need – as a common property resource (common good)
(b) Agency of management	Civil society and state	Private user/owner (individual consumer)	Community and voluntary agencies (civil society)
(c) Role of market	No	Full and free	Restrained
(d) Role of state	Partial (to conserve water)	Facilitator to private consumers	Facilitator and subservient to the community/ society
(e) Equity	Partial	No (Inequity)	Full
(f) Sustainability	Full	Unsustainable	Full

Concluding Remarks: Policy Implications

From the above, it is quite clear that water is exploited excessively and even commoditized in India as elsewhere. The following pragmatic measures may be taken easily to conserve and use water in a sustainable manner:

(a) We should put a brake on our consumerist culture of using more and more water for domestic purposes; e.g. using a bucket and a mug for bathing instead of a shower, using cloth for car washing, replacing flush, using a mug of water for brushing of teeth instead of using an open tap.

(b) Recycling and reuse of water for different purposes like washing, cleansing of utensils and garden irrigation should be promoted, and water-saving and water-audit devices should be developed.

(c) Rainwater harvesting on roofs and its use for different purposes should be promoted.

(d) Use sprinklers/drip for irrigation of crops; develop short-term and new varieties of foodgrains/vegetables/fruits requiring less water; and in water-logged areas new water-logging-resistant paddy varieties should be developed. Fortunately, India has the suitable context for organic farming and the 'System of Rice Intensification' (SRI) has been developed (2002–03) here, wherein water requirement is reduced by 50 per cent but productivity may be increased doubly. Besides, in SRI, for increasing the capacity of soil, the plants are given more physical space and organic atmosphere. Tamil Nadu and later Bihar gained substantially in rice production and productivity due to SRI.

(e) Not to throw dirt, filth, corpses and carcasses in rivers/ponds.

(f) Reasonable water charges be levied to avoid misuse by urban dwellers.

(g) Ensuring suitable action for leakage, damage, theft and over-use/exploitation of water (e.g. for cold drinks); local community and Gram Panchayat be the appropriate authority for allowing or not allowing groundwater use by outside agency.

(h) Traditional water reservoirs like *Ahar, pyne, pokhra, baori* and lake should be rejuvenated for conservation of surface water as well as for helping recharge of groundwater in nearby areas.

(i) There should be a massive drive to generate mass awareness in both rural and urban areas for conservation and reasonable use of water for different purposes through better practices and techniques. Water education should be part of the school curricula. Teachers should use transformation methods like sensitizing learners to their environment, develop learners' critical thinking faculties, encourage creativity, ensure to take practical steps (like soil conservation and diagnosing diseases), and encourage to evaluate the outcome of their decisions and actions. Ultimately, vision is to be reflected in action.

(j) *Pucca* constructions in parks (including pavements) should not be more than 5 per cent of the total area for rainwater harvesting.

(k) Sustainability and sanitation should be kept in mind for the different stages of drinking water system: raw procurement stage, production stage (pre-sedimentation, mixing, filtration, absorption and disinfection) and supply stage (storage, pumping and distribution network).

(l) Collective participatory methods are usually more useful and effective, hence self-help groups, community-based organizations, NGOs and panchayati raj institutions should be encouraged more and more for water conservation at local level because they are more and better informed, adequately organized, more confident, contextual, sharing, experienced and pragmatic.

(m) Potential water leaders for future generations should be identified at different levels and, after encouraging them for a creative vision, a functional network between young leaders and established leaders should be promoted.

(n) Since most of the water is used in India for irrigation in agriculture, it is necessary to have effective 'participatory irrigation management' (PIM) for developing a sense of economy in water use among users, to make best use of natural precipitation and groundwater compatible with canal water and facilitate them to have sustainable choices in terms of crops, sequence of crops, timing and frequency of water supply, conflict resolution and equity. For this, genuine water users' associations have to be involved effectively in all aspects and at all levels of irrigation management. Preferably, a bottom-up approach should be followed (as in The Philippines) with an intensive and progressive interaction and dialogue of institutional development officers and farmers' associations with a flexibility to adapt a gradual phase-wise approach (as done in Bihar, Gujarat, Maharashtra, UP, Rajasthan and Karnataka), not 'big bang' approach with uniform water users' association and participatory irrigation management (as in MP and Andhra

Pradesh). Only in Andhra Pradesh, Manipur, Kerala, Himachal Pradesh, Madhya Pradesh, Goa and Tamil Nadu have water users' associations been visible and effective (2000), covering 91.6 per cent, 75.8 per cent, 41.6 per cent, 33.3 per cent, 23.4 per cent, 20 per cent, and 14.7 per cent area, respectively, as percentage of the total net area in the states concerned. Unfortunately, in states like Bihar, UP and Jammu and Kashmir, only one water user association had been formed by 2000 and in Assam there were just two such associations.[18]

Thus, we may conclude that water is not merely a natural resource for commodification but also an elixir of life – life itself. Hence, it has to be conserved with safety and purity if life is to be made safe, sustainable, healthy and hygienic. Water cannot be reduced to a mere commodity to be sold and bought in a market. It is one of the five *Mahabhutas* (basic elements of life), as the Indian tradition rightly tells us. It is unfortunate that as we are becoming more advanced materially, we are taking a negative perspective towards rivers (most of the civilizations flourished in the ancient period along their banks) and ponds. As an environmental activist, Anupam Mishra perceptively remarks: 'When we were uncivilized, rivers were sacred. When we became civilized, rivers began to be profane. Due to our ego we have reduced rivers from mothers to maids.'[19] In fact, the entire humanity requires a new kind of development where the whole ecology (including the water resource) is to be addressed on a priority basis for its sustainability in consonance with social equity and social development. In order to assess the sustainability of water projects, it is essential to undergo both social impact assessment (SIA) and environmental impact assessment (EIA) simultaneously but these should be completed fairly well before the sanctioning of such a project. Policy planners have to go with people's social, economic, cultural, technological and participatory preferences for the locale, size, form and structure of water projects, because that ensures 'development without destruction'. Often, some political representatives have different and contrary opinions (against the marginalized people they represent) on various water projects from the viewpoint of profit-making or vote-bank politics.

Undoubtedly, globalization is not a uniform process. It has both integrative and marginalizing consequences. As Takahasi et al., have pointed out, it is of two types: 'market-based globalization' (MBG) and 'civil society globalization' (CSG).[20] We have to opt for the latter in the interest of the humanity, equity for present and future generations as well as the marginalized classes, and ecological sustainability because deregulation, sweeping absolutely free trade through competition and privatization under the MBG would lead to the total destruction of local and traditional water systems on the one hand, and new conflicts due to increasing socio-economic inequality on the other. Korten rightly observes that development is a process by which people enhance their human, institutional and technical capacities to produce the goods and services for improvement in their quality of life sustainably using the available resources – it is 'people-centred development' where the marginalized people's participation and direct benefits with distributive justice are the core issues.[21] To him, poverty is the deprivation associated with lack of money – lack of access to water, food, clothing and shelter. This requires locally produced goods at a small scale and at a low cost in consonance with the cultural preferences (social adaptive capacity) of the poor. Capacity-building through learning by doing through stakeholders' participation in water use and management has correlation with many types of sustainability – environmental, technical, financial, social and institutional. Hence, water projects should ultimately become 'change agents' directed towards building the local people's capacity. That is, global vision (thinking globally) should be accompanied with local action (acting locally) for water ethics and equity. Thus, a kind of local, or at the most regional, water development paradigm is called for where water knowledge-sharing will be a multidimensional, more comprehensive and down-to-earth process.

Notes

1. Government of India (2007) *Annual Report 2006–07*, Ministry of Water Resources, New Delhi, p. 5.
2. Wazha Tema (2001) 'Water Education in African Cities', in UNCHS, *Water Education in African Cities*, Nairobi, pp. 45–46.
3. Ibid., p. 46.
4. Kripa Shankar (2008) 'Siyasat Ke Raste Nilam Hota Pani', *Pratham Impact*, 5, 16–29 February, p. 25.
5. M.M. Jana (2005) 'Water Resource in India and its Sustainable Management', in A. Kumar (ed.), *Sustainable Water Management*, SPM Govt Degree College, Phaphamau, Allahabad, p. 42.
6. B.N. Pandey (2005) 'Is Third World War Inevitable for Water Crisis in 21st Century?', in A. Kumar (ed.), *Sustainable Water Management*, SPM Government Degree College, Phaphamau, Allahabad, p. 363.
7. Jana, op. cit., p. 43.

8. Government of India, op. cit., p. 5.
9. A.S. Foster (1998) 'Ground Water in Urban Development', World Bank Technical Paper No. 390, World Bank, Washington, D.C.
10. Aravind Kumar (2005) 'Sustainable Water Management with Special Reference to Ganga and Allahabad: An Appraisal', in Aravind Kumar (ed.), *Sustainable Water Management*, SPM Government Degree College, Phaphamau, Allahabad, p. 428.
11. Jana, op. cit, p. 48.
12. Narayan P. Murthi and V.K. Shunglu (2000) *Audit Report of Ganga Action Plan 2000*, Publications Division, New Delhi, 13 December.
13. Shankar, op. cit., p. 26.
14. C. Bosch et al. (2000) 'Water, Sanitation and Poverty', in World Bank, *Poverty Reduction Strategy Source Book* (Draft), World Bank, Washington, D.C.
15. S. Rose-Ackerman (1996) 'The Political Economy of Corruption: Causes and Consequences', World Bank Public Policy for Private Sector, Note No. 74, World Bank, Washington, D.C.
16. E. Lobina and D. Hall (2001) *Potential for Public Sector Water Operations in Developing Countries*, Public Service International Research Unit, London.
17. www.world-psi.org
18. Asian Development Bank (2008) *Irrigation Management Transfer*, Sage Publications, New Delhi, p. 19.
19. Cited in Rajesh Sirothia (2008) 'Jal Bachane Par Hua Manthan', *Outlook Saptahik* (Hindi), 9, 4–10 March, p. 41.
20. K. Takahasi et al. (2002) 'Driving Forces and Incentives for Change: Towards Sustainable Water Development', *Water Science and Technology*, 45 (8), pp. 141–44.
21. D.C. Korten (1990) *Getting to 21st Century: Voluntary Action and the Global Agenda*, Kumarian Press, West Hartford.

5

Poverty Eradication in Rural India

Microfinance and Beyond

In this chapter, poverty has been conceptualized holistically, taking into account its multiple dimensions, viz., economic, social, spatial, political and demographic. The norm of calorie intake (for both food and non-food items) and well-being has been ignored in defining official poverty line in India over the years. Hence, there is a need to emphasize on it again because the practice of taking only per capita GNP into account to measure poverty has certain limitations. Besides, globalization, liberalization and privatization have affected the poor adversely in terms of rising prices of essential food items, growing unemployment, inequality, assetlessness and development-induced displacement; even the rate of development aid from the developed countries like the US has declined. Therefore, microfinance may play a significant role in reducing poverty. This may be done either through SHG–Bank linkage or through Micro Finance Institutions (MFIs). Grameen Bank succeeded in Bangladesh because of certain specific attributes like bank going to the client, prioritization for the absolute poor, dedicated bank staff, and so on. But, unfortunately, these features are missing in the Indian context. Microfinance, therefore, cannot provide a holistic solution to the gigantic problem of poverty (though it brings incremental change, meeting the immediate needs of survival) because of its high transaction costs, commercialization and lack of transparency. Many MFIs have become new incarnations of traditional moneylenders and, therefore, many loanees have either fled their villages or were compelled to commit suicide due to various sorts of coercion. Thus, public policy should endeavour for inclusive and real social development with equity and ecological sustainability.

Since India's Independence in 1947, various Five Year Plans have perceived and focused on poverty in different ways. However, about six decades of planning have not been able to eradicate it. Rather, the absolute number of the poor in India remains the same, around three hundred million. To be precise, there have been unending debates on defining *poverty line,* officially and unofficially, for several decades. It is now more or less accepted that India did not succeed to make a real dent on poverty because of not according a consistently high priority to agriculture and allied activities in a holistic manner. It is also a fact that only the economists have ruled the roost in the entire planning process, neglecting the views of the sociologists, political scientists, geographers, demographers, and so on, and this has led to lop-sided development – high growth rate without adequate jobs as well as development-induced displacement resulting into the worsening of the misery of the masses.

Further, a wide range and depth of corruption (in terms of cuts) is prevailing in the implementation of poverty alleviation programmes, including MNREGA. Therefore, all the genuine rural poor have not got employment. Nor have they been given unemployment allowance. Even those who got employment did not get full wages in time. However, MNREGA is better conceived than earlier poverty alleviation programmes in the sense that it has slowed down the pace of migration from rural to urban areas. Further, self-employment of the rural poor by taking loans from banks or MFIs has also not been successful because of lack of dedication among the staff as well as lack of transparency. Hence, a genuine attempt for poverty eradication requires radical socio-economic and political measures (like redistribution of land, enhancing the quantity and quality of wage employment under MNREGA, massive public investment in agriculture and allied activities, providing housing, free education and health services as well as expanding social security to the poor), not merely a technical measure, because poverty is not just a technical problem.

Therefore, we take here an inter-disciplinary perspective in order to understand the issue of poverty in all its dimensions. In fact, poverty is a multiple deprivation (economic, political, social, demographic and spatial); therefore, one should not restrict only to income poverty. Similarly, it would be a parochial view to focus on the individual's incapacities, 'flawed character', curse of gods or bad luck as the cause of poverty. Rather, a holistic and systemic view is to be taken where lack of adequate socio-economic and political opportunities, policy shortcomings, lack of political and administrative will and defects in implementation of various programmes are to be emphasized, because these aspects of reality are not within the control of the poor households. Nowadays, microfinance is the buzzword in development discourse but it only mitigates the pangs of poverty; it does not succeed in eradicating poverty totally.

This chapter is divided into four sections. The first section deals with the issue of defining and estimating poverty (especially rural poverty). The second section deals with the various perspectives on poverty. The third section deals with the role of microfinance in poverty eradication. Finally, we discuss other necessary strategies beyond microfinance in order to tackle the gigantic problem of rural poverty.

Defining and Estimating Poverty

In early twenty-first century, India is perceived and described by different bodies, organizations and scholars differently. While the UNDP categorizes India as a 'low income country', the World Bank sees it as a 'low income economy' (one of the 53 countries in the world), while putting China in the category of 55 lower-middle income countries. The US sees it as a 'transforming' rather than a developing country and decided to cut aid to India by 35 per cent, others see it as a 'developing' country. ILO sees India as a 'medium-income developing country,' better than the 'least developed countries'. However, some enthusiastic scholars (including Robert Zoellick, the then President of World Bank, *The Indian Express*, 8 October 2008) see India as an 'emerging economic power', along with China and Brazil, forgetting its 'darkness at noon'.

The then Indian Prime Minister's Economic Advisory Council estimated India's per capita income in July 2007 as $1,021 against the same being $561 in 2003–04, thus becoming a middle-income country (per capita income ranging from $906 to $3,595). India's Gross Domestic Product (GDP) was growing at the rate of 9 per cent (2007–08), yet it did not succeed in making a big dent on hunger, poverty and inequality. Its track record in Human Development Index (HDI) and Human Poverty Index (HPI) is pathetic. In the Global Prosperity Index (GPI), India ranked 46 out of 50 countries in 2007 – India scores better in political freedom, comfort of religious faiths, and family and community bonds, but it scores badly in social and economic indices like health care, education, job, housing and clothing. On the other hand, Norway, Sweden and the US occupied the first, second and third positions, respectively in the GPI. In Sweden and Norway, the economic disparity was far less but their social security is the highest in the world. India ranked 70th among 104 nations in the World Prosperity Index (WPI) 2008 due to the bad quality of secondary education, the cost of starting a business (due to excessive bureaucracy) and lack of government effectiveness (*The Indian Express*, 22 October 2008).

Poverty may be defined as a multiple deprivation consisting of food, education, health, housing, clothing and social security deprivations. If we look at the global scenario of poverty, the following facts draw our attention:

(a) 1.2 billion persons lived on less than one dollar a day in 2000, thus they couldn't make both ends meet; but, as per the new international poverty line ($1.25 per day per head), the number of poor people increased to 1.4 billion in 2005; 50,000 children die daily due to poverty-related causes.

(b) 1.5 billion persons don't have access to safe drinking water.

(c) 880 million people don't have access to health services; 10 million children die every year due to lack of vaccination and 14 million persons die every year due to infectious diseases.

(d) 40,000 people die daily because of preventable diseases; 2.8 million children and 0.3 million women die annually in developing countries.

(e) One woman dies for every 260 live births – one woman dying every minute – because of non-availability of medical facilities and trained nurses/doctors at the time of delivery or due to chronic anaemia, etc. of the pregnant women.

(f) 125 million children have no access to school education and more than 500 million women are illiterate.

(g) 840 million people worldwide are malnourished – about 30 per cent of the world population; there are 13.2 million refugees worldwide.

(h) 925 million persons suffer from hunger and 1.5 billion people are affected by desertification and drought.

(i) As the demand for food exceeds the supply (because of better/new food habits, better purchasing power, less production/productivity and less quantity available in the market due to national governments' restrictions in order to ensure domestic food security), food prices have soared, resulting into food riots in some countries of Africa and Asia.

(j) AIDS has already killed 20 million people and at present 34 million people (23 million in Africa) are infected with AIDS/HIV – 15,000 persons are infected with AIDS/HIV daily.

(k) Though the proponents of globalization talk of the global village and the shrinking of world distance due to better information technology, communication, transport and global trade, they forget that during 1980–2000 the share of developing countries in world trade declined from 0.8 per cent to 0.4 per cent. Similarly, a city like Manhattan has more Internet connections than the entire Africa – an instance of 'communication inequality', indeed.

This may be seen in Table 1.

The first of the Millennium Development Goals (MDGs) is to halve the number of people living below the extreme poverty line (one dollar per day per head) in the world as well as to halve proportion of people suffering from hunger by 2015. The second goal is to achieve universal primary education. The third goal is to eliminate gender disparity in primary and secondary education by 2005 and at all educational levels by 2015. The fourth goal is to reduce child mortality by two-thirds. The fifth goal is to reduce maternal mortality rate by three-fourths. The sixth goal is to halt and reverse the spread of AIDS/HIV, malaria and other major diseases. The seventh goal is to reverse the loss of environmental resources and integrate the principle of sustainable development in the national policy, to halve the proportion of people without sustainable access to safe drinking water and sanitation by 2015, and to have significant improvement in the lives of at least 100 million slum dwellers. The eighth goal is to have an open and fair trading and financial system, to address special needs of the least developed countries (tariff – and quota-free access to their exports) and of landlocked countries/small islands, to ease debt problems, to develop decent and productive work for youth and, in cooperation with pharmaceutical companies provide, access to affordable essential drugs in developing countries, and, in cooperation with the private sector, make available the benefits of new technologies, especially information and communications.

Thus, the MDGs recognize the multi-dimensionality of chronic poverty. But all these goals are not really noble because disaster relief, a temporary measure, has been placed in a permanent form in MDGs. Actually, huge foreign aid puts several nations permanently 'on the dole' (Reinert, 2007). The MDGs do not focus on causes of poverty. Rather, they concentrate on attacking the symptoms of poverty whereas the need of the hour is to attack the sources of poverty from the inside through the production system, to diversify the economy, to raise the competitiveness of farmers of developing countries, and to globalize the labour.

Despite a high growth rate (9%) in India in the first decade of twentieth century, poverty has not been eradicated, though, according to some scholars, it has declined. Still, a huge population in India lives below the poverty line. Various estimates about poverty in India may be seen in Table 2.

Thus, from the perusal of Table 2, it is clear that the number of the poor in India is estimated differently, ranging from 260 million to 724.32 million, depending on the varying definitions of poverty line (proportion varying from 24% to 70%). Estimates by Arjun Sengupta et. al. and Utsa Patnaik are more comprehensive but these too have not taken all aspects of poverty, especially the unquantifiable ones. As per the Planning Commission of India, the share of all the poor in India's entire population declined from 54.9 per cent in 1973 to 27.5 per cent in 2004–05 and 20.4 per cent in 2005–06. In rural areas also, it declined from 56.4 per cent (1973–74) to 28.3 per cent (2004–05). However, the absolute number of the poor in India only marginally declined from 321.34 million in 1973 to 301.7 million in 2004–05. Similarly, in rural areas, the absolute number of the poor declined from 261.3 million in 1973 to 220.9 million in 2004–05. The absolute number of the urban poor increased from 60 million to 80 million partly because of the migration of the rural poor to urban areas during the same period. Surprisingly, the absolute number of the poor increased during 1973–74 to 2004–05 in the following states of India: in UP (including Uttarakhand), from 53.57 million to 62.6 million; in Rajasthan, from 12.85 million to 13.49 million; in Maharashtra, from 28.74 million to 31.74 million; in Nagaland, from 0.29 million to 0.4 million; in MP (including Chhattisgarh), from 27.6 million to 34.1 million; and in Bihar (including Jharkhand), from 37 million to 48.55 million. But West Bengal and four southern states (AP, Kerala, Karnataka and Tamil Nadu) were able to reduce the absolute number of the rural poor substantially during the same period: Andhra Pradesh from 17.82 million to 6.47 million, Karnataka from 12.84 million to 7.5 million, Kerala from 11.14 million to 3.24 million, Tamil Nadu from 17.26 million to 7.65 million, and West Bengal from 25.79 million to 17.32

Table 1

A Profile of Multidimensional Global Poverty

Aspects	*Estimated No./Per Cent*	*Remarks*
(a) No access to adequate food	(a) 1.20 billion (b) 1.40 billion	(a) based on $1 daily per head (World Bank 2000) (b) based on $1.25 daily per head (World Bank 2008)
(b) Worldwide refugees	13.2 million	
(c) Desertification and drought-affected worldwide	l.5 billion	
(d) No access to safe drinking water	1.5 billion	
(e) No access to health services	880 million	
(f) People dying of infectious diseases/year	14.0 million	ICMR, 2008
(g) Children dying due to lack of vaccination/year	10.0 million	
(h) Malnourished people	840 million	
(i) No access to school education	125 million	
(j) Illiterate women	500 million	
(k) People suffering from hunger	963 million	14 per cent of world population (FAO, State of Food Insecurity in the World 2008)

Cont'd ...

... Cont'd

(l)	Persons dying daily due to preventable diseases	40,000–2.8 million children and 0.3 million women dying annually	
(m)	Woman dying every 260 live births	1	1 woman dying every minute
(n)	Persons killed by AIDS	20 million	
(o)	Persons affected by AIDS/HIV	34 million	
(p)	Decline of developing countries' share in global trade (1980–2000)	From 0.8 per cent to 0.4 per cent	Failure of globalization.

Source: Karlsson (2001); Sharma (2008); World Bank's Chen and Ravallion (2008); *TOI*, 20 September and 11 November 2008; UNDP (1998)

Table 2

Various Estimates of Poverty in India

Source (Agency/author)	*Year*	*People Below Poverty Line (millions)*	*Estimated Per Cent (Head Count Ratio)*	*Remarks*
(a) Planning Commission of India	2001	260	26%	193 million in rural areas (27%) (less than 2400 calorie per day per head in rural areas; living in Kachcha single room, spending less than ₹ 373 per capita per month)
(b) World Bank	2008	456	42%	Below international poverty line of $1.25 a day
(c) Asian Development Bank	2008	724.32	63.9%	Less than $1.35 a day (Asian Poverty Line)
(d) World Bank	2006	—	35%	$1PPP daily
(e) Arjun Sengupta et al.	2004–05	69.7	6.4%	(i) extremely poor with per capita consumption of 75% of official poverty line
		167.3	15.4%	(ii) poor – as per official poverty line
		207.0	19.0%	(iii) marginally poor – 25% above official poverty line
		392.0	36.0%	(iv) vulnerable – between 1.25 and 2 times of official poverty line
		836	76.8%	
(f) Planning Commission of India	2005–06		20.4%	

Cont'd ...

... *Cont'd*

(g) U. Patnaik	2008		70% to 87% (2004–5)	Less than ₹ 20 daily spending for 2200 calorie per head in rural areas; 87% on 2400 kcal basis
(h) K. Shankar	2007		60%	Below landholdings of 0.4 hectare
(i) Planning Commission of India	2004–05	301.72	27.5%	Population increase keeps number of poor high and constant (220.9 million in rural areas, 28.3%)

Source: *TOI* 27 August 2008, *Business Standard* 28 August 2008; Planning Commission of India (2008); Shankar (2007); Patnaik (2008); Sengupta et al. (2008)

million. Assam and Gujarat were also able to reduce the absolute number of the rural poor but not that substantially: from 7.64 million to 5.45 million and from 9.46 million to 6.35 million, respectively (see Table 3).

Table 3

Improvement and Deterioration in Poverty in States in India

Position	*State*	*No. (1973–74)*	*No. (2004–05)*
Improvement	Andhra Pradesh	17.82 million	6.47 million
	Karnataka	12.84 million	7.5 million
	Kerala	11.14 million	3.24 million
	Tamil Nadu	17.26 million	7.65 million
	West Bengal	25.79 million	17.32 million
	Assam	7.64 million	5.45 million
	Gujarat	9.46 million	6.35 million
Deterioration	UP (including Uttarakhand)	53.57 million	62.6 million
	Rajasthan	12.85 million	13.49 million
	Maharashtra	28.74 million	31.74 million
	Nagaland	0.29 million	0.4 million
	MP (including Chhattisgarh)	27.6 million	34.1 million
	Bihar (including Jharkhand)	37 million	48.55 million

Source: Based on Planning Commission of India

In a study by the International Food Policy Research Institute (*The Times of India*, 15 October 2008), India ranked 66th out of 88 countries in the world (Mauritius 1, China 15, Surinam 17, Sri Lanka 39, Pakistan 61, Burkina Faso 65). Seventeen states measured in India were found as follows:

I. *Extremely Alarming*: Madhya Pradesh

II. *Alarming*: Andhra Pradesh, UP, Tamil Nadu, Rajasthan, West Bengal, Karnataka, Odisha, Maharashtra, Gujarat, Chhattisgarh, Bihar and Jharkhand

III. *Serious*: Punjab, Kerala, Haryana and Assam

It was found that 60 per cent of children (below 5 years) in MP were underweight, 56 per cent children in Bihar were malnourished and even in Punjab 25 per cent children were underweight. MP ranks between Ethiopia and Chad and even the developed Punjab ranks below Gabon, Honduras and Vietnam. India, with 200 million hungry people, scores worse than 25 Sub-Saharan African countries and South Asia (except Bangladesh – due to better agricultural productivity in India than Bangladesh). Thus, the finding is that better economic growth does not necessarily translate into lower hunger levels (as in Gujarat and Maharashtra). In fact, hunger and malnutrition are rooted in poverty.

Social Composition

If we look at the social composition of the poor in rural India, we find that the SCs, STs and backward castes accounted for 80 per cent of the rural poor in 2004–05: 36.8 per cent SC, 47.3 per cent ST and 26.7 per cent OBC were found living below the poverty line by the Planning Commission of India (2008). Further, in rural population, the incidence of poverty among the STs declined at a slower rate from 51.9 per cent in 1993–94 to 47.3 per cent in 2004–05, while it declined from 37 per cent to 27.5 per cent in the total population. In terms of asset ownership too, the position of the SCs and STs is pathetic: though among the total population 60 per cent of rural households are cultivators, only 47 per cent of the SCs are cultivators while 25 per cent of the SCs are agricultural labourers. In terms of percentage of area owned by different social groups in rural areas, the position of the OBCs is the best (43.5%), followed by 'others' (36.3%), ST (11.2%) and SC (9%). Thus the position of OBCs is better than the general category (others). However, the percentage of households is unfavourable to SC (21.6%), compared to ST (10.6%), OBC (41.6%) and others (26.3%).

In terms of one of the health indicators – infant and child mortality – the position of SC/ST children/infants is adverse. In rural India, the infant mortality rate in 2005–06 for SCs was 71, for STs 64, for OBCs 61 and for 'others' 56, while the child mortality (below 5 years) was 95 for SCs, 100 for STs, 79 for OBCs and 68 for 'others'. Further, 42 per cent of the SC women and 46 per cent of the ST women had a Body Mass Index (BMI) less than 18.5 (cut-off for malnutrition). That is much higher than that for 'other' women

(30%) but it clearly shows a discrimination against women of all social groups. Again, maternal mortality rate in rural India is very high. Further, due to regional disparity, poverty is more pronounced in some states like Bihar, UP, Chhattisgarh, Jharkhand, Madhya Pradesh and Odisha, which account for 61 per cent (1999) of the number of the poor in India (increasing from 53% in 1993–94). However, unfortunately, even some developed states like Gujarat and Maharashtra could not reduce poverty significantly as the trickle-down theory did not work in practice. Second, it is also notable that the share of the agricultural labour households among the poor increased from 41 per cent in 1993–94 to 47 per cent in 1999–2000 whereas the share of self-employed in agriculture among the poor decreased from 33 per cent to 28 per cent during the same period (as the 55th round of NSS data reveal). Third, Jharkhand, Gujarat, Odisha, Chhattisgarh and Maharashtra account for more than three-fourths of the rural poor STs – the maximum percentage of rural poor tribes live in Odisha (73%).

Regarding the definition of poverty line, there is no agreed formula. Some scholars focus on minimum calorie intake (thus converting it into minimum earning per month), with food items only or food and non-food items like clothing, shelter, etc. (Planning Commission of India, 2008). Others emphasize on reasonable income based on purchasing power parity (PPP) or market exchange rates (World Bank). Still others underline basic needs like food, shelter, clothing, nutrition, sanitation, safe drinking water, primary education and primary health (Streeten et al., 1981). Paul Streeten et al., focus on 'first things first', i.e. for the eradication of poverty, the basic human needs of the poor in developing countries should be met. Hence, in addition to the income aspect, the consumption aspect for adequate standards of nutrition, health, shelter, water and sanitation, education and other essentials is emphasized. Thus, four issues are highlighted in the basic needs approach:

(a) Better education, nutrition and health are beneficial in reducing fertility, raising labour productivity, enhancing people's adaptability and capacity for change, and creating a political environment for stable development.

(b) The basic needs can be met even at a quite low level of income per head, without sacrificing economic growth; e.g. Sri Lanka achieved higher life expectancy than other South Asian countries though their per capita income was the same in the late 1970s.

(c) Even in the short term, the basic needs can be met by better reallocation and management of resources (from defence to food to education) – external assistance may help such redeployment.

(d) Though public policies are to be changed/redirected for meeting the basic needs, various political systems have succeeded in achieving these; e.g. market economy in South Korea, mixed economy in Sri Lanka, centrally planned economy in China and Cuba, and decentralized socialist economy in Yugoslavia successfully ensured a fairly equitable distribution of physical assets (e.g. land), a decentralized administration and delegation of decision-making to the local level, and appropriate policies. The role of women in households for meeting basic needs was also recognized.

They emphasize the line of ILO that in developing countries (unlike developed countries), in order to afford to be unemployed, a worker has to be fairly well-off. The root problem is poverty or 'low-productivity employment', not unemployment. Thus, poverty is the problem of 'the working poor', not of the unemployed.

The Ministry of Rural Development got its first quinquennial survey done for identifying the poor in 1992, using the income criterion. In the second survey (1997), it used consumption criterion and in the third (2002) it used a 13-criteria questionnaire (equal weightage to each). In fact, poverty is a multiple deprivation (making one unable to live a dignified life) involving the economic dimension (lack of assets like land and water, no access to forest produces, absence of job-led growth policies, providing doles leading to dependency syndrome) that affects mostly the agricultural labour, marginal/small farmers and the self-employed, the geographical/spatial dimension (pockets of rural areas of some states like Bihar, Odisha, UP, MP, Chhattisgarh, Jharkhand and Uttarakhand), the social dimension with discrimination based on caste and sex (like SC/ST groups and women) as well as lack of access to education, health and nutrition, the political dimension (lack of good governance to provide opportunities for livelihood and social security as well as ensuring peace), and the demographic dimension. This may be seen in Table 4.

Table 4

Multiple Dimensions of Poverty in India

Dimensions		*Ingredients*
(a) Economic	(i)	lack of access to livelihood sources (land, water, forest produces)
	(ii)	absence of job-led growth policies
	(iii)	self-employment scheme more as doles, leading to dependency syndrome
	(iv)	food insecurity
	(v)	lack of infrastructure – roads, electricity, irrigation facility and transport.
(b) Social	(i)	discrimination on the basis of caste and gender
	(ii)	lack of adequate access to education and technical skills
	(iii)	lack of adequate access to health services
	(iv)	lack of adequate social security to the aged, widows and destitutes
(c) Spatial	(i)	pockets of poverty (east UP, Bihar, MP, Chhattisgarh, Uttarakhand, Rajasthan and Odisha)
	(ii)	adverse ecological situations (flood, droughts, and soil degradation)
	(iii)	deforestation depriving the local people from food, fruits, fertilizers, fibre, fodder, etc.
	(iv)	politics of regionalism against the poor north Indians in Maharashtra and the North-East India
(d) Political	(i)	lack of good governance to provide opportunities for livelihood, social security and ensuring peace
	(ii)	absence of right to work as a fundamental right in the Constitution
	(iii)	MNREGA as mere peanuts in view of the enormous demand
	(iv)	policy of large dams or SEZs leading to mass displacement without adequate rehabilitation, destruction of flora, fauna, cultural heritage and sources of livelihood
	(v)	lack of development as freedom
	(vi)	lack of genuine participation in the governance
(e) Demographic	(i)	lack of family planning methods on time – leading to dependency syndrome
	(ii)	higher maternal mortality rate
	(iii)	higher infant and child mortality rate

A public interest litigation (PIL) was filed in the Supreme Court of India against the criteria used for defining the poverty line in India. Hence, the Planning Commission of India took a broad view to define poverty line with a multidimensional approach consisting of 27 targets in different sectors like (*Hindustan Times*, 19 August 2008):

(a) sustained 9 per cent growth rate;

(b) agricultural growth rate of 4 per cent (leading to 20% increase in wages of unskilled workers);

(c) education sector: lowering the drop-out rate by 20 per cent by 2011–12;

(d) developing a minimum education standard for all schools;

(e) increasing the literacy rate for persons of 7 years or more to 85 per cent;

(f) increasing the enrolment ratio in higher education to 15 per cent;

(g) health sector: halving the malnutrition rate to 40.4 per cent;

(h) providing clean drinking water to all by 2009;

(i) reducing total fertility rate to 2.1;

(j) infrastructure: providing electricity to all families below poverty line by 2009; and

(k) providing broadband facilities to all villages by 2015.

No doubt, it is a more comprehensive perspective to define poverty. The calorie norm has now almost taken a back seat. Needless to say that the calorie norm of 2,400 per head per day in rural India for estimating poverty by the Planning Commission of India in 1973–74 provided a total expenditure of ₹ 49 per month or ₹ 1.63 per day (for food and non-food items). As per the estimate by this official poverty line, 56 per cent of the rural population was found living below the poverty line in 1973–74 in India. Hence, Utsa Patnaik (2008) rightly observes that directly applying the calorie norm (food and non-food items) for defining poverty line was given up subsequently and the initially assessed minimum monthly expenditure of ₹ 49 for 2,400 calories was updated from time to time with a price index, but unfortunately it has resulted into 'an absurdly low official rural poverty line' of ₹ 12 per day by 2004–05. About 28 per cent of the rural Indian population spent less than ₹ 12 per day in 2004–05, but by that amount at the most 1,800 calories could be availed. According to Utsa Patnaik, availing 2,200 calories daily per head (the officially accepted norm in India in 1973–74) required a spending of ₹ 20 in 2004–05, but 70 per cent of India's rural population could not avail that then (an increase from 59 per cent in 1993–94 on the same basis). On the basis of 2,400 calories daily per head (the theoretically accepted norm in India in 1973–74), 87 per cent of the rural people lived below the poverty line in 2004–05 (a rise from 75 per cent in 1993–94 on the same basis). She finds even the World Bank's view of considering $1.25 (per day per head) for poverty line for 2005 as unrealistically low.

T.N. Srinivasan (2007) traces the history of defining the poverty line in India in four ways: First, in 1876, Dadabhai Naoroji defined poverty as living below subsistence: 'what is necessary for the bare wants of a human being, to keep him in ordinary good health and decency.' He calculated the costs on the basis of the diet prescribed by the Medical Inspector of Emigrants, a diet scale (including rice or flour, pulse, mutton, vegetables, ghee, oil and salt but excluding fuel, tobacco and spices) that did not take into account energy requirements for work. Thus, his subsistence costs–based poverty line varied from ₹ 16 to ₹ 35 per capita per year in different regions of India (at 1867–68 prices). Second, the National Planning Committee (1938) – with J. Nehru as its Chairman and K.T. Shah as its Secretary – talked of an irreducible minimum standard of living, varying from ₹ 15 to ₹ 20 per capita per month at current prices. It prescribed four tests: (a) improvement of nutrition with calories from 2,400 to 2,800 per adult worker; (b) improvement of clothing from the present consumption of 15 yards to 30 yards per capita per year; (c) housing standards to reach at least 100 sq feet per capita; (d) increase in agricultural and industrial production, and elimination of unemployment and illiteracy. Third, the Bombay Plan (prepared by P. Thakurdas, J.R.D. Tata, G.D. Birla, A. Dalal, S. Ram, A.D. Shroff and J. Mathai in 1944) prescribed a per capita annual income of ₹ 75 for the poverty line (at prices prevailing before the outbreak of the Second World War in 1939). Fourth, in 1962, a working group of economists prescribed three criteria of 'minimum level of living': (a) a national minimum of ₹ 20 per capita per month at 1960–61 prices; (b) the national minimum excludes expenditures on health and education (to be provided by the state); (c) an element of subsidy in urban housing is to be provided after taking ₹ 10, or 10 per cent of the national minimum of ₹ 100 per household (of 5 persons at the rate of ₹ 20 each) as rent. This 'minimum level of living (or poverty line) was at the heart of the Perspective Planning Division of the Planning Commission.

Thus, except for the Bombay Plan, these three perspectives focused on a basket of goods and talked of a minimum per capita (nutritional) daily energy requirement but did not link poverty lines to it rigidly. Later, the Task Force of Planning Commission (1979), using the NSS data of the 28th round (1973–74) prescribed the energy norm of 2,400 calories in rural areas (per capita per day) and 2,100 calories in urban areas (for both food and non-food items). Later, in 1993, poverty lines were updated for changes in prices by using the wholesale price index and later by using the private consumption deflation in the National Accounts Statistics. However, the 26th round (1971–72) of the NSS used a norm of 2,700 calories daily per head (for both rural and urban areas). That is why as per the NSS data, poverty increased significantly in rural India from 1993–94 to 2004–05, while as per the official poverty line it declined during the same period. Hence, Srinivasan argues for broadening of the concept of poverty – more than expenditure, a rights-based approach in the light of the Directive Principles of State Policy, but he distinguishes between 'private sphere responsibilities' (household) and 'public sphere responsibilities' (state). To him, the state is to focus on the health and education of the poor, and income transfer (through wage employment). Sanjay G. Reddy (2007) is rightly of the view that food consumption pattern of a group 'may reflect economic duress as well as tastes or prices' or a change in consumption pattern may result from increase/decrease in real income or from temporal change in tastes or prices, complicating the interpretation of poverty lines constructed at different times for the same group. Hence, both the direct and the indirect approaches to define poverty line are not satisfactory. Therefore, he argues for a broader and contextually sensitive approach to synthesize evaluative judgments and empirical evidence concerning preferences and opportunities. He notes the following facts on this account:

(a) In many parts of India, people now purchase items like fuel wood which were available free earlier as common property resource (now depleted).
(b) The possibility that poorer Indians are now better off cannot and should not be discounted; nor can it be assumed.

(c) Confusion arose due to the change of the recall period for select commodities in the 55th round (1999–2000) of the NSS – from the traditional 30-day period to either a 365-day period (for low-frequency expenditure items such as durables, footwear, clothing, education and medical expenses) or both a 7 and a 30-day recall period (for high-frequency expenditure items like food, *paan* and tobacco).

(d) It should be recognized that consumption (or income) poverty is the failure to possess elementary capabilities as a direct result of inadequate command over resources. Hence, Reddy follows Amartya Sen's conception of non-deprivation that is '*absolute* in the space of *capabilities* and *relative* in the space of *commodities*'; therefore, a capability-based approach should draw on evaluative judgments and on empirical information.

Similarly, using the 61st round of the NSS data (2003), Kripa Shankar (2007) explains that the bottom 51 per cent of the rural households in India had land holdings of less than 0.2 hectare, accounting for only 2 per cent of the total land; 60 per cent of the households had land holdings of less than 0.4 hectare; and 80 per cent of the households had land holdings of less than one hectare (while the top 1 per cent households had 15 per cent of the land). To him, 60 per cent of the rural households with less than 0.4 hectare can earn about ₹ 12,000 in a year from agriculture, ₹ 2,000 from livestock and ₹ 4,000 from wage labour at the most; hence, they are not above the poverty line. As per the World Bank's report by Chen and Ravallion (2008), 468 million more people became poor in 2005, and in India the percentage of poor increased from 22 to 30 during 1990–2005 while in China, it declined from 38 to 12 during the same period.

Further, the practice of GNP per capita as a measure of poverty (or prosperity) has three limitations (Thomas, 2000). First, it is an average measure not disclosing the distribution within a country. Second, using market valuations for measuring income per capita gives rise to at least two different problems with relating this measure to poverty levels: GNP is a measure of production and the value is given in a currency which can be freely converted internationally. Third, well-being is not entirely a matter of purchasing power, e.g. production for use – subsistence or 'direct entitlement' – by peasants.

Similarly, Maxwell (1999) rightly points out nine *faultlines* in the poverty debate:

(a) Individual or household measure: Earlier, only the household was taken into account for measuring poverty, ignoring the intra-household discrimination based on gender, age, disability, etc.

(b) Private consumption only or private consumption plus publicly provided goods/services (the social wage).

(c) Monetary or monetary plus non-monetary components of poverty (like autonomy, self-esteem or participation)

(d) Snapshot (point in time) or timeline, i.e. life-cycle experience, seasonal stress and shocks (illness, drought, flood, war, etc.).

(e) Actual or potential poverty: The current income may be adequate but the vulnerability is high.

(f) Stock of resources (land, jewellery and cash) or flow measures of poverty: The flow of resources that comes from social capital (contacts, networks, reciprocal relationships, community membership and entitlements) may derive not only from the current income but also from the past investments, stores or social claims on others (including the state).

(g) Input or output measures: Poverty measured as a shortfall in income essentially captures an input to an individual's capability and functioning rather than a direct measure of well-being. Often, some scholars wrongly assume an automatic link between income and participation.

(h) Absolute or relative poverty: The World Bank uses one dollar per head per day for absolute poverty while the relative deprivation is half the mean income or exclusion from participation in the society.

(i) Objective or subjective perceptions: The exposure to domestic violence may be important in one community; dependency on traditional structure may be so in another community.

We should take these aspects into account while defining poverty. Jeffrey D. Sachs (2005) thinks that the extreme poor lack six major types of capital:

(i) *Human capital* – health, nutrition, and skills to be economically productive;

(ii) *Business capital* – machinery facilities, motor transport used in agriculture, industry and services;

(iii) *Infrastructure* – roads, power, water and sanitation, airports and seaports, and telecommunications systems as critical inputs in business productivity;

(iv) *Natural capital* – arable land, healthy soils, biodiversity, and well-functioning ecosystems to provide environmental services;

(v) *Public institutional capital* – commercial law, judicial systems, government services and policing for peaceful and prosperous division of labour;

(vi) *Knowledge capital* – scientific and technological know-how that raises productivity in business output and the promotion of physical and natural capital.

Obviously, he thinks that these six types of capital should be made available to the poor in developing countries to get their feet on 'the ladder of development'. But we do not fully agree with him because developing countries like India have by and large adequate business capital, natural capital, public institutional capital and knowledge capital. We lack in human capital and infrastructure in rural areas, where even educated persons don't have the required skills. Our public policy needs to reallocate maximum resources to this on the one hand, and the administration should implement it and employment generation schemes in letter and spirit, on the other.

Impact of Globalization

What the outcome of globalization, liberalization and privatization on the poverty in developing countries has been, especially since the 1990s, is the moot question today. The first and foremost lesson is that higher economic growth may be a necessary but not sufficient condition. A higher growth rate with a higher per capita income does not lead to social equity and distributive justice on its own. On the other hand, even a moderate growth rate may lead to more social equity and distributive justice if it is accompanied with decentralization and better allocation of resources (out of the small kitty) for the poor, as in Sri Lanka, Kerala, China and Cuba. That is, the 'trickle down' theory does not hold good for all developing countries. Rather, the distribution (who gets what) matters as much as, if not more than, the size (how much is available) of the cake. It is most probable that if the vast majority duly knows about their share, they would be involved with more dedication for more production and better productivity.

Second, in practice, the market is neither fully free nor fully efficient, and, therefore, the market is unable to reduce poverty drastically without state intervention. Markets are usually imperfect due to imperfect information and imperfect competition, being corrupt and grabbed by the well-off traders. In fact, small farmers and labourers are 'compulsorily involved' in the market (to use Krishna Bharadwaj's term).

Third, global trade is not equally shared and mutually beneficial in a truly interdependent manner. The World Trade Organisation (WTO) has made such built-in mechanisms structurally that developed countries always benefit from these vis-à-vis the developing ones. For instance, developed countries provide a huge subsidy to their farmers (both to foodgrains and cotton growers), but they unjustly pressure the developing countries to drastically reduce or remove such subsidies. Earlier, the US had agreed to cut cotton subsidy by 70 per cent but at Geneva (July 2008) it refused to do so. Hence, the fate of Doha Round went in doldrums. On the other hand, the US insisted that developing countries should evolve a mechanism not to protect themselves against import surges in agricultural items. Similarly, the developing countries' demand for special safeguards for agriculture due to serious injury is not considered positively by the developed countries though the former should be allowed to raise the tariff above the 'bound' level as once damage/injury is done in agriculture, it cannot be recouped like in industry (because of its very seasonal nature and process). In fact, the wholesale application of West-supplied-and-inspired technology and global trade under the WTO regime has not benefitted the poor in the developing countries. Rather, a dependency syndrome has developed. Susan George (1981) remarks perceptively: 'Development has been the password for imposing a new kind of dependency, for enriching the already rich world and for shaping other societies to meet its commercial and political needs.' Consequently, the share of developing countries in global trade declined from 0.8 per cent to 0.4 per cent during 1980–2000.

Fourth, there has been a decline in the rate of development aid by the developed countries. For instance, in 1998, the US foreign aid totalled $8.8 billion (0.11% of GNP) and of this, only one-sixth went to the least developed countries – amounting to $5 per American in a year. This was so when the average per capita income of the US was more than $30,000! On the other hand, from the recipient's view, in 1998 about 600 million people in least developed countries received such US aid at the rate of $2.2 per head; in all low income countries (with per capita GNP being below $765 in 1995), 3.36 billion persons received US aid of $3.7 billion amounting to $1.13 per head (Sachs, 2001)! On the other hand, the US enthusiastically spent $8 billion to fight the 79-day war in Kosovo! This is the priority principle of the US that claims to champion peace and democracy everywhere in the world. Needless to say that development aid is often tied with various sorts of conditionality like structural adjustment, downsizing of government, disinvestment and other policy changes (that developing countries consider against their national interest) for the developing countries.

Fifth, there is a fast trend of assetlessness of the marginal people in the developing countries – more so, in the name of 'development' that displaces people by constructing big dams (like the Sardar Sarovar Project in MP), big power projects (Dadri, UP), industrial complexes (special economic zones like Singur, Nandigram), housing projects (Greater Noida), big stores and malls, huge roads/bridges, etc. without providing them adequate rehabilitation, just compensation at market rates, land for land, share in the company, etc. About 40 million poor Indians have been displaced due to such projects since 1947. The conditionality of structural adjustment lending was that aid can buy policy reform, but it has failed miserably in reality. On the other hand, such aid has developed a 'dependency syndrome'.

Sixth, the state under pressure from donors has withdrawn from its welfare role in most of the developing countries in the name of liberalization, economic reforms, privatization (public–private partnership is the buzzword) or structural adjustment. In many developing countries, repression by the state or its apparatuses (army, police, ideology, public institutions, etc.) has increased to the extent that the voice of dissent is suppressed in various ways and the protestors against unemployment, corruption, violation of human rights, etc. are tortured. Social security/safety net has been declining in many countries and under the manifest or latent instructions and guidance of multilateral financial institutions like World Bank, IMF, Asian Development Bank, to name the prominent ones, a substantial 'user fee' is being charged even for basic services like primary education, primary health and irrigation. Consequently, bad health, lack of education and lack of access to water for crops quickly drag the marginal people deeper into poverty. Rapid commercialization has further eroded the traditional social fabric and moral economy based on kinship. However, China successfully followed the economic reform strategy based on the dual tracks of gradualism and experimentation tailored to pre-existing institutions that matter and altering which takes time and genuine effort. Even Rodrik (2001) admits that development requires solid public institutions. For instance, Japan, the US and the Western European nations follow development model with similar focus on private property, sound money and rule of law but they have dissimilar practices in labour market relations, social insurance, corporate governance, product market regulation and taxation.

Seventh, in most of the developing countries, the middle class is much poorer in absolute terms than the upper class in their own countries and the middle class in the developed countries. For instance, in Brazil and Poland, middle-class households have a tenth of income (in purchasing power parity or PPP terms) of their counterparts in the US. So is the difference in education; e.g. in Costa Rica, adults in middle-class households have only six years of education, in Brazil only four years of education, while their counterparts in the US have 13 years of education. In addition, middle-class households in most of the developing countries are closer to poverty line and more downwardly mobile; e.g. in Indonesia 30 per cent of the non-poor households, and in Peru 22 per cent, are likely to become poor in next three-six years, based on the three-year fluctuation in the reported per capita household expenditure (2000). Poverty eradication, therefore, requires sustainable growth that, in turn, requires adequate public institutions, whose bedrock is usually the middle class in a democratic polity. Hence, a market-friendly middle class is ultimately required for poverty reduction in most of the developing countries, says Birdsall (2001). We think that the withdrawal of the state from its welfare role gives way to such requirement. This trend has emerged because of contractualization, casualization and informalization of most of the new emerging jobs (hire-and-fire basis, without protection and security). More often than not, women workers are the worst victims, thus leading to the feminization of poverty.

II
Perspectives on Poverty

There are various theories of and perspectives on poverty which have been categorized into three as follows (Goldsmith and Blakely, 1992):

(a) Poverty as pathology

(b) Poverty as incident or accident

(c) Poverty as structure

Further, Barry R. Schiller (1976) categorizes these into two points of view: (i) 'flawed character' view and (ii) 'restricted opportunity' view. The first view sees the incidence of poverty as a natural concomitant of individual defects in aspiration or ability or even a punishment for vice, sin or immorality (by a law of providence). This view, shared by many upper-class Americans, western Europeans and Indians, sees insufficient effort, lack of ability, weak motivation, immoderation, loose morals and drunkenness as causes of poverty. On the other hand, the 'restricted opportunity' view proposes that 'the poor are poor because they do not have adequate access to good schools, jobs and income because they are discriminated against on the basis of colour, sex, income or class and because they are not furnished with a fair share of government protection, subsidy or services' (Schiller, 1976: 40).

In another perspective of culture as the root cause of poverty, Edward C. Banfield (1973) argues that the innate cultural ethos of some groups prevents them from acquiring the proper work habits, moral disposition, attitudes and cultural norms necessary for social mobility. Taking a conservative view, he suggests that government should not waste resources trying to change the cultural weaknesses of such groups; rather, it should constrain their physical mobility and ability to damage others' chances. Similarly, George Gilder (1989) holds that the real problem is not poverty but a 'collapse of family discipline and sexual morality'. He further suggests that poverty is inevitable for some persons due to their moral character – the poor have rejected hard work, marriage, family, and religious faith. In his book *Wealth and Poverty*, Gilder (1981) holds that the only assured way out from poverty is hard work, family and faith. Thus, like Banfield, he is also of the view that poverty reflects immorality and lack of hard work. The first view, thus, focuses wrongly on individual behaviour and the second view rightly on social, political and economic structures or situations. To the question why poverty has continued among the blacks for a long time, Jay R. Mandel (1978) finds the answer in the plantation economy in the South. W.E.B. DuBois (1985) is more forthright, blaming the state policy for keeping the blacks poor to confine them to menial occupations to make them surplus labour reservoir and force them to 'peonage and unpaid toil'.

Similarly, Henry George (1958) finds that in America, poverty has been the result of socio-economic forces and the concomitant absence of the political base for impacted groups – poverty being related to the rise in land values and the poor did not own land at all. Low wages and lack of jobs at decent wages are the significant causes of poverty for all groups. Barry Bluestone (1969) found a strong correlation between poverty and low wages. Similarly, Linda R. Martin and K.D. Giannaros (1990) found that in relative terms the real minimum wages plays a major role in explaining the feminization of poverty. Similarly, David Osborne (1990) holds that economic decline, especially decline in manufacturing jobs, is the root cause of poverty and it reflects the ill health of the economy from which a large number of people are disconnected – they are caught in a downward spiral of disinvestments, increasing poverty and further disinvestments. As Vijay P. Singh (1991) points out, in America, the massive elimination of blue-collar entry-level jobs and the emergence of knowledge-based jobs have not favoured many blacks who do not have adequate level of education, skill or work experience. Hence, their unemployment and growing isolation has led to unwed parenting, dependency, lawlessness, joblessness and school failure among the blacks.

The 'culture of poverty' thesis of neo-conservatives like Charles Murray (1984), Gilder, Banfield and others has rightly been questioned by scholars like William J. Wilson (1987), who points out 'social isolation' as the root cause of poverty because the poor do not conform to the norms of middle-class expectations as they are detached and isolated from the latter. Famous sociologist Charles A. Valentine (1968) has taken the same view in his book *Culture and Poverty*, arguing that cultural explanation is a 'subtle form of social class and racial snobbery and ignorance.' Therefore, he calls for more social welfare programmes for the poor, on the one hand, and their political mobilization, on the other. Manning Marable (1983, 1987) and Cornel West (1987) are also of the view that those scholars who emphasize on fatalistic or culture-focused perspectives to explain black poverty, represent the interests of political, social, economic and cultural status quo that are antithetical to the well-being of the poor or to poverty eradication.

Similarly, some scholars like P.A. Baran and P.M. Sweezy (1966) focus on lack of political power as the cause of poverty. According to them, the system has two poles: wealth, privilege and power at one pole; and poverty, deprivation and powerlessness at the other.

Hence, both poles should be abolished, and a new society with shared wealth and power is the need of the hour. Similarly, Martin Luther King, Jr (1967) found persistent poverty as a reflection of the political power and moral will of the wealthy and better-off sectors in society and, therefore, only 'power can transform the ghetto'. According to him, growing militarization and imperialism of the US government are to be confronted. Besides, he felt, the US capitalism produces and is responsible for poverty of the blacks. Martha Nussbaun has taken capabilities approach – e.g. the ability to live a full life, engage in recreational activities and participate in political affairs – as a framework of development. She has improved Amartya Sen's approach on substantial freedoms in contrast with the liberal classical view of seeing development in terms of economic growth and accumulation of wealth only (implying poverty simply as a lack of growth and wealth). To her, if someone is deprived of 10 human capabilities, he/she is poor and not able to live a decent and dignified human life. Her approach has elements of Amartya Sen, young Karl Marx (who talked of leisure, sociability and humanness required for workers) and the Universal Declaration of Human Rights, 1948.

From the above, it transpires that poverty is a multi-dimensional problem where various social, economic, spatial and political aspects of deprivation cause poverty. The public policy of liberalization, privatization and globalization excludes the marginal people from the mainstream of the economy, polity and society by depriving them of sustainable livelihood, health and hygiene, education, subsidized food and water, nutrition, and labour-intensive technology in agriculture and industry. Amartya Sen (2008) talks of a shift from 'arrangement-focused' view of justice (*niti*) to *'realization-focused'* view of justice (*nyaya*) as being central for the practice of democracy being more than the sum of its parts.

It is not out of context to mention here that a UN Millennium Campaign was launched on 17–19 October 2008 – 'Stand Up: Take Action Against Poverty Campaign' – in which 116.99 million people from 110 countries (15 million from India) participated to press the policy makers to alleviate poverty as per the UN Millennium Development Goals. The US gave a package of $700 billion overnight to bail out the richest bankers like Wall Street, Lehmann Brothers, AIG, etc. in October 2008 and $1,000 billion is spent by the US on one war, but the UN falls short of only $18 billion to meet the MDGs and yet this fund does not come by (*The Hindu*, 23 October 2008).

III
Microfinance to the Poor

Here we discuss microfinance as a strategy to eradicate rural poverty in India. The microfinance movement began in the 1970s under the leadership of Mohammad Yunus with the creation of the Grameen Bank in 1976 as a response to fight the extreme poverty during the 1974 famine in Bangladesh. He found various economic theories of no practical use to understand 'the real-life economics played out everyday in villages' (Yunus, 2008). In Jobra village, then, moneylenders were charging an interest rate of 10 per cent per week. So, he gave the first loan of just $27 from his own pocket and since then, Grameen Bank has given credit to 7 million villagers (including 1,00,000 beggars) without any collateral and its 97 per cent women loanees have repaid up to 98 per cent. Now, he also talks of 'social business' with profits to be returned to the poor owners. Thus, there are two types of micro credit programme in the Grameen Bank (Bangladesh):

Type I: Poverty-focused micro credit programme: Poverty-focused, collateral-free and low-interest micro credits where interest rate does not exceed (a) cost of fund plus 10 per cent (green rate) or (b) cost of fund plus 15 per cent (yellow rate).

Type II: Profit-maximizing micro credit programme: Interest rate above cost of fund plus 15 per cent (red rate); it is actually a moneylending programme under the garb of micro credit.

The Grameen Bank claims itself to be sustainable as it has also created employment for 25,000 staff with long-term job security. But this is not fully true because many of the staff have left their jobs due to less salary and rigorous cycling in villages for a long distance. Besides, the Grameen Bank succeeded in Bangladesh because of certain special features there: (i) bank going to the client, not vice versa; (ii) practice of prioritizing single female-headed households, the absolutely landless or those owning only homestead land; (iii) bank's goals of bringing of self-reliance, obligations to society and health care like tree plantation, using latrines, educating children, no dowry, mutual help, etc.; (iv) no provision of subsidy; and (v) dedicated bank staff working in rural areas. Microfinance has spread to many developing countries and in South Asia, microfinance has covered about 50 million families, meeting 15 per cent of the credit need of the poor families, but in Bangladesh and Sri Lanka, microfinance services have covered 60 per cent of the poor, while India and Nepal have the minimum coverage, and Pakistan and Afghanistan have a low coverage. As per one estimate (December 2007), the size of microfinance in India is ₹ 27,000 millions and is expected to rise up to ₹ 2,50,000 millions by 2012 (*Jansatta*, 21 May 2008).

The concept of microfinance is broader than that of micro credit in degree and magnitude, range and depth. The Reserve Bank of India (1999) has defined microfinance as 'the provision of thrift, credit and other financial services and products of very small amount to the poor enabling them to raise their income levels and improve living standards.' Now the questions arise: Why microfinance? How to give microfinance and for what? And microfinance for whom? First, microfinance emerged to fill up the credit vacuum created by the commercial banks in rural areas. In India, the coverage of institutional finance in rural areas is very limited. As per NSS 59th round (2003), only 27 per cent of the total cultivator households received credit from formal (institutional) sources, 22 per cent from informal sources and the remaining 51 per cent of marginal and small farmers as well as the landless labourers have no access to credit in rural India. Second, the village moneylenders charge a very high rate of interest. Third, the institutions (banks and cooperatives) do not trust the poor (declaring them not bankable); their lending processes and procedures are cumbersome; and they indulge in corrupt practices at different stages. So, the credit–deposit (CD) ratio declined over the years (Table 5).

Table 5

Region-wise Decline in Credit–Deposit Ratio (1981–2001)

Region	*1981*	*1991*	*2001*
(a) Eastern	54	50	37
(b) Central (MP, UP)	47	50	33
(c) North Eastern	43	50	28

Source: Shetty (2005)

Thus, it is clear that in all these regions, the CD ratio declined during 1981–2001, the North-Eastern region suffering the most (28%). In Bihar, it was about 25 per cent, depriving the local people of their 75 per cent deposits in banks. Further, with the background of an increase in population growth as well as the deteriorating condition of farmers and labourers in most of rural India, it was expected that more and more bank branches would be opened in rural areas, but the reality is otherwise. Forget opening of new branches; even the several existing bank branches in rural areas were closed, merged with others or shifted to urban areas. For instance, the number of Regional Rural Banks (RRBs) declined from 196 in 1990 to 104 in 2006. Further, the total number of loan accounts fell from 65.9 million in 1991 to 52.4 million in 2001, while both the credit and deposits in private banks increased from about 4 per cent each in 1990 to 18–19 per cent each in 2005 (RBI, 2006; Shah et al., 2007). However, since new NDA government in June 2014, Prime Minister started 'Jan Dhan Yojana' wherein crores of new accounts of the poor persons were opened liberally for financial inclusion. Therefore many new branches of banks were also opened. Hence, microfinance evolved as a mode of small loans to the needy and poor for self-employment through income-generating activities and provided for backward and forward linkages. That is, the assetless poor people were trusted and treated as bankable without collaterals. Moreover, the commercial public sector banks do not provide any consumption loan or health and school education loan to the rural poor, but microfinance did not hesitate to cover such human needs of the rural poor. In India, the evolution of microfinance has taken two major models of processing:

(a) *Self-help Group–Bank Linkage* (SBL)

(b) *Micro Finance Institutions* (MFIs)

The SBL model was started in India in 1992 by NABARD with a pilot project of 500 self-help groups (SHGs) and later it worked in partnership with three non-governmental organizations (NGOs), namely, MYRADA, PRADAN and DHAN. By March 2006, more than 2.2 million SHGs had been disbursed loans of ₹ 1,13,980 millions covering 30 million families, thus accounting for 6.5 per cent of the total rural credit of commercial banks (NABARD, 2006). There are five major SBL models (Sharma, 2008):

(a) *Model I:* The bank deals with the SHG directly by providing finance for on-lending to the individual members of the group.

(b) *Model II:* The bank gives direct finance to the SHG while an NGO provides training and guidance as a facilitator to the group.

(c) *Model III:* An NGO may be a financial intermediary between the bank and several SHGs. It accepts contractual responsibility for loan repayment to the bank. The linkage between the bank and the SHGs remains indirect as it is the NGO that takes loans from the bank.

(d) *Model IV:* The bank gives loans directly to the members of an SHG on recommendation of that SHG and an NGO assists the bank in the monitoring, supervision and recovery of loans.

(e) *Model V:* Foreign donors finance the NGOs and the latter, in turn, extend the loan to the SHGs.

It has been found that the SBL mode of finance has been uneven across India as more than 54 per cent of credit-linked SHGs and 75 per cent of cumulative SHG loans were disbursed in south India; that is, the north and the north-east have been covered very poorly. While the number of rural bank branches (as per the RBI) increased during 1969–1990 from 1,443 to 34,867, it declined afterwards to 30,572 in 2006. Second, their share in total credit outstanding decreased from 14.2 per cent to 8.1 per cent. Third, interestingly, the deposits of rural bank branches during 1990–2006 increased from ₹ 2,86,090 millions to ₹ 22,60,490 millions.

On the other hand, the MFIs came into being to intermediate the financial resources and services between (a) investors, banks, donors and depositors on the one hand and (b) the poor people on the other. Since the transaction costs of MFIs are high as their coverage is in remote areas and account sizes are small, it has taken three to seven years for the MFIs to become financially strong enough to attract commercial risk capital. Hence, donors' funding has played a significant role of 'venture capital' in stimulating micro-finance investment and promoting microfinance markets. In India, 162 MFIs disbursed loans to the tune of ₹ 16 billion by March 2006 (Ghate, 2006). It has been growing further in leaps and bounds.

One such enterprise, SKS Micro Finance, having a staff of 3,000, led by Vikram Akula, covered 0.65 million women borrowers exclusively and aspired to cover 5 million clients across India. To him, 'the poor look for opportunity and not charity. Give them opportunity and they will protect it, use loans productively.' Besides, like other MFIs, it charged a higher interest rate of 25 per cent annually and even then its recovery rate was 99 per cent. It justified the higher interest rate on two counts: (a) though regional rural banks charge nominally at 7 per cent or so, the cost of borrowing from them is too high due to bribes, lack of collateral among the poor making them ineligible, cumbersome process of bank loans, and so on; and (b) to scale-up microfinance with commercial capital, profit-oriented model needs to be adopted. SKS Micro Finance took funds from Citibank (800 million rupees), ICICI bank and Stanchart as venture capital, and it has financed the poor women in 11 states from Andhra Pradesh to Bihar. Akula sees microfinance as a 'ticket out of poverty' and C.K. Prahlad calls it a 'fortune at the bottom of the pyramid' (Gupta, 2007). SKS Micro Finance lends exclusively to women due to three reasons:

(a) Women tend to invest money back in their households, while men spend a part of the loan for personal consumption also.

(b) Women are actually more risk-averse than men, hence more careful and successful.

(c) In group loans, more inter-personal cooperation is required as everybody is a guarantor for other members of the group and women fulfil this requirement better than men.

However, it is also a fact that many farmers' suicides have been taking place in Andhra Pradesh and Maharashtra, suggesting thereby that Akula's model of MFI has not been successful everywhere. Hence, ultimately it was wound up.

Self-Help Groups in Bihar

In Bihar, Mahila Vikas Nigam (Women's Development Corporation) is the nodal agency for women's empowerment through SHGs. It implements three SHG-oriented projects of Government of India – *Swayamsiddha, Swawalamban* and *Deep* (for SC women). In fact, the SHG approach is adopted for self-confidence-building through community action. For this purpose, the Government of India allocated ₹ 0.6 million to each block, but the SHGs are free to avail funds from other agencies like the state government and local *panchayats*, amounting to 60 per cent as institutional share of the project and 40 per cent SHGs' share.

An SHG passes through three phases – formation, stabilization and growth, and sustainability and self-reliance. Under the aegis of Mahila Vikas Nigam, Bihar, 10,181 SHGs had been formed in Bihar by 2006 with cumulative savings of ₹ 38.35 million and 7,520 bank accounts opened, but the SHG–Bank linkage materialized only in 896 cases. Banks gave loan to the tune of ₹ 15.44 million. On the other hand, MFIs gave loans to the tune of ₹ 1.25 million only. Thus, we find that the SHG–Bank linkage is not satisfactory but it also shows that the coverage of MFIs is worse – hardly a seventh of the SBL mode. By 2005, 80 blocks of 22 districts (out of 38) had been covered in the formation of SHGs. Though more SHGs were formed in Gaya, Samastipur, Vaishali and Rohtas, the quality of such groups was pronounced in Muzaffarpur and Madhubani districts probably because of the availability of better NGOs in the latter.

Table 6

A Profile of Successful SHGs in Muzaffarpur (Bihar)

Name of SHG	Activities	Mobilization Process	Outcome
(1) Hina, Haraun (Motipur block)	Fishery	(a) village lake being captured by the feudal lord deprived the poor of fishing (b) fisherwomen protested; they dug 10 ponds and put seedlings there out of their savings (c) one local NGO helped	(a) additional income of ₹ 8,000 (from an investment of ₹ 2,500) per year (b) self-confidence-building (c) development as freedom from local exploitation (d) capability-building
(2) Pankhuri, Marwan (Marwan block)	Lac bangle-making	(a) savings habit (b) training and visit to bangle-making sites (c) publicity of work attracted a few buyers, then sale in local market, festivals and fairs (d) improvement in the quality of bangles (e) trying to scale up (f) help from an NGO	(a) additional income of ₹ 1,000 per month per head (b) self-confidence-building (c) exposure to the outside world (d) skill development (capability-building)

Cont'd ...

... *Cont'd*

(3)	Santoshi, Alineura, (Minapur block)	Lac bangle-making	(a) training (b) help of an NGO	(a) additional income (b) skill upgradation: trainee becomes trainer (c) self-confidence-building (d) exposure to the outside world
(4)	Yamuna, Maidapur (Bochahan block)	Sheep/goat-reari ng, dairy, poultry, blanket-weaving, shops	(a) regular meetings of the group (b) savings habit due to the meetings (c) meetings led to problem – identification (d) search for solution (e) help from an NGO (Sansarg)	(a) earning additional income (b) capability-building (c) self-confidence-building (d) repayment regular

Cont'd ...

... Cont'd

(5)	Saraswati, Marwan Bhoj (Marwan block)	Dairy	(a) regular meetings led to savings habit (b) help from an NGO (Nirdesh) (c) mobilization for solving social problem – personal is political: Munni Kumari (daughter of a member) was deserted by her husband; panchayat and SHG helped to solve the problem	(a) self-confidence-building (b) women's empowerment – challenging patriarchy for gender justice (c) development as freedom (d) earning additional income

Table 6 gives a glimpse of the success stories of the SHGs in Muzaffarpur (Bihar).

Limitations of the MFIs

But, all said and done, MFIs suffer from various limitations:

(i) High transaction costs due to small sizes of loans.

(ii) High interest rates, often leading to more cost than benefit from loans.

(iii) High pressure to lend somewhat in order to maximize profit: 'dumping money on borrowers' (Ghate, 2006).

(iv) Lack of transparency: Unfortunately, they charge interest for the entire remaining period, irrespective of its repayment earlier or adjusting overdues against the security deposit.

(v) Usually, MFIs use all types of coercive methods of recovery like frequent visit, holding meetings or sit-ins before borrower's home, abusing/insulting the borrowers in public or pasting notice on the borrower's house, pressurizing to sign blank cheques or even using physical coercion. Consequently, some borrowers abscond and migrate to other areas with families or even commit suicide (e.g. in AP, Maharashtra, etc.).

(vi) Due to the commercialization of microfinance, the missionary human welfare zeal of providing credit to the needy to come out of poverty is giving way to the so-called financial viability and expansion. The unhealthy competition between the MFIs is resulting into benefit to wealthy borrowers. In the Telangana region of Andhra Pradesh, the SHGs excluded the poorest and perpetuated the existing caste and class hierarchies (Rao, 2005).

(vii) MFIs' management capacity is often low; hence they are unable to attract adequate finance from equity investors, financial institutions and voluntary depositors for long term.

(viii) Due to pressure to repay at a particular time, the poor borrowers are often compelled to borrow, on adverse terms from the moneylenders in order to pay back the MFIs.

(ix) MFIs like SEWA Bank also suffer from the problem of overdues, ranging 20–28 per cent during 1996–97–1998–99, while the same ranged 16–18 per cent during 1995–96–1997–98 in public sector banks.

Limitations of the SBL Mode

The following deficiencies have cropped up in the SBL mode:

(i) Like earlier self-employment programmes (e.g. Integrated Rural Development Programme), the SBL mode often suffers from cumbersome process and procedure. On the one hand, the SHGs have their own by-laws regarding minimum monthly savings, conditions of lending, holding meetings, penal provisions for violation of rules, and so on. On the other hand, banks also have a plethora of formal procedures for eligibility, selection of activities, feasibility of project, training, record-keeping, etc. So, most of the illiterate or semi-literate poor farmers and landless labourers get bogged down and are, hence, usually excluded from this micro-credit facility.

(ii) Unfortunately, the SBL mode, too, suffers from the target syndrome as it is usually a 'govt-pushed model' of microfinance – too many targets at a given time for a unit of administration (panchayat or block) costs the quality of the SHGs. This may result into a 'macro debt' in due course (Shah et al., 2007).

(iii) The negative attitude of banks in processing microfinance to the poor still persists due to corruption, apathy, misunderstanding, feudal mentality (calling borrowers to the bank frequently) and passivity (not doing field visits to assess projects). In 2000–01, as per the RBI, total lending under the SBL mode was less than 0.5 per cent of the total amount disbursed by banks for agriculture and allied activities. Further, there is a huge gap between the number of loan applications sent to banks and the number of applications sanctioned (hardly 50 per cent of the total). The Eleventh Five Year Plan (Planning Commission of India, 2008) itself admits that under the Swarnajayanti Gram Swarozgar Yojana (SGSY), 2.6 million SHGs have been formed since its inception, of which 1.6 million SHGs crossed the Grade I stage (entitling revolving fund of ₹ 10,000) and 0.8 million SHGs crossed the Grade II stage and of the latter less than 0.5 million (60%) took up economic activities but the remaining 40 per cent are waiting for financial assistance. Of about ₹ 250 billion credit flow targeted under SGSY, less than 50 per cent has been achieved. Hence, there is a need to review the graded system of fund flow to SHGs thoroughly.

(iv) The government offices like Blocks, DRDAs (District Rural Development Agencies) or Zila Parishads, from where applications are forwarded and recommended (to banks) or subsidies granted, are also not sensitive and transparent in selection of borrowers, preparation of projects, training of borrowers, backward and forward linkages (from input to marketing stages). Often, the subsidy portion is cornered by the village level worker (VLW), Block Development Officer (BDO), bank manager and his staff as a birthright. This is popularly known as *'Suvidha Shulk'* (speed money) in north India and *'mamool'* in south India.

(v) In most of the states in India, except Andhra Pradesh, Kerala and Tamil Nadu (Kudumshree linked with panchayats in Kerala), there is no genuine effort to mobilize the SHGs both in terms of evolving institutions like federation of SHGs at district or state level for sharing of knowledge and better practices/success stories about reducing transaction and promotional costs, provision of value added services, creating better and more human capital, and also socially empowering the members of SHGs for bringing social change in the relations of production, developing collective bargaining power and collective self-reliance of groups. In fact, the motive and potential of group dynamics to compensate for the weaknesses of the individual rural poor has not been realized in most of rural India yet.

(vi) There is a provision for innovative and alternative projects under SGSY but it is hardly implemented. In the entire country, only 231 such innovative projects were sanctioned and only 29 were completed due to inefficiency and indifference, admits the Planning Commission in the Eleventh Five Year Plan (2008).

(vii) Usually, the transaction costs of SHGs are high because of frequent meetings locally as well as with banks (and sometimes with NGOs if they are involved as catalysts or intermediaries). No doubt, time is money and most of the rural SHG members are poor farmers or labourers or local artisans; hence they also lose their wages due to frequent meetings.

(viii) SHGs can not be substitutes to public sector banks. While banks need SHGs for promoting their products, the SHGs also need the banks for adequate microfinance in order to flourish.

(ix) It is also a fact that there is a new dishonest trend among a section of the rural poor of misusing the microfinance (individually or collectively). The common perception (that has emerged from dishonest situations) that loan is not to be repaid due to some expected government debt relief scheme or absence of regular monitoring from public sector banks makes the borrowers passive (either spending for non-priority consumption or not bothering in giving the bribe to Block and bank staff). This is also because of the wrong selection process or lack of training of borrowers to raise their motivation and commitment. In some people's common perception, there is a vast gap between taking personal '*karja*' (debt) and taking public loan (from banks, cooperatives, etc.). While the non-repayment of the former is considered sinful and is to be repaid with heavy interest even in the next birth, the non-repayment of public loan is not considered sinful and may, hence, be spent carelessly.

We can depict a comparative profile of SBL, MFIs and moneylenders in Table 7.

From Table 7, it transpires that financing by moneylenders leads to pauperization and semi-bondage of loanees due to economic and social costs, lack of transparency, high pressure of recovery, and a very high interest rate, but it is highly informal and flexible. On the other hand, the SBL mode is moderately transparent, has no social costs and less pressure of recovery, provides long and medium term loan for income-generating activities, has low interest rates, and is more inclusive, but it is formal in structure and procedure, bribe is taken by staff, has a high transaction cost but low recovery rate, and insensitive red-tapism. MFI credit is informal and more flexible, has a high recovery rate and wide coverage but it has high transaction costs, a high interest rate, pressure for recovery and profit motive (commercialization).

IV
Beyond Microfinance

As we have seen in the preceding section, both modes of microfinance have, inter alia, limitations as their vision is not far-sighted. Rather, working within the socio-economic system, they intend to bring about only functional and incremental changes in the system slowly, not change it structurally, viz., change in production relations and distribution system. In fact, the fundamental social, economic and political changes may be brought about only through measures of structural change like comprehensive land reforms and restoration of Common Property Rights (CPRs), especially in states like

Table 7

Comparison of Modes of Microfinancing

Aspects	*SBL*	*MFI*	*Moneylenders*
Structure	Mix of formal (bank) and informal (SHG)	Informal	Informal
Transaction Cost	High	High	No cost to very low cost
Formality	Complex, more	Simple, little	Simple, very little
Rate of Interest (annual)	Low to moderate (7–10%) simple interest rate	High (25%) simple interest rate, but charging for entire period, even if paid earlier	Very high (60 per cent+), cumulative rate
Social Cost	Little	Little	High (forced labour, non-payment for hens, fruits, vegetables, sexual abuse of women)
Flexibility	Moderate	High	High
Area of operation	Scattered in remote villages	Scattered in remote villages	Compact
Collateral	No, only group guarantee	No, only group guarantee	Yes, ornaments, land on *rehan* (mortgage), costly utensils
Size of loan	Small	Small	Small to large
Gender of loanees	Mostly females	Mostly females	Mostly males
state of recovery/ repayment	Moderate (greater frequency of small amounts)	High (greater frequency of small amounts)	High (greater frequency of small amounts)

Cont'd ...

... Cont'd

Nature of loan	Group	Group	Individual
Transparency	Moderate (cut by bank, block staff)	Less	Least (manipulation maximum, forgery)
Mode of recovery	Notice, recovery certificate	Notice, demonstration, drum beating, abuse, pressurizing to sign blank cheque, physical coercion – leading to migration/suicide	*Dharna* (sit-in), abuse, insult in public, physical coercion
Category of loanees	Poor labourers, marginal and small farmers, artisans, women	Poor labourers, marginal and small farmers, artisans, mostly women	Poor labourers, small and marginal farmers, artisans, hardly women
Type of loan activities	Mostly income-generating activities	Mostly income-generating activities	Mostly for consumption, rarely for production
Duration of credit	For long/medium-term needs	For long/medium-term needs	Short-term needs (traditional)
Motive of financing	Govt-pushed, target oriented with insensitivity but non-profit	Profit	Profit
Outcome	Relatively positive – reducing poverty, reducing moneylender's pressure	Mixed (positive and negative both) – reducing poverty without compromising on profit	Negative (pauperization and semi-bondage of the loanee and enrichment of the money lender)

Bihar and Jharkhand, where there still prevails the practice of absentee landlordism, *benami* lands, sharecropping, suppression/grabbing of ceiling surplus and Bhoodan lands, the practice of non-payment of minimum wages, etc. leading to various socio-economic conflicts (in rural areas) and attacks by the naxalites. It has been found in Bihar (Sharma, 2008) that 0.39 million acres of Bhoodan lands are pending for confirmation and distribution for several decades; so is the case of ceiling surplus lands (0.11 million acres) and other public (government) lands.

The Government of India itself admits that MNREGA 'supplements income' of the poor. But where is the income that would be supplemented? If the poor get land, only then MNREGA may supplement the income earned from land. The truth is that for the eradication of poverty in rural areas, 'land matters' because despite the growth rate of Indian economy at 9 per cent per annum, neither industry nor non-agricultural activities in rural India are able to provide livelihood to the teeming millions. Rural violence has highlighted the major issue of the rural poor's access to land, water, forest produce, etc. (Bandhyopadhyay, 2008). More than 150 districts in 12 states in India are affected by the naxals, known as 'fish in water' (Mao Zedong) – the fish are the naxals and water symbolizes the disgruntled peasants and agricultural labourers. In fact, the possession of even a small piece of land – say homestead land – gives the poor a sense of dignity, self-confidence, freedom from bondage, legal entitlement (for opening a bank account, taking a loan, being benefited from Indira Awas Yojana, etc.). Deshkal, an NGO, conducted a survey in the Gaya district of Bihar with the help of a ₹ 4.2 million funding from DFID (Deptt for International Development, UK). Thirty-three per cent of the state's dalits live in Gaya and among these dalits, 60 per cent are *Musahars* living in 200 villages – the poorest of the poor. Out of the 20,000 households of *Musahars* surveyed there, 13,000 had no homestead lands in their names. With the help of the local administration, Deshkal was successful in distributing homestead lands with legal *Vasgit parchas* to 1,800 *Musahar* households in 2006–07.

Second, there is a big scope of public investment in agriculture and allied activities, especially in watershed management, soil conservation, agro-forestry, sustainability of common property resources and infrastructure in villages. Needless to say the increase in public investment in agriculture and allied activities triggers increase in private investment there directly and quickly. The Green

Revolution in the mid-1960s reduced poverty through better productivity and higher production, more employment and more income. But since Green Revolution has some negative consequences like soil degradation, lowering of water table, salinization of soil, etc. there is a need for 'evergreen revolution', as Swaminathan rightly says, with eco-sustainability (sustainable agriculture through integration of traditional knowledge and modern science). The goal of Green Revolution in India was to strike a balance between population growth and food production. It demystified the myth of food production (at arithmetic rate) lagging far behind the over-population (geometric progression) by establishing a synergy between the innovative technology (high-yielding varieties of seeds, assured irrigation, chemical fertilizers, and pesticides/insecticides), proactive public policy of field demonstrations/extension (from lab to land) as well as subsidies and the positive response from farmers.

Since the 1990s, however, there has been a perceptible decline in the rate of growth of food production, probably due to 'a fatigue of green revolution' (Swaminathan, 2008). As per his estimate, by 2050, cereal yield and net irrigation is to be increased by 40 per cent in India and an additional 100–200 million hectares of land may be required to meet the then food demand. The evergreen revolution is based on eco-technology – eco-agriculture (organic farming), bio-fertilizers, bio-pesticides, integrated crop–livestock production system, integrated pest management, integrated nutrient supply, and integrated resource management – unlike commodity-centred increase in productivity through heavy doses and more frequencies of chemical fertilizers and water under Green Revolution. For the success of the evergreen revolution, one village resource centre (VRC) linked to satellites in every block, one village knowledge centre (Gyan Chaupal) in every panchayat, a food and water bank in every panchayat and 'last mile–last person connectivity' through FM/Community radio or mobile phone would be ensured for capability-building. We should, therefore, critically develop and sharpen the indigenous rural knowledge system in the light of public interest for better and sustainable production and productivity.

Third, since poverty in most of the developing countries like India is multi-dimensional and a multiple deprivation, it requires multiple inclusion by giving priority to primary education (full enrolment and retention), nutrition (to children and pregnant/lactating women), basic health like appropriate BMI, preventive (immunization) and curative medical treatment so that the real social development of the marginalized may be ensured. In fact, 'specific egalitarianism' (Tobin, 1970) is the need of the hour, i.e. 'non-market, egalitarian distribution of commodities essential to life and citizenship,' so that the domain of inequality and poverty may be eradicated drastically, going beyond Tobin's proposal of 'limiting the domain of inequality'. Government authorities should ensure that the poor children are not excluded from schools on any count.

Unfortunately, Transparency International, India–CMS, in a survey of 22,728 families in 31 states, found (in 2007) that 0.7 million poor families in India paid bribes to the tune of ₹ 120 millions in the previous one year to avail school education (admission and promotion); 0.9 million poor families used contacts to get their wards admitted to schools; and about 0.5 million poor families could not get their children admitted to schools because they could neither pay bribes nor had any contacts. The level of such corruption in Bihar, UP, Meghalaya and Goa was found 'alarming'; J&K, Manipur, Assam and MP reported 'very high corruption' standards; while Chandigarh, Delhi, Kerala, Tamil Nadu, Chhattisgarh and Rajasthan reported 'high corruption'. Odisha, Arunachal Pradesh, Tripura and West Bengal reported 'moderate' corruption, thanks to 'active citizenry or social pressure' (*The Times of India*, July 2008). Similarly, Transparency International India–CMS (2007) also found that the poor living below the poverty line paid ₹ 870 million as bribe to hospital staff for medical treatment during the previous one year, and that one million people were not treated because they did not pay bribe (*Jansatta*, 18 July 2008). The need of the hour is that the government should ensure, in a transparent manner, useful vocational school education in order to develop suitable job skills. Leakage in developmental schemes is a very significant issue that requires strong action against the corrupt.

Fourth, the initiation of a rural employment guarantee scheme as a right to employment under the Mahatma Gandhi National Rural Employment Guarantee Act (MNREGA), 2005, is undoubtedly pro-poor and bottom-up people-centred development for poverty eradication. It covers, since 1 April 2008, the entire rural area of 34 states/Union Territories, 614 districts, 6,096 blocks and 2.65 lakh Gram Panchayats. It provided employment in 330 districts of India to 33.7 million households for 1,416.2 million person-days in 2007–08; out of this, 56 per cent were SCs/STs and 43 per cent were women; and ₹ 1,26,103.9 millions was spent. Earlier, in 2006–07, only 21 million households got employment for 900 million person-days.

The performance of MNREGA is better than that of earlier rural wage employment schemes like Jawahar Rozgar Yojana, Employment Assurance Scheme and Sampoorna Rozgar Yojana. In fact, under MNREGA, the Centre's share in wages for unskilled manual work is 100 per cent, while that for skilled/semi-skilled labour and cost of materials is 75 per cent and the remaining 25 per cent is borne by the states. Now, all job card holders living below the poverty line are given employment for at least 100 days in a year and unemployment allowance is given by the state if work is not provided for 15 days continuously. Panchayats play a key role in execution (minimum 50%) of the scheme.

Yet, MNREGA requires improvement in terms of the following:

(a) Employment should be provided for 200 days in a year to at least one adult in the family. The Ministry of Rural Development admits the average employment per household is 42–43 days only at present (2006–07 to 2007–08).

(b) Social audit should be made proactive and mandatory: Any attempt to prevent or circumvent social audit (as in the case of the killings of two social activists in Palamu and Giridih in Jharkhand) should be dealt with firmly. Further routine pre-fixed inspections should be replaced by sudden and serious inspections.

(c) Wages should be increased at market rates in view of the high inflation rates and paid regularly in a transparent way at least weekly. In some states, even the minimum wages fixed is not being paid.

(d) All eligible wage workers who do not get employment under MNREGA must be paid allowance (as per provision) without loss of time. In fact, they are not getting more than 50 days' employment in a year, yet no allowance is paid by state governments.

(e) The quality of construction work/earth work should be ensured better through increasing the number of technical/supervisory staff as well as training of government and panchayat functionaries about the basics of accountancy and estimates of construction works to be taken. The schedule of rates should be revised and made pro-labour from pro-contractor. Unfortunately, the proportion of completion of works taken up is unsatisfactory; e.g. under MNREGA, the number of works taken up in 2006–07 was 8,28,160, but only 3,87,133 (46.7%) were completed. Similarly, in 2007–08, against 17,76,041 works taken up only, 8,05,260 (45%) were completed. This shows lack of proper planning and monitoring of such works.

(f) Annual perspective plans and shelf of projects should be prepared realistically and transparently by the local people/gram panchayats and meetings should be held on fixed dates.

(g) MNREGA requires ₹ 530 billions of expenditure even for providing 100 days' work to the existing 50 million agricultural labour families – the number of the landless increased from 22 per cent in 1992 to 33 per cent in 2003, as per NSS data 2003. Only then it will guarantee empowerment of the rural poor.

(h) Often, works are not taken in all villages/hamlets (*tolas, purwas*) in proportion to their population. Thus, labourers of some villages are deprived of wage employment. This should be addressed soon.

(i) Panchayati Raj System has not been functioning up to the mark because of lack of 'funds, functions and functionaries', on the one hand, and lack of transparency and accountability, on the other.

Such employment should mean both income (demand side) and actual asset creation or production on the ground (supply side) – wage as income to the worker and as labour cost to the employer. Though the growth rate in India is about 9 per cent at present, yet due to an inflation rate of 12–13 per cent, there is an alarming rise in the prices of basic commodities and no full employment is ensured. According to the FAO, food prices rose 52 per cent during 2007–08 and prices of fertilizers doubled during the same period. This pushed 75 million poor to hunger and, thus, 925 million poor now suffer from hunger and chronic poverty in the world (*The Times of India*, 20 September 2008). Hence, as per the FAO, food should be made accessible to the most vulnerable, and small farmers should be helped to raise their output. As pointed out by Amit Bhaduri (2005), 'development with dignity' of the poor requires their full employment as well as full participation in the production and distribution of commodities – by real decentralization of socio-economic and political power to the poor, who should not be seen as a part of the problem, but as a part of the solution. Earlier, in rural India, 'spatial identity' was more pronounced than caste, class and religious identity. The entire village was often perceived by the outside world as educated, peace-loving, cooperative and developed or otherwise;

hence 'development with dignity and identity' (spatial-cultural identity is to be preferred to the narrow forms of caste, class and religious identity). In a village, the local people know it very well as to who is poor, who is not so poor and who is rich. Therefore, the revitalization of 'spatial (village) identity' would be more meaningful for both identification of the actual poor as well as being conceived as an appropriate unit of planning from below through full participation of the local people. In order to realize this, the cooperation of civil society organizations active at the local level should be taken so that they may work as catalyst for social mobilization.

Fifth, social security/safety nets like the National Family Benefit Scheme (providing ₹ 10,000 if the main bread-earner of the family dies between the age of 18–64 years), the National Maternity Benefit Scheme (providing ₹ 500 to poor pregnant women up to two pregnancies and renamed since 2001–02 as Janani Bal Suraksha Yojana as a part of the National Rural Health Mission), and the National Old Age Pension Scheme (₹ 200 is given to senior citizens by the central government and equal or more amount by the state government) should be strengthened by increasing the amount and rationalized progressively by including all the eligible persons and removing the names of the ineligible persons, so that social protection as a Directive Principle of State Policy (as provided in Article 41 of the Indian Constitution) may be fully realized. In fact, safety nets should include anti-monopolistic laws to protect small farmers from the demands of globalization, especially contract farming or the practice of paying more for buying inputs without gaining higher prices for selling their produce.

Sixth, housing for the rural poor also needs to be given a priority because a substantial part of rural workers' wages is spent on construction or maintenance of their houses and, therefore, Indira Awas Yojana needs revamping on four counts: (a) its allocation should be increased to cover all the chronic/extreme poor (irrespective of their caste or religion) by 2020; (b) its unit cost fixed should be enhanced; (c) though beneficiaries are given the amount directly, yet its progress is very worrisome; hence, better monitoring and supervision should be ensured by local civil society organizations/community-based organizations and also by the block/panchayat concerned; and (d) useful common work sheds and homestead lands for kitchen garden or poultry, piggery, goatry, etc. should also be made available along with the houses to the poor for ensuring a harmony between living and livelihood. In fact, a huge number of the poorest of the poor like Musahars in Bihar have no homestead lands to live and earn sustainable livelihood on. For this, appropriate technology, sharpening of skills (e.g. masonry, preparation of compost and green bio-fertilizers), market linkage, availability of inputs at reasonable prices (from nearest markets), infrastructure and enabling institutions are required so that 'livelihood finance' (Mahajan, 2005), not merely micro credit, may be meaningfully realized.

Some scholars like Arvind Subramanian, Devesh Kapur and Partha Mukhopadhyay (*EPW*, 12 March 2008) talk of 'direct cash transfer' to the poor in case of Public Distribution System, Indira Awas Yojana, food, fuel and fertilizer subsidies (to the tune of ₹ 700 billion in the 2008–09 budget of the Government of India) to transfer ₹ 10 million to each Panchayat and also to poor individuals directly every year as the best option. But it is not so simple and always useful, as Mihir Shah (2008) has correctly argued, due to the following facts: (a) There is already direct cash transfer (DCT) in the Indira Awas Yojana but it has not succeeded because of the amount being inadequate, the fund being diverted by the beneficiary for other urgencies, the beneficiary not having skilled masons, etc. (b) There is direct cash transfer in the Swarnajayanti Gram Swarozgar Yojana (SGSY) but due to target-driven government-pushed model of microfinancing, lack of feasibility study, red-tapism and market linkage and its being 'no magic bullet', most of such loanees become defaulters to banks. (c) The coverage of the public distribution system (PDS) shops is 'the weakest in the neediest regions' and food grains preferred in many poor pockets are not sold in the PDS shops. Further, PDS dealers are rampantly engaged in malpractices like not lifting the total quantity, selling in black market, giving less than the quantity fixed, charging more than the rates fixed, etc. (d) MNREGA is wrongly shown as a case of DCT – it is not a dole-out but a development initiative to create guaranteed job as well as permanent asset as required and decided locally through panchayats.

Seventh, some scholars (like Jeffrey D. Sachs, 2005) talk of foreign aid as poor people in developing countries start with a very low level of capital per person, and it declines due to population increase being higher than capital accumulation. Therefore, in Sachs' view, the solution to such 'poverty trap' lies in foreign aid that feeds into three channels: (a) a little bit goes directly to households as food aid during drought/flood; (b) a substantial part goes to the budget to finance public investments; and (c) some part is directed to private businesses (e.g. farmers) through microfinance programmes, etc. If the foreign aid is substantial enough, and lasts long enough, the capital stock rises to lift households above subsistence; it is then, in his view, that the 'poverty trap' is broken. But it is not so simple because almost all foreign aids have certain conditions that often go against the aid-receiving developing country's national interest. The example of structural adjustment or economic reforms in India in the 1990 is noteworthy here. Various pro-capitalist/industrialist/trader decisions were taken; for instance, contractualization of labour force, conditions for lock-outs by industrialists in industries made easier but labour strike made tougher, downsizing of government offices, charging user fee for services like hospitals and schools, and disinvestments in public sector enterprises.

In fact, the World Bank, IMF and 'Washington Consensus' focus on 'getting the prices right' on the macro-economic scale of aligning the domestic relative prices of goods and services with the international relative prices. But the Trade and Development Report or TDR (2008) of UNCTAD focuses on macro-economic prices like exchange rate, interest rate and wage rate as policy variables strongly affected by government policy. Thus, unlike the World Bank, IMF and 'Washington Consensus', TDR (2008) is of the view that macro-economic issues cannot be analysed with the same tools as used in micro-economics, quoting Kaldor (1983): Anthropomorphic economics applies 'to the national economy the same principles and rules of conduct as have been found appropriate to a single individual or family – paying your way, trimming your expenditure to fit your earnings, avoiding living beyond your means and avoiding getting into debt. These are well-worn principles of prudent conduct for an individual, but when applied as policy prescriptions to a national economy they lead to absurdities. If an individual cuts his expenditure he will not thereby reduce his income. However, if a government cut their expenditure programme in relation to tax rates and charges, they will reduce the total spending in an economy and, hence, the level of production and income.' A major initiative for poverty eradication is, therefore, possible through land reforms, better reallocation of resources, and more production and productivity with sustainable livelihood, but foreign aid should be taken selectively without compromising the interests of the nation and its poor people.

The process of aid, with palliative effects in the era of globalization, has created a kind of 'welfare colonialism' (Robert Paine) with the following features (Reinert, 2007):

(a) A reversal of the colonial drain of the old days, with the net flow of funds to the colony, rather than to the mother country;
(b) Integration of the native population in ways that radically undermine their previous livelihoods; and
(c) The native population is put on what is essentially 'unemployment benefits'.

Thus, welfare becomes the vehicle for a stable 'governing at a distance', through the exercise of a particular subtle, 'non-demonstrative', and dependency-generating form of neo-colonial social control that pre-empts local autonomy. Needless to say that the World Bank has often financed large dam projects like the Sardar Sarovar Project, which led to the displacement of more than 100,000 people as a result of the disappearance of the Harsud town and several villages without adequate rehabilitation. In fact, before the preparation of the Environmental Impact Assessment, the work on that dam was started under the pressure of the politician-bureaucrat-contractor-industrialist nexus at the cost of the local rural poor, most of whom were tribals in Madhya Pradesh. Hence, for poverty eradication, 'think globally, act locally' (local bottom-up planning with appropriate adaptable technology) is called for to create 'job-led growth' with social equity and inclusiveness as well as a 'shared public space' for the poor. Therefore, the creation of Special Economic Zones (SEZs) by acquiring lands forcefully from local farmers at cheaper rates (and providing tax holiday to industrialists) in Singur, Nandigram (resulting in 14 deaths), Dadri, Odisha (Posco firing resulting in many deaths) and elsewhere in the name of 'public purpose' has led to people's protests because their main source of livelihood is snatched, leading to their poverty. Hence, the Special Economic Zones should be replaced by 'Special Agricultural Zones' (as M.S. Swaminathan correctly argues) to increase production and productivity, in consonance with ecological sustainability, thus helping the poor in food security.

Finally, for realizing the noble objective of inclusive and 'real social development' with equity and ecological sustainability, the market in itself cannot be sufficient due to various fetters like unhealthy competition from everyone at every place and time, imperfection of information, and fallacy of rational behaviour of all individuals all the time in the so-called free market. Similarly, due to the vast resources required for such development as well as inertia, red-tapism and corrupt practices prevalent in large sections of the state machinery in different forms, the state alone cannot meet this lofty ideal goal. Therefore, a proactive facilitator state and a tamed and regulated market should work in a complementary and interdependent way to provide maximum opportunities to the rural poor in India. Similarly, too much economics in planning for the poor has often been one-dimensional and unrealistic. Hence, as the problem of poverty is multi-dimensional, it requires a multi-dimensional solution, with an inter-disciplinary approach, by involving sociologists, geographers, demographers, educationists and political scientists along with economists for a sustained planning for eradication of rural poverty in India in a holistic manner and in the shortest time.

We may conclude undoubtedly that poverty is not a technical problem, rather a socio-economic, spatial and political problem; hence it urgently requires a radical socio-economic, spatial and political solution, not merely a technical solution (that will bring only cosmetic changes). Hence, an alternative development paradigm with a genuine decentralized planning with an adequate space for the local poor people's active participation with adequate funds, functions and functionaries is required to drastically eradicate the chronic poverty and inequality in rural India. For this, political and administrative will is equally required as it is a gigantic task. The state cannot shirk from its 'public domain responsibility' to eradicate multidimensional rural poverty in India as has been shown feasible by China, Cuba, Sri Lanka and Kerala in their own ways.

References

Bandhyopadhyay, D. (2008) 'Does Land Still Matter?', *Economic and Political Weekly*, XLIII (10), 8 March.

Banfield, Edward C. (1973) *The Unheavenly City*, Little Brown, Boston.

Baran, P.A. and P.M. Sweezy (1966) *Monopoly Capital*, Monthly Review Press, New York.

Bhaduri, Amit (2005) *Development with Dignity*, National Book Trust, New Delhi.

Birdsall, Nancy (2001) 'Comments', in B. Plescovic and N. Stern (eds), *Annual Conference on Development Economics*, World Bank, Washington, D.C.

Bluestone, Barry (1969) 'Lower-Income Works and Marginal Industries', in Louis A. Ferman et al. (eds), *Poverty in America*, University of Michigan Press, Ann Arbor.

Chen, S. and Martin Ravallion (2008) 'The Developing World is Poorer Than We Thought, But No Less Successful in the Fight Against Poverty', Policy Research Working Paper 4703, Development Research Group, World Bank, August.

DuBois, W.E.B. (1985) *Black Reconstruction in America 1860–1880*, Atheneun, New York (1st ed. 1935).

George, Henry (1958) *Progress and Poverty*, Robert S. Foundation, New York (1st ed. 1879).

George, Susan (1983) *How the Other Half Dies*, Penguin Books, Harmondsworth, Middlesex.

Ghate, P. (2006) *Micro Finance in India: A State of the Sector Report 2006*, Care and Ford Foundation, New Delhi.

Gilder, George (1981) *Wealth and Poverty*, Basic Books, New York.

— (1989) 'The Nature of Poverty', in I.C. Colby (ed.), *Social Welfare Policy*, Dorsey Press, Chicago.

Goldsmith, William W. and Edward J. Blakely (1992) *Separate Societies*, Temple University Press, Philadelphia.

Gupta, Shekhar (2007) 'Walk the Talk with Vikram Akula', *The Indian Express*, 4 June.

Karlsson, Mats (2001) 'Opening Address', in B. Plescovic and Nicholas Stern (eds), *Annual World Bank Conference on Development Economics*, World Bank, Washington, D.C.

King, M.L. Jr. (1967) *Where Do We Go From Here: Chaos or Community?*, Beacon Press, Boston.

Mahajan, V. (2005) 'From Micro Credit to Livelihood Finance', *Economic and Political Weekly*, 8 October.

Mandel, Jay R. (1978) *The Roots of Black Poverty*, Duke University Press, Durham, NC.

Marable, Manning (1983) *How Capitalism Underdeveloped Black America?*, South End Press, Boston.

— (1987) 'The Contradictory Contours of Black Political Culture', in Mike Davis et al. (eds), *The Year Left 2*, Verso, London.

Martin, Linda R. and D. Giannaros (1990) 'Would a Higher Minimum Wage Help Poor Families Headed by Women?', *Monthly Labour Review*, 113 (8), August.

Maxwell, S. (1999) *The Measuring and Measurement of Poverty*, ODI Poverty Briefing 3, Overseas Development Institute, London.

Murray, Charles A. (1984) *Losing Ground: American Social Policy, 1950–1980*, Basic Books, New York.

NABARD (2006) *Annual Report*.

Osborne, David (1990) *Laboratories of Democracy*, Harvard Business School Press, Cambridge, Mass.

Patnaik, Utsa (2008) 'Reconceptualising Poverty', *The Hindu*, 3 September, p. 13.

Planning Commission of India (2008) *Eleventh Five Year Plan*, Vol. I, Oxford University Press, New Delhi.

Rao, Smriti (2005) 'Women's SHGs and Credit for the Poor: A Case Study from Andhra Pradesh', in V.K. Ramchandran and Madhura Swaminathan (eds), *Financial Liberalisation and Rural Credit in India*, Tulika Books, New Delhi.

RBI (1999) *Report on Micro Credit*, Micro Credit Special Cell, Reserve Bank of India, Mumbai.

— (2006) *Quarterly Statistics on Deposits and Credit of Scheduled Commercial Banks*, Reserve Bank of India, Mumbai, March.

Reddy, Sanjay G. (2007) 'Poverty Estimates: How Great is the Debate?', *Economic and Political Weekly*, 10 February.

Reinert, Erik S. (2007) *How Rich Countries Got Rich ... and Why Poor Countries Stay Poor*, Carroll and Graf Publishers, New York.

Rodrik, Dani (2001) 'Development Strategies for the 21st Century', in B. Plescovic and N. Stern (eds), *Annual World Bank Conference on Development Economics*, World Bank, Washington, D.C.

Sachs, J. (2001) 'A New Global Consensus on Helping the Poorest of the Poor', in B. Plescovic and N. Stern (eds), *Annual World Bank Conference on Development Economics*, World Bank, Washington, D.C.

Sachs, Jeffrey D. (2005) *The End of Poverty*, Penguin Press, New York.

Schiller, Barry R. (1976) *The Economics of Poverty and Discrimination*, Prentice Hall, Englewood Cliffs, NJ.

Sen, Amartya (2008) 'Democracy is More Than the Sum of Its Parts', *The Indian Express*.

Sengupta, Arjun et al. (2008) 'India's Common People', *Economic and Political Weekly*, 15 March.

Shah, Mihir (2008) 'Direct Cash Transfer No Panacea by Itself', *The Hindu*, 20 September.

Shah, Mihir, Raghu Rao and P.S. Vijay Kumar (2007) 'Rural Credit in 20th Century India', *Economic and Political Weekly*, XLII (15), 14–20 April.

Shankar, Kripa (2007) 'Poverty in India', *Mainstream*, 19–25 October.

Sharma, Subhash (2007) 'Dynamics of Violence in Rural South Bihar', in B.K. Choudhary (ed.), *Readings in the History of Rural South Bihar*, K.P. Jayaswal Research Institute, Patna.

— (2008) 'Micro Finance for Rural Women's Empowerment', *Management in Government*, XXXIX (4), January–March.

— (2008a) 'Dynamics of Use and Abuse of Water', *Management in Government*, 6, July–September.

Shetty, S.L. (2005) 'Regional, Sectoral and Functional Distribution of Bank Credit', in V.K. Ramchandran and M.S. Swaminathan (eds), *Financial Liberalisation and Rural Credit in India*, Tulika Books, New Delhi.

Singh, Vijay P. (1991) 'The Underclass in the US', *Sociological Inquiry*, 61 (4).

Srinivasan, T.N. (2007) 'Poverty Lines in India', *Economic and Political Weekly*, 13 October.

Streeten, Paul et al. (1981) *First Things First*, Oxford University Press, New York.

Swaminathan, M.S. (2008) 'Beyond the Green Revolution', *Seminar*, 589, September.

Thomas, Alan (2000) 'Poverty and the End of Development', in Tim Allen and Alan Thomas (eds), *Poverty and Development into 21st Century*, Open University/Oxford University Press, New York.

Tobin, J. (1970) 'On Limiting the Domain of Inequality', *Journal of Law and Economics*, 13 (2).

UNCTAD (2008) *Trade and Development Report*, Geneva.

UNDP (1998) *Human Development Report 1998*, Oxford University Press, New York.

Valentine, Charles A. (1968) *Culture and Poverty*, University of Chicago Press, Chicago.

West, Cornel (1987) 'Race and Social Theory', in Mike Davis et al. (eds), *The Year Left 2*, Verso, London.

Wilson, William J. (1987) *The Truly Disadvantaged*, University of Chicago Press, Chicago.

Yunus, M. (2008) 'Give the Man Credit', *Yojana*, 52, January.

6

Higher Education in India

Core Issues and Policy Implications

India is undoubtedly the largest democracy in the whole world. But is it also the greatest democracy? No, not at all. What makes a democracy great is the quality of its citizens and transparency in its governance. The lack of access as well as quality of higher education in particular, and education in general, is one of the factors responsible for such a sordid state of affairs. In ancient India, Nalanda, Vikramshila, Dharanikota, Takshashila, Benares and Navadvipa were seats of higher learning 'responsible for developing the higher mind of the country, its conscience and its ideals' and produced 'a community of cultural ideas' (Radhakrishnan). During the British period, first three universities were established in 1857 in Calcutta, Madras and Bombay to produce necessary bureaucratic staff for the colonial system with British attitude and mindset. It lacked the spirit of adventure and freedom from fear. Their medium of instruction was English and these universities followed the curriculum of University of London. These were examination-oriented teaching centres, not research-oriented and, therefore, had affiliated several colleges. At the time of independence of India, there were 3.69 lakh students studying in 27 universities and 695 colleges (Agarwal, 2009). Then higher education remained an elitist, teaching-centred, western-oriented and self-serving colonial system. Jawaharlal Nehru wanted to make Indian universities the ivory towers of innovative and modern ideas, concepts and theories. In this context W. Churchill had rightly remarked, 'The empires of the future are going to be the empires of the mind.' D.S. Kothari Commission report (1968) had called the universities 'the organs of civilization', allowing openness, questioning and dissent in letter and spirit. But Indian universities are in their 'death throes' (Upendra Baxi), 'at the very centre of politics' (Deepak Nayyar), 'democrazy' (Ritty Lukose), 'an immobile colossus ... insensitive, unresponsive and absorbed so completely in trying to preserve its structural form that it does not have the time to consider its own large purpose' (S.C. Dube). Amrik Singh rightly observed that more than half the expanding network of Indian colleges was 'intellectual and social slums' (Nilekani, 2008). Actually the individual goals of education have been cognitive, affective (character, attitudes and values) and skill. But the proportion of these three domains have varied from time to time and place to place in terms of focus on state or market or civil society, as well as in terms of stages of societal development (developed or post-colonial developing societies). Undoubtedly education, as both perfection of inherent powers as well as the socialization of the children, is the best investment in future development of individuals and society. Though India has the third largest scientific and technical manpower in the world (after US and China), yet it has the largest number of illiterate persons in the whole world. Its ambition to become a knowledge super power and a developed country by 2020 (as APJ Abdul Kalam's vision of India is) does not seem to be realistic and realizable because of pathologies of inaccessibility, poor quality, social and gender-inequity, irrelevance and lack of intellectual ambience in Indian universities and colleges which are infested with these 'banana problems' for long – stakeholders don't know when and where to stop. We will discuss these problematic issues one by one in second section and try to suggest some policy implications in short and long terms in third section.

II
Access

At the time of independence of India, there were only 27 universities in India. In 2011 there were 42 central universities, 296 state universities and 130 institutions deemed to be universities, as declared by Central Government on the advice of University Grants Commission (UGC), that enjoy the autonomy and privileges of universities though not declared universities by any law. Further there were 33,000 colleges too. In 2008, in total 13 million students were enrolled in higher education in India. All central universities (except two, IGNOU, New Delhi and Central Agricultural University, Imphal) are given development maintenance grants directly by UGC. Out of 296 state universities (including 53 state private universities), 130 state universities are provided budgetary support by UGC as per norms and procedures – state medical and agricultural universities are funded by the Ministry of Health and the Ministry of Agriculture, respectively. Out of 130 deemed to be universities 10 institutions are provided both development and maintenance grants and 23 institutions are provided only development grants. There are 33 institutions of national importance in India. At present, there are 25,951 colleges. Colleges recognized and declared fit (5,997 in 2009–10) under section 12 (B) of UGC Act 1956, get financial support for undergraduate and post-graduate programmes. The objectives of such development assistance are (GOI, 2010):

(a) To strengthen basic infrastructure and meet basic needs like books, journals, scientific equipment, staff, campus development, teaching aids, etc;

(b) To provide special assistance to colleges catering to the needs of marginalized groups;

(c) To develop colleges situated in the backward, rural or hilly areas to remove/reduce disparities and regional imbalances; and

(d) To support financially the uncovered state colleges, etc.

Government of India allocated to UGC for higher education the general plan budget of ₹ 3,439.95 crores for 2009–10 and out of this ₹ 2,654.66 crores was provided for enhancing aggregate access that accounts for 77.2 per cent of the total budgetary provisions for higher education. Undoubtedly the budgetary allocation for education in Eleventh plan is 19 per cent against only 7.7 per cent during Tenth Plan. Similarly, allocation for higher education has for the first time crossed one per cent of GDP (Gross Domestic Product). But we are still far behind to achieve the budgetary allocation for all sectors of education to the tune of 6 per cent of GDP (as suggested by Kothari Commission). We may get a glimpse of sub-sectoral allocation in 2009–10 higher education budget in Table 1.

Though Government of India is providing more than three-fourth of its allocation for higher education on enhancing aggregate access, it is still far less than required per student in view of the rising expectations and more demand for higher education. As Asha Gupta (2008: 1) perceptively remarks, 'Whereas the demand for higher education is constantly rising, which is likely to be 160 million by 2025, the state support in terms of funding per student as unit is declining. We find shifts in expenditure from the state to the market and from the market to the household. In some cases, household is spending up to 33 per cent on higher education as it is seen as an embodiment of personal growth, social and global mobility, and political and economic power.' Needless to say that every year a large number of Indian students (either on getting fellowships or paying the huge fee on their own) go abroad for higher studies – in 2008 this number was two lakhs (then 8.92 lakh Chinese students were studying abroad). Many Indian students are going even to China for higher education.

Table 1

Sub-Sectoral Allocation for Higher Education (2009–10)

S. No.	*Sub-sectors*	*Allocation (₹ in crores)*	*% of Total Allocation*
1.	Enhancing aggregate access	2,654.66	77.2
2.	Equity	243.34	07.1
3.	Quality and excellence	324.50	09.4
4.	Research	72.00	02.1
5.	Relevance and value-based education	39.00	01.1
6.	ICT integration	53.95	01.6
7.	Governance and efficiency improvement	18.50	0.5
8.	Others (new schemes and committed liability of Tenth Plan)	34.00	1.0
	Total	3,439.95	100.0

Source: GOI (2010)

Regarding accessibility, the best indicator is enrolment in higher educational institutions. Unfortunately, it ranges between 13 and 14 per cent of eligible age group whereas it is, at present, 50 per cent in developed countries on an average. In China, gross enrolment rate for higher education is 23 per cent while in Japan it is 58 per cent, in South Korea 50 per cent plus, in UK 59 per cent and in US 82 per cent (highest in the world). Government of India is aspiring for 30 per cent enrolment by 2020. At present world average in this regard is 23 per cent. It appears that India will take several decades to reach the level of such enrolment prevailing in UK, not to talk of US. In number, China's enrolment in higher education is 27 million whereas in India it is 13 million. As India's 70 per cent population is under 35 years and 54 per cent population under 25 years, India has a 'demographic dividend' of youthful citizens, but it will become a detriment 'unless there are sufficient highly educated citizens to lead, take charge in science, technology, business and the professions' (Vickery, 2010). However, it is also a fact that public universities are no more perceived as 'the sole custodians of culture and disseminators of knowledge', as private universities and colleges have emerged on the national and international horizon. Some scholars are of the view that private universities/colleges easily adapt to the market needs at a faster speed than the public universities/colleges which lack autonomy. However, private universities and colleges charge very high fee and commercialize education and allied services with profit-motive. Regarding Other Backward Classes (OBCs), Government of India has made a reservation of 27 per cent in higher educational institutions since 2008 as a policy response to the 'perceived deficit' due to low access and participation of the so-called backward classes in higher education. Now the pertinent point emerges: Whether 'attainment' is a better indicator or 'enrolment'? In this regard two factors need to be considered (Basant, 2008):

(a) Attainment captures 'the segment that has completed graduation or post graduation education', while enrolment focuses on the segment that is currently studying for graduation or higher courses;

(b) While attainment is a 'stock measure' (already graduated) and carries the 'burden of history', enrolment is a 'flow measure' that captures the current situation and provides indications for the future.

Here it may also be added, as pointed out by 'Youth for Equality' and others, that most of the castes collectively branded as 'OBCs' did not historically suffer the pangs of untouchability and other types of social discrimination. Further, from the analysis of NSSO data, Basant (2008) proves that deficits for the under-privileged groups are lower when 'flow measures' are considered and decline dramatically when we consider only the eligible population. For instance, the OBCs' share in the eligible population in the age groups of 18–25 years is 30 per cent while their share in the currently studying population is 28.5 per cent. His overall finding is that scheduled castes and Muslims are still somewhat disadvantaged but OBCs are not disadvantaged in any significant way, in terms of participation in higher education. Rather the economic background (the poor) and location (rural areas) are significant factors regarding access to higher education. But even the spirit of 'creamy layer' (as stipulated by the Supreme Court) was diluted when its ceiling was increased up to the family income of ₹ 4 lakhs per annum.

Equity

The issue of gender-equity is of prime importance not only because women account for almost half (48%) of India's population but also because of constitutional protection, especially under fundamental rights, fundamental duties and Directive Principles of State Policy. Women's enrolment in higher education was less than 10 per cent on the eve of Independence but it has risen to 41.4 per cent in the beginning of the academic year 2009–10. However, as per latest government data, there are regional variations as women's enrolment as a percentage of total enrolment in a state is the highest in Goa (59%) and the lowest in Bihar (30%). In addition, in terms of absolute number of women's enrolment Uttar Pradesh (UP) tops the list of states with 8 lakhs, followed by Maharashtra with 7.8 lakhs. However, 49 per cent women are enrolled in arts, 4.9 per cent in engineering, 3.50 per cent in medicine and only 1.58 per cent in law (Table 2):

Table 2

Faculty-wise Women's Enrolment in India (2009–10)

S. No.	*Faculty*	*Women Enrolment*	*% of Total Women Enrolment*
1.	Arts	27,72,580	49.08
2.	Science	11,29,255	19.99
3.	Commerce/Management	9,15,719	16.21
4.	Education	1,80,771	3.20
5.	Engineering/Technology	2,76,806	4.90
6.	Medicine	2,02,803	3.59
7.	Agriculture	15,253	0.27
8.	Veterinary Science	4,519	0.08
9.	Law	89,256	1.58
10.	Others	62,140	1.10
	Total	56,49,102	100.00

Source: GOI, (2009–10) Annual Report, MHRD.

From Table 2 it amply transpires that women's enrolment in higher education, both in terms of total enrolment (men and women) and against Women's eligible population in the relevant age group (18–25 yrs), is less than satisfactory due to following factors:

(a) Still a large section of the poor stratum in India is deprived of elementary/secondary education, hence they are unable to join higher education.

(b) Many school pass outs are unable to join and continue higher education due to economic compulsions to do some jobs to make both ends meet.

(c) There is a substantial percentage of failure at higher secondary (plus two) level, hence they are unable to study further.

(d) Still there is a social custom to believe that daughters are '*paraya dhan*' (others' property), hence it is not considered economically sound to enroll daughters for higher education.

(e) Early marriage is still prevalent in most of north India, hence marriage of daughters are preferred to their higher education.

(f) Higher educational institutions are not situated near homes, hence the enrolling of daughters in distant cities/towns is not digestible in rural families.

(g) There is a shortage of girls' colleges, hence often many parents don't enrol their daughters in co-educational institutions.

(h) Due to the shortage of quality educational institutions, many parents are disillusioned with mediocre institutions taking high fees, unsatisfactory infrastructure, poor teaching–learning environment and no guarantee of placement after graduation.

(i) Due to cut-throat competition for job-oriented professional courses (engineering, medicine, management, law), many girls drop out.

(j) Lack of incentives, like scholarship, also restricts women's higher education. Though there is a scheme of Indira Gandhi Scholarship for Single Girl Child at the rate of ₹ 2,000 per month for 20 months but the budgetary allocation is meagre on this count (only 1,200 slots in a year); secondly, due to prevalence of two or more children in a household, it is more restrictive in nature.

Other schemes for gender equity are: Construction of women hostels in colleges, to establish and/or strengthen centres for women's studies (at present 51 such centres in universities and 16 centres in colleges), – ₹ 25 lakhs for universities and ₹ 15 lakhs for colleges in Phase I, ₹ 40 lakhs and 20 lakhs, respectively, in Phase II, and ₹ 60 lakhs and ₹ 40 lakhs respectively, in Phase III, capacity-building for women managers in higher education (faculty, staff and administration, to sensitize the system for gender-equity), and providing post-doctoral fellowships for women (100 in a year) at the rate of 6,000 per month for fresh PhD candidates and ₹ 8,000 for those with 5 years' experience after PhD. Equity principle also has another dimension. For deprived sections like SC/ST, following steps have been taken by the government:

(a) Providing reservation both in appointment of teachers as well as seats for students;
(b) Providing scholarships for students for post-graduation professional courses (5,000 per month) and research;
(c) Establishing residential coaching academies for preparing for civil services examinations and NET;
(d) Providing post-doctoral fellowships – a slot of 100 per year – (₹ 16,000 per month plus a contingency of ₹ 30,000).
(e) Establishing of equal opportunity cell in universities/colleges to oversee the effective implementation of policies for the disadvantaged groups (SC/ST/Minorities/OBCs).

Quality and Excellence

In June 2007, the then Prime Minister of India, Dr Manmohan Singh, admitted the poor quality of higher education, while addressing 150th anniversary function of University of Mumbai: 'Our education system is, in many parts, in a state of disrepair. In almost half the districts in the country, higher education enrolments are abysmally low, almost two-thirds of our universities and 90 per cent of our colleges are rated as below average on quality parameters ... . I am concerned that in many states university appointments, including that of Vice Chancellors, have been politicized and have become subject to caste and communal considerations; there are complaints of favouritism and corruption.'

First and foremost step adopted by the UGC is to grant autonomous status to colleges of quality – during 11th Plan the target is granting autonomous status to at least 10 per cent of eligible colleges. Autonomous colleges have autonomy to (GOI, 2010):

(a) prescribe new course of study – restructure/redesign syllabi to suit local needs;

(b) prescribe rules for admission in consonance with the reservation policy;

(c) evolve methods of assessment of students' performance, conduct of examinations and notification of results;

(d) use modern tools/technology to achieve higher standards and better quality.

Actually, an autonomous college is managed by its governing body, academic council, board of studies, and finance committee. Further, during the Ninth Plan, UGC gave the status of University with 'potential for excellence' to five universities (JNU, Hyderabad, Madras, Pune and Jadavpur) and during the Tenth Plan to four universities (NEHU, Madurai Kamraj, Mumbai and Calcutta) were given such status. During the Eleventh Plan, six such universities were identified. Such universities are given additional funds for ensuring excellence. In addition, autonomous colleges or colleges being more than 10 years old as well as accredited by National Assessment and Accreditation Council (NAAC) are eligible for potential for excellence. By 2009–10, 246 colleges were accorded such status and were given additional grants to improve their academic/physical infrastructure, adopt innovation in teaching modern methods in learning/evaluation, etc. Again Special Assistance Programme (SAP) has been launched with six objectives (GOI, 2010):

(a) To identify and support university departments that have the potential to undertake quality teaching and research;

(b) Programme to be relevant to societal needs and have society and industry interaction;

(c) To make research a catalyst for good teaching and introduction of new course;

(d) To enhance infrastructural facilities to utilise the output of research for the development of nation and society;

(e) To train and create quality human resource in the identified thrust areas; and

(f) To search for new/generic areas, its promotion and nurturing.

For SAP, departments with one professor, two readers and three lecturers are eligible. By 31 December 2009, 723 departments in

India were assisted under SAP. Further 66 Academic Staff Colleges have been set up in universities for orientation programmes of four weeks for new teachers and refresher courses of three weeks for in-service teachers. In the entire country, 15 universities/institutions have been identified as UGC Refresher Course Centres. By December 2009, 223 orientation programmes, 702 Refresher courses and 77 workshops were approved by UGC.

UGC also provides travel grant (50% of admissible expenditure to college teachers and 100% to VCs and UGC members) to present research papers at international conferences abroad for enriching their knowledge. During 2009–10, 583 college teachers and two VCs were given travel grants. Further, there are six inter-university centres to provide common advanced centralized services/facilities to play a vital role in offering the best expertise in each field, and to provide state–of-the-art equipment and excellent library facilities. In addition, there are four centres of National Facilities (Mumbai, Tirupati, Chennai and Shimla). UGC also provides fund on 100 per cent basis for laboratory equipment, contingency, etc. for teaching and research in innovative and inter-disciplinary areas. Further, under faculty improvement programme, UGC provides opportunity for research as well as to participate in seminars/workshops/conferences for updating research and pedagogy skills. UGC has also cultural and educational exchange programmes with 44 countries. Moreover, UGC conducts National Eligibility Test (NET) for recruiting lecturers or providing Junior Research Fellowships at 12,000 per month for first two years and ₹ 14,000 per month for remaining years along with contingency of ₹ 10,000 (₹ 12,000 for science) per year for first two years and ₹ 20,500 (₹ 25,500 per year for science) for remaining years in order to ensure minimum standards. To promote excellence in research, the number of JRF is 1000 in a year for the whole country which is far less. UGC also provides financial support for major research project (₹ 12 lakhs in science and engineering and ₹ 10 lakhs for others) and minor research project (₹ 2 lakhs) in any discipline. About 900 research projects were selected in science/engineering and 600 projects in humanities and social sciences in 2009–10.

The moot point is that excellence is to be promoted and measured differently at different levels (primary, secondary and tertiary sectors), in different countries (developed/developing), at different periods of time (mid-twentieth century with focus on public higher educational institutions vis-à-vis last two decades of twentieth century and early twenty-first century), and with different perspectives (like charging full user fee versus subsidizing higher education). Actually excellence is required in all stakeholders – students, teachers, environment, teaching and research policies/programmes and outcomes. Quality products in all streams in Indian universities, especially in the state universities, are hardly noteworthy. Parliamentary Committee on Estimates has held the UGC primarily responsible for the 'prevailing low/mediocre standards of the majorities of universities and colleges in the country' – only 30 per cent of the universities and 10 per cent of the colleges are of quality because UGC's financial support to state universities is 'extremely inadequate' (*The Economic Times*, 2 August 2010). As per McKinsey report, 75 per cent of engineering graduates in India are too poorly educated to function effectively in the economy without additional on the job training (Jha, 2009). Similarly not a single Indian university ranks in the top 100 universities of the world, as per 2010 Shanghai Jiao Tong University's academic rankings based on research productivity, or as per Times Higher Education rankings (2010–11) and QS World University rankings (2010). As per Times Higher Education World University rankings, five top universities are: Harvard university, California Institute of Technology, Massachusetts Institute of Technology, Stanford University, and Princeton University. As per QS World University rankings five top universities are: University of Cambridge, Harvard University, Yale University, University College London, and Massachusetts Institute of Technology. QS WU rankings consist of 100 score with academic score, employer reputation score, faculty-student ratio and citations per faculty. In QS rankings, many Asian universities (from China, Japan, South Korea, Singapore, Israel, Taiwan, Thailand etc.) rank much higher than Indian universities. For instance, University of Hong Kong ranks 23rd and Peking University ranks 47th while IIT Bombay ranks 187th, IIT Delhi 202, IIT Kanpur 249, IIT Madras 262, IIT Kharagpur 311, Delhi University 371, IIT Roorkee 401, and Bombay University 451 (*The Indian Express*, 15 September 2010). The ranking status has not improved even thereafter. That is why after Independence none of Indian professors/researches received the prestigious Nobel Prize in difference academic disciplines, though before Independence scholars like Rabindra Nath Tagore and C.V. Raman had got Nobel Prize in literature and physics, respectively. Often the instances of plagiarism, repetition, duplication and mediocrity of research come to public notice. This actually reflects the lack of sincerity on the part of researchers (not concerned with range and depth of issues), lack of vision of research supervisors, lack of qualitative facilities as well as lack of conducive environment. As Elliot has rightly observed: 'Where is the wisdom we have lost in knowledge? Where is the knowledge lost in information?' Thus, nowadays in most of Indian universities and colleges, wisdom and knowledge are sacrificed at the altar of the information, hence there is hardly creativity, originality and innovation in our research (Table 3):

Table 3

Comparison of Wisdom, Knowledge and Information

Level	*Parameters*	*Core Attributes*	*Outcome*
1. Higher	Wisdom	Originality, innovation and creativity	Holistic qualitative decisiveness, ethics – orientation, IQ, EQ and Spiritual quotient
2. Middle	Knowledge	Explanatory/ analytical (cause – effect)	Scientific temper, synthesis of quality and quantity, IQ and EQ
3. Lower	Information	Facts and figures	Quantitative cognitive resource, IQ only
4. Below	No information	Inaccessibility	Cognitive deprivation – no quantity, no quality – ignorance

Relevance

OECD Economic Survey India (2007) points out that researches from Indian universities published very low number of articles in top-quality international journals (about 25 per million population) while researchers from Korea published (about 700 per million population) articles in that year.

UGC duly recognizes the relevance of higher education and, therefore, it has Area Studies Programme for promoting holistic understanding of the area with cultural, social, economic and strategic facilities and also to promote alternate paradigm from the perspective of post-colonial societies as well as to promote inter-regional comparative perspective. UGC provides fund for this to 46 centres in 25 universities (2009–10) with three levels – Level 1 (up to ₹ 60 lakhs), Level 2 (up to ₹ 40 lakhs) and Level 3 (up to ₹ 25 lakhs). Second, career-oriented courses have been launched – certificate/diploma/advanced diploma. UGC provides ₹ 7 lakhs per course as one time seed money in humanities/commerce streams and ₹ 10 lakhs per course for five years in science stream. Third, in order to study discrimination, exclusion and inclusion, UGC has selected 35 universities for establishment of centre for studies in social exclusion and inclusive policy. Fourth, for understanding thoughts of socio-political leaders like Gandhi, Ambedkar, Nehru, Vivekanand, Guru Nanak, Zakir Hussain, Aurobindo and others, UGC has sanctioned 191 study centres and each receive ₹ 3 lakh as non-recurring grant and ₹ 7.50 lakhs as recurring grant every year. Fifth, for ensuring adult, continuing education and extension, UGC has sanctioned 86 centres of lifelong learning. They promote total education, integrate formal and non-formal education to enrich the learning process through extension activities. Such centres get recurring grant of ₹ 10 lakhs and non-recurring grant of ₹ 5 lakhs per year during the Eleventh Plan period. Sixth, Human Rights Education is another important and relevant dimension of higher education with three components – human rights and duties, human rights and values, and human rights and human development. It has five objectives (GOI, 2010):

(a) To humanize and democratize all power relations through restructuring of rights and duties;

(b) To create awareness and commitment to values where individualistic self-interest is properly reconciled with the collective and common good;

(c) To search for universal values in a globalizing but fragmented world;

(d) To promote and sustain the values like pluralism, respect for all religions, scientific temper, open mind, public reasoning etc;

(e) To promote and enforce rights and to envision rights approach to development by the states.

UGC provides fund for foundation/certificate/diploma/undergraduate/post-graduate courses, for conducting seminars/workshops, and also for publication of books/journals on human rights education. Financial assistance varies for different purposes. In addition, 157 universities in India were provided internet connection of bandwidth under UGC connectivity programme during 2002–2009.

Academic Environment

Academic environment of most Indian universities and colleges is not conducive to free and frank dissemination of knowledge due to the following reasons:

(a) Poor and ill-maintained infrastructure in terms of class rooms, library, labs, teaching aids, etc.

(b) Politicization of the campus – most of students/teachers' organizations are attached to national/regional political parties whose goal is politicking, rather than reasoning; as Deepak Nayyar, ex-VC of Delhi University perceptively observes: 'Our deans and administrators now hang on the spoken word of our politicians, and student unions and teachers beat to their drum. It's so entrenched that asserting independence in appointments and day-to-day decisions turns you into a radical, a rebel in the system' (Nilekani, 2008: 338).

(c) Fossilization of a large number of teachers and administrators.

(d) Prevalence of short cut methods in teaching and research – 'jugar' to get quick results in examinations.

(e) Lack of adequate courage to choose the road less travelled.

(f) No focus on creating leaders, no search for excellence.

(g) No transparency in functioning of either higher educational institutions, or their regulators.

(h) Prevalence of hyper – Darwinian selection process with 'quota mindset' (reservation for OBCs) and 'Kota mindset' (coaching institutes in Kota being successful in admission to IITs and IIMs).

Further, National Knowledge Commission of India (2009) has rightly diagnosed ten ailments of higher education:

(a) curricula have 'almost unchanged for decades, have not kept pace with the times';

(b) learning and creativity are at a discount in assessment system that 'places premium on memory rather than understanding';

(c) the milieu is not conducive to anything beyond the class;

(d) academic calendar is no longer sacrosanct for classes or for examinations;

(e) the infrastructure is on the verge of collapse;

(f) the boundaries between disciplines have become 'dividing walls';

(g) the importance of research has eroded;

(h) decline in the volume of research (frequency of publication) and quality of research;

(i) little accountability – no rewards for performance and no penalties for non-performance;

(j) governance structure not responsive to changing times and circumstances that the system is readily subverted by vested interests.

If we look at the higher education in the entire country, we find that 5–7 per cent brilliant students despite the 'system', are comparable in quality and excellence to top ranking students in the world-class universities. Arvind Panagariya (2008) rightly calls it 'a paradox of brilliant graduates and a dysfunctional system' in India due to three factors:

(i) India has a large number of men and women interested in higher education because of a huge young population as well as tradition of highest value to intellectual pursuits.

(ii) Due to a sizeable number of quality private secondary schools in urban India, many students are well prepared for higher education.

(iii) Still many Indian universities/colleges have standardized curricula and centralized examination system, hence a small segment (5%–7%) of students succeeds with flying colours.

III
Policy Implications

It is often talked of allowing the entry of foreign higher education institutions in India for excellence, expansion, credibility, better reference group, saving of foreign exchange, synergy between internal and external talents, avoiding brain-drain and also avoiding racial discrimination prevalent in many foreign countries (like Australia). China's aggressive policy has attracted more than 2 lakh international students to study in China (2007) whereas in India only about 20,000 international students study (2008). Second, in China, 76 per cent international students hail from Asia, 12 per cent from Europe, 9 per cent from America, 2 per cent from Africa and one per cent from Oceania, while in India international students mostly come form south Asia, Africa and Indian Diaspora. Third, about 1000 foreign educational institutions have some kind of collaborative arrangement (including joint degree) in China (including Johns Hopkins University, University of Michigan, full-fledged branch campuses of two British Universities). On the other hand, only 150 foreign educational institutions (66 from US and 59 from UK) have collaborative arrangements in India. Finally, while China has regulatory laws to regulate foreign collaboration since 2003, India has not legislated in this regard so far (Altbach, 2010). However, all foreign universities are not excellent and qualitative and they, too, have certain costs, as Tilak (2010) points out:

(a) foreign universities are more interested in taking students to home campuses to get more revenue or through twinning arrangement desire to utilize campuses/facilities of domestic universities – thus not interested in capital investment in inviting (developing) countries;
(b) no top ranking university is willing to come to India or other developing countries to offer quality education;
(c) students going abroad for study also want to get work permit there; the percentage of Indians obtaining PhDs in science and engineering who had 'definite plans to stay' in the US increased from 56.3 per cent in 1994–97 to 62.7 per cent in 2002–05, though the number of Indians obtaining PhDs in science and engineering there declined by 30 per cent (from 5014 to 3587) in that period (Kapur, 2008) and, on the other hand, the foreign universities prefer their products in jobs;
(d) entry of foreign universities will result into a fierce competition between unequals without providing a level playing field as domestic universities are starved of resources and are subject to a plethora of regulations while foreign universities will be free of these impediments;
(e) foreign universities will not solve domestic problems of inequitable access, falling standards and scarcity of public finance.

Further, even in famous US universities like Harvard 'Z List' makes the 'A List', that is, admission policy 'compromises standards in the interests of alumni and donors, enabling their children to enter America's most famous university by a side door. The Z list consists of 25 to 50 well-connected but often borderline applicants accepted on condition they defer enrolment until the following fall – when they occupy slots that could otherwise be given to outstanding but unhooked applicants' (Golden, 2006: 37) that is, some students are adjudged by their parentage and wealth, not by merit. Second, as Golden points out, more than 90 per cent of students at elite universities graduate, simply being 'qualified' to meet the minimum standards, not being the best for the slot.

However, all such criticisms may be controlled by a proactive and transparent regulatory agency if there is a strong political and administrative will to do so. Actually it also depends on the type of model – hard or soft – that is to be adopted by India or other developing countries. A comparative paradigm of models of entry of foreign universities may be seen in Table 4.

Table 4

A Comparative Paradigm of Models of Entry of Foreign Universities

Type of Model	*Positive*	*Negative (Distorted)*
(A) Hard Model	Competition-oriented	Conflict-Oriented
	(i) enhancing quality of curricula, teaching content/method with high costs.	(i) more focus on quantity than quality – publish or perish
	(ii) fierce search for excellence through fierce competition	(ii) profit-motive to prevail over excellence
	(iii) right-sizing of faculty for accountability and performance	(iii) high motive to minimize costs by compromising size, status and quality of faculty
	(iv) assigning independent research projects of industries to the most deserving	(iv) research in back gear – taking projects for profit only
	(v) striving for institution-industry interface in a balanced way	(v) dominance of industry over institution
	(vi) rare regulation	(vi) excessive regulation/control
	(vii) reasonable corporate culture for fee, selection of teachers, students/staff – need – blind	(vii) dominance of corporate culture

Cont'd ...

... Cont'd

	(viii) unconcerned with local culture	(viii) aggressive attitude to local culture, a kind of neo-imperialism
	(ix) not sharing success stories/best practices with local institutions	(ix) not much to share with local institutions
	(x) competition between unequals – no level playing field	(x) competing situations between unequals sharpened
(B) Soft Model	Collaboration-Oriented	Connivance-Oriented
	(i) sensitive/respectful to local socio-cultural norms/practices of diversity	(i) misusing of local cultural norms/practices – conversion
	(ii) enhancing quality of curricula, teaching content/method with low costs	(ii) copying, repetitive research in more quantity with corrupt practices
	(iii) search for excellence through healthy competition with local institutions	(iii) no concern for excellence – enhancing mediocrity
	(iv) taking relevant research projects – problem of local people to be given top priority	(iv) taking research projects with profit motive
	(v) selecting creative and critical faculty to produce leaders – 'intellectual discovery' of ideas	(v) selecting faculty for networking for more students
	(vi) striving for a balanced interface between industry, institution and civil society	(vi) interests of industry to prevail over institution
	(vii) reasonable regulation and more cooperation	(vii) violating regulations in connivance with regulators
	(viii) openness, transparency and accountability	(viii) lack of openness, transparency and accountability

Cont'd ...

... Cont'd

	(ix) sharing of success stories/best practices with local institutions – mutual exchange of guest faculty and amenities	(ix) sharing negative (corrupt) practices (like taking contract for thesis-writing, highly charging for placement)
	(x) providing level-playing field to local institutions to grow	(x) declining level-playing field encouraging dating, fashion, consumerism, gay culture, etc.

Thus, it is clear form Table 4 that a soft model with positive features is to be preferred. Entry of only excellent foreign institutions should be allowed and they should be reasonably regulated to invest here, to respect indigenous culture and follow merit-based selection of students, teachers and staff and to pay local taxes. On the other hand, India's premier institutions should be allowed to open their centres/branches abroad with transparency and accountability. But we must keep this point in mind that our scattered talents should be pooled together at the earliest to make conducive environment for excellence in higher educational institutions. In our view, to be a future educational leader, India should not wait for the future. We do not agree with the recommendation of National Knowledge Commission (2009) to open 1500 universities because already state universities are in disrepair and their arena of operation is quite small but they are not doing well. Capacity of colleges should be enhanced to increase enrolment of students at degree level. Still many deserving colleges have not been made autonomous. This aspect needs to be focused in letter and spirit.

Undoubtedly establishing and promoting world-class top universities is a tough task. It takes very long time to assemble global leaders in their fields of specialization. On the other hand, to attract world-level academics, a very high salary structure and necessary facilities would also be required in world class universities. Two top private universities of US, Harvard and Yale, took centuries to achieve parity with Oxford and Cambridge, and Stanford and Chicago took more than half a century to become world class. Only one Asian University, namely Tokyo (established in 1877) has been ranked into top 25 in global ranking so far. Entry of foreign universities in India should be considered only as an opportunity for win-win situation. However, reasonable regulation is required otherwise there is possibility of neo-imperialistic tendencies among foreign universities. Actually, we agree with the recommendation of National Knowledge Commission to open 50 national universities of excellence and to establish national knowledge network with gigabit capabilities to connect all libraries, laboratories, hospitals and agricultural institutions.

Second, in India regulatory authorities like AICTE, MCI, UGC, Bar Council, etc. have been reportedly dens of corruption for several decades, hence Union Ministry of Human Resource Development's initiative to establish an inclusive regulatory agency like National Commission for Higher Education and Research (NCHER) is appreciable to cut multiplicity of agencies as well as for making it transparent and accountable. However, it should be clearly spelt out as to how NCHER would deal with state universities which are quite large in number – and these are governed by separate state laws. Needless to say that state universities require various kinds of resources for enhancing their quality of teaching and research. Though they cater the needs of a large number of students, they get only a small portion of UGC grants, compared to central universities. All universities should revise their curricula once in three years; there should be continuous internal assessment (with weightage up to 50%), there should be transition to a course credit system (with choices), synergy between research and teaching, and better working conditions and incentives to retain faculty. Finally, a genuine search committee of experts should select the meritorious and worthy Vice-Chancellors of universities to avoid political and bureaucratic control. Often, many unworthy Vice-Chancellors centralize power disproportionately and create a coterie to serve their narrow vested interests. It results into cornering and disregard for deserving teachers who don't believe in sycophancy and cheap caucus or lobbying politics.

Third, though working conditions and salary structure of teachers in central universities have been improved over the years, there is a decline in their standard of teaching and research, what to talk of state universities! The number of quality papers in international journals of repute has been declining in most of the disciplines. In terms of publications output, India's rank has dropped from 8th in 1985 to 14th in 2006. Annual number of PhD engineers in India is half per engineering college per year. If we analyse the number of university teachers invited every year by reputed foreign universities for delivering lectures or participating in serious technical deliberations, they may be counted on fingers. Among the top 100 intellectuals of the world, only two are from India – Ramchandra Guha and Ashis Nandy – the first being a freelance writer! Unfortunately many university teachers are busy in teaching in coaching classes or giving tuition or writing theses on contract for others or in petty party politics. Many of them do not go to universities/colleges in time or they return soon from there after completing formalities. Moreover the vacancies in faculties compound the problem. In this regard, disincentives should also be provided to non-performing teachers, especially in terms of restraining promotion or even forcing pre-mature retirement. However, before giving disincentives, teachers should be evaluated by students and peers (teachers) every year, as National Knowledge Commission rightly suggests. Orientation programmes and refresher courses launched so far have not been adequate and dynamic. Without accountability, inertia and anarchy prevails in the vast arena of higher education in India. Government of Bihar took a drastic step (June 2010) to demote 873 teachers as lecturers (in Magadh University) who had illegally and undeservingly taken promotion to the posts of professors. In some departments in some Bihar universities, there are more teachers than students – e.g. in Patna University's Maithili Department Further, all the funding of non-defence research should be thoroughly peer reviewed as is the prevailing practice in developed countries – in US 75 per cent of funding of non-defence research is peer reviewed to ensure quality and relevance. Similarly, the teachers are required to ensure 'learning to read and reading to learn' and, on the other hand, they should redefine their teaching style by making it student–centred learning in a creative and critical conducive environment. As Albert Einstein rightly observed, 'The significant problems we face, can not be solved at the same level of thinking we were at when we created them.' But unfortunately, in India, in most of the universities and Indian Institutes of Technology, priority is not given to intensive and quality research whereas in many western universities like Oxford, Cambridge, Harvard, Yale and so on, research is given the top-most priority. This is reflected in far less number of patents by Indian scholars in Indian universities and IITs in the arenas of medicine, engineering, technology, life sciences, environmental sciences, computer sciences and agricultural sciences. The then President of India, Smt Pratibha Patil expressed great concern on the occasion of golden jubilee of IIT, Delhi (16 August 2010): as per World Intellectual Property Organisation 2009, India has got only 761 patents so far, while China has got more than 7900 patents so far. For achieving this, it is the need of the hour to ensure transparent and objective selection process of teachers, so that 'brain-drain' is also restrained. The retirement age of teachers in central universities has already been increased to 65 years, the same should be extended to state universities. Similarly non-academics (freelancers, NGOs, bureaucracy, innovative farmers) who have contributed to any field of knowledge in original, innovative or qualitative way, should be absorbed in academics for a synergy of theory and practice, inter-disciplinary approach and out of box thinking or action (e.g. participatory or action research). In addition, fruits of researches should reach to the people without loss of time. Education is too important to be left to the educationists alone! Though some rare talents come up despite the fossilized and obsolete teaching system, yet there is an urgent need to bring fundamental systemic change in teaching/research system in universities/colleges.

Fourth, unfortunately there is mismatch between higher educational institutions' products and employers' required skilled manpower. It is so because of following reasons as pointed out by the second National Commission on Labour in 2002 (Mukhopadhyay, 2008):

(a) A mismatch in supply of training and skills in demand due to inadequate coverage of skill requirement, mismatch in demand and supply relation, and inability of small firms to hire apprentices.

(b) Inadequate and poor quality of training facilities as well as training staff.

(c) Procedural problems in public ownership – lack of flexibility in engaging trade apprentices within the same trade group, lengthy and clumsy administrative process for record keeping and filling up returns, and lack of incentives to encourage industries to modernise their training facilities.

Hence the second National Commission on Labour recommended a stronger link between industry and vocational training, as well as private involvement in the improvement of training facilities. Therefore, instead of learning to learn, higher educational institutions should shift to learning to work – linking education to production, productivity and livelihood. Unfortunately, because of not providing adequate skills, even postgraduates in arts, commerce and science aspire to become group 'C' or even group 'D' government employees! Therefore, it is required that at post-secondary level there should be one or two applied courses to impart practical skills for ensuring at least self-employment. In Indian education as a whole there is 'IAS deficit' – Institutional, Accreditation and Skill. We should stop the high rate and volume of wastage created by higher education system. However, as Radhakrishnan observes, university should propagate right ideals: 'If man makes history, ideas make man. What is our objective with regard to the training of youth? Are we to prepare them for life or death?' (Munshi and Diwakar, 1990: 509).

Finally, human capital through higher education can be improved by more financial allocation in the budget – in 11th plan it was 1 per cent of GDP, whereas National Knowledge Commission rightly recommended 1.5 per cent of GDP. The OECD countries are spending about 1.5 per cent of GDP on higher education. Further this allocation needs to be judiciously distributed among central universities and state universities by focusing on the backward regions like Hindi belt as well as the gender-equity. For making India a knowledge society, perhaps the public funding (by Union and state governments) would not be sufficient. Hence, private sector is also to be roped in with reasonable terms and conditions for higher education. But not like Chhatisgarh where more than 100 private universities were opened by taking the benefit of the loopholes of the state law in 2002 and those were functioning in one room like stationary shops or in a garage for purely commercial purposes. Later, with the intervention of Supreme Court, in a Public Interest Litigation (PIL) filed by Yashpal, those private universities were abolished and UGC was given full power of regulation to ensure minimum requirements in terms of courses, curricula, faculty, infrastructure, and financial viability. Supreme Court observed that mere conferment of degrees by universities is not enough, these must be recognized. However, UGC has been very causal and liberal in granting deemed university status to private sector, especially in the first decade of 21st century. A committee constituted by the Union Ministry of Human Resource Development found in 2010 that 44 deemed universities were functioning without observing minimum quality and manpower norms and the Ministry wanted to take stern action but because of a case filed by such deemed universities in Supreme Court, necessary legal action could not be taken against such malfunctioning deemed universities in different parts of India. But consequently, five unfit deemed universities sought affiliation from other universities – National Museum Institute of History of Art, Conservation and Museology, Nava Nalanda Mavihara, Rajiv Gandhi National Institute of Youth Development (these three are government deemed universities), Tilak Maharashtra Vidyapeeth, Pune and Gurukul Kangri Vishwavidyalaya (these two are private deemed universities) (*The Times of India*, 28 July 2010).

After universalization of elementary education, the universalization of secondary education and tertiary education are needed in a chain of sequences because elementary school teachers usually possess secondary education certificates and secondary school teachers possess tertiary education degrees. All the three sub-sectors of education are interrelated. Though elementary education is to be given top priority (in view of illiteracy of a large number of children) by the state, the secondary and tertiary education cannot be ignored. Moreover, the accreditation started by the National Assessment and Accreditation Council (NAAC) has a good impact in terms of awareness generation among students, guardians and teachers. But, unfortunately, UGC has adopted a wrong policy that the accreditation will have no implications for funding and salaries, thus making NAAC a teethless tiger. This needs to be reversed at the earliest.

We may conclude that higher education in India needs a thorough surgery to make it fully accessible, quality-conscious, gender-just and egalitarian, structurally and functionally transparent, and relevant to the needs in national interests, keeping in view the future demands. We lag far behind China as far as patents are concerned; we somehow managed to get patents of basmati rice, *neem* and *haldi* after a long legal battle with developed countries. Higher education in India has not reached the take-off stage so far because there is no top priority on innovative research even in the fields of pure sciences, bio-technology, environmental sciences, medical sciences, agricultural sciences and life sciences, not to speak of social sciences. Probably the new 14 innovative universities by the Government of India will sow the seeds of inventions in different arenas of life without compromising the merit and excellence.

References

Agarwal, P. (2009) *Indian Higher Education: Envisioning the Future*, Sage Publications, New Delhi.

Altbach, Philip G. (2010) 'The Giants Awake: Higher Education Systems in China and India', *Economic and Political Weekly*, XLIV (23), 6 June, pp. 39–51.

Basant, Rakesh (2008) 'Decoding Access', *Seminar*, 587, July, pp. 19–22.

GOI (2010) *Annual Report 2009–10*, Ministry of Human Resource Development, New Delhi.

Golden, Daniel (2006) *The Price of Admission*, Three Rivers Press, New York.

Gupta, Asha (2008) 'Introduction', in Asha Gupta, D.C. Levy and K.B. Powar (eds), *Private Higher Education*, Shipra Publications, New Delhi.

Jha, A. (2009) 'Abysmal Global Ranking of India's Best University', *Education World*, February, pp. 64–72.

Kapur, Devesh (2008) 'The Supply Mix', *Seminar*, 587, July, pp. 14–18.

Mukhopadhyay, Partha (2008) 'Learning to Work', *Seminar*, 587, July, pp. 52–57.

Munshi, K.M. and R.R. Diwakar (eds) (1990) *Radhakrishnan Reader: An Anthology*, Bhartiya Vidya Bhawan, Bombay.

National Knowledge Commission (2009) *Report to the Nation 2006–09*, Government of India, New Delhi.

Nilekani, Nandan (2008) *Imagining India: Ideas for the New Century*, Penguin, New Delhi.

Panagariya, Arvind (2008) *India: The Emerging Giant*, Oxford University Press, New York.

Tilak, J.B.G. (2010) 'The Foreign Educational Institutions Bill: A Critique', *Economic and Political Weekly*, XLV (19), 8 May, pp. 12–15.

Vickery, R.E. Jr (2010) 'Obama's India Opportunity in Higher Education', *The Guardian Weekly*, 16 July.

7

School Education of the Marginalized

A Critical Study of Tharu Tribals' Education in West Champaran (Bihar)

Here, in this chapter, we would try to present an overview and then demystify the following myths:

- There is a monolithic unity of *dalits* and tribals in rural Bihar (India).
- There exists a binding unity and homogeneity within a tribal community.
- The political leadership from backward castes is more concerned towards the tribals' development in general and their education in particular.
- The teachers would improve their performance in school if their pay and perks were improved.
- The extremists disrupt and disturb the school system, especially the teachers.

We will then look at the concept of school education at different levels in theory (policy) and practice (implementation), especially in the context of the marginalized. Finally, we will point out the emerging issues and policy implications.

Overview

As every person is a social being, his or her education is also a socio-cultural process. But, unfortunately, a large number of marginal children are deprived of their childhood in general and the right to education in particular. Long back, Albert Einstein rightly remarked: 'Nothing in this world is great till a single child is in grief.' In 1948, the Universal Declaration of Human Rights, the Magna Carta (originated in 1215 in England) of the entire humankind, perceptively provided that all human beings are born equal and have dignity and entitlement to all *indivisible* and *inalienable* human rights simply because of being born as humans, irrespective of their social background, status, caste, class, race, place of birth, sex, language, ideology and so on. Later, the Convention on Rights of Child (CRC), 1989, made various fundamental provisions for the all-round development of children of the whole world. India ratified this Convention on 11 December 1992 and 191 countries have ratified it. Various rights of children provided by CRC are put into four categories:[1]

(i) right to survival

(ii) right to protection

(iii) right to development

(iv) right to participation.

The CRC is undoubtedly the most comprehensive treaty on the rights of children under 18 years and ensures a wide range of their human rights, including the right to be protected from economic exploitation and from performing any work that interferes with their education or is harmful to their health, or physical, mental, spiritual, moral or social development. Thus, the CRC believes in *'putting the children first'*. India's ratification of CRC had this rider: 'It is not practical to immediately prescribe minimum age for admission to each and every area of employment in India.' More than 15 years have elapsed since that ratification. The Child Labour (Prohibition and Regulation) Act 1986 provides that children below 14 years are prohibited from working in hazardous occupations and industrial processes. Eighteen occupations and sixty-five industrial processes are declared by the Government of India as harmful and hazardous for children below 14 years. Thus, though CRC defines child as a person below 18 years, the Child Labour Act (1986) of India defines a child as a person below 14 years of age. Besides, Article 21A provides that children of 6 to 14 years will be given free and compulsory education, leaving children below 6 years and those in the age group 15–18 years. Further, in practice, even children of 6–14 years are not given free and compulsory education in the real sense of the term. Let us see what the actual status of children's rights, especially tribals', in India is.

First, one in 11 children dies before the age of five from preventable diseases and/or malnutrition – 2.1 million children in India die before the age of five out of 9.7 million dying in the world (in 2006) from preventable diseases.

Second, 50 per cent of India's children (6–14 years) did not attend school, according to the Campaign Against Child Labour (CACL), whereas according to the Ministry of Human Resource Development (GOI), only 5 per cent of all the children (6–14 years), numbering 7 million (in 2006), were out of schools in India.[2] Further, according to official estimates (2004–05) 29 per cent children drop out by the fifth standard, 51 per cent by the eighth standard and about 62 per cent by the tenth standard. Dropout rates are the highest among the STs – 42.3 per cent by the fifth standard, 66 per cent by the eighth standard, and 79 per cent by the tenth standard.

Third, 1.26 crores (12.6 million) of children below 14 years work as child labourers in India, as per the 2001 Census. Among the child labourers, most of the children belong to the marginal communities.

Fourth, 47 per cent of children suffer from malnutrition; hence they are stunted and/or underweight.

Fifth, almost half of the children get married before attaining the age of 18. This deprives them of their childhood and education as the responsibilities of adults are thrust upon them. Early child marriage is common among the marginalized.

Sixth, gross enrolment ratio (2004–05) of all categories for Class 1–8 (6–14 years) is 93.5 per cent, for Class 9–10 (14–16 years) is 51.7 per cent and for Class 11–12 (16–18 years) is 27.8 per cent, while that of ST students is 102.4 per cent, 37.2 per cent and 17.2 per cent, respectively.

Seventh, if we look at the number of girls enrolled against per hundred boys, the situation is quite unsatisfactory. The number of girls enrolled per hundred boys in all categories (2004–05) for Class 1–8 is 85, for Class 9–10 is 71 and for Class 11–12 is 71, while that in ST category is 83, 64 and 62, respectively.[3] Thus, the overall educational status of the tribals is the worst among the children in India.

Finally, if we look at the gross enrolment ratio of ST students in Bihar (2004–05), it is 65.2 for boys and 42.3 for girls (total 54.5) for Class 1–8, 16.45 for boys and 8.46 for girls (total 12.78) for Class 9–10, and 3.7 for boys and 4.1 for girls (total 3.9) for Class 11–12. Similarly, for the ST category in Bihar, the number of girls per hundred boys (2004–05) is 57 for Class 1–8, 44 for Class 9–10, and 51 for Class 11–12. On the other hand, the dropout rates of ST students in Bihar is very high: 59.2 per cent for boys and 63 per cent for girls for Class 1–5 (total 60.8%), 76.3 per cent for boys and 76.1 per cent for girls for

Class 1–8 (total 76.2%), and 88 per cent for boys and 90.3 per cent for girls in Class 1–10 (total 89%). That is, in Bihar only 41 per cent boys and only 37 per cent girls in ST category are able to complete primary education, while only 24 per cent tribal boys and girls are able to complete upper primary or elementary level in Bihar. It is rare for tribal students to complete the tenth class – only 12 per cent tribal boys and only 9.7 per cent tribal girls are able to reach the tenth class in Bihar. This fact shows the glaring example of tribal students being at the bottom for most of the educational indicators.

As early as March 1990, during an international conference on 'Education for All' (in Jometien, Thailand), it was expected from all member nations and international agencies to ensure effective ways and means to fulfil the target of 'Education for All' by 2000. Subsequently, in 2002, Sarva Shiksha Abhiyan (SSA) was launched in India for the universalization of elementary education as a centrally-sponsored scheme (centre and states' ratio being 75:25). SSA intended to cover about 200 million children in more than 1.1 million settlements covering 0.973 million existing primary/upper primary schools, and a large number of non-formal initiatives like Education Guarantee Schemes (EGS) and Alternative Innovative Education (AIE) centres in the whole country. It focused on 'decentralized, participative and consultative planning' with the opening of new schools or the strengthening of the existing schools' infrastructure like additional classrooms, drinking water facilities and maintenance, providing additional teachers, their training, teaching–learning materials, etc. An allocation of ₹ 17,000 crores (₹ 170,000 millions) was provided for SSA in the Tenth Plan (2002–07). Further, for mid-day meals (MDM), ₹ 59,000 millions was provided in the Tenth Plan. Again, for out-of-school girls, 2,075 residential schools (Kasturba Gandhi Balika Vidyalayas) in educationally backward blocks were sanctioned on the CSS pattern of 75:25 ratio between the centre and the states. These intend to cater to the educational needs of girls from SC/ST and minority communities in backward blocks (3,427 such blocks exist in India with lower female literacy than national average, and high gender gap). A minimum of three-fourths of the seats are reserved for the girls from marginalized and minority communities and the rest for the girls from families below the poverty line. In all, 444 Kasturba Gandhi Balika Vidyalayas (KGBVs) were opened in tribal blocks and by December 2006, 6,400 girls were enrolled in all in 1039 KGBVs, out of which 30 per cent were tribal girls.

Further, the National Development Council fixed 11 monitorable targets, out of which three relate to education as follows:

(a) All children in school by 2003 (extended to 2005–06) and all children to complete 5 years of schooling by 2007.

(b) Reduction in gender gap in literacy by at least 50 per cent.

(c) Increasing functional literacy to 75 per cent.

But none of these goals could be achieved by 2007 despite pious intention. The draft of the Eleventh Five Year Plan (Government of India)[4] points out the following vision for secondary education:

(i) It should aim at a progressive rise in the *maximum* level of education towards high school level (Class X).

(ii) It must evolve strategies for secondary schooling that will emphasize the '*primacy of public responsibility* for providing secondary schooling but also allow scope for private schools to expand if they *complement* the public effort.'

(iii) Government must ensure that public schools are available 'to provide *competition* to private schools and, of course, in areas *unserved* and *underserved* by private schools'.

(iv) Special efforts must be made to cater to the educational needs of the SCs, STs, minorities and girls '*whose enrolment depicts a wide gap*'.

We will subsequently see as to what happens to this vision.

Now, the question arises about the ingredients, methods and goals of education. The United Nations' International Commission on Education (headed by Jacque Delors) in its report, 'Learning: The Treasure Within' (1996) defines education as 'a necessary utopia' and points out its four pillars:[5]

(a) *Learning to know*: Knowledge of environment and occupational skills. Since it is not possible to learn everything in one go, one should learn the technique of attaining knowledge.

(b) *Learning to do:* Practising the learnt things – from skill to competence in order to control the uncertainty.

(c) *Learning to live together:* To discover others and work for common goals so that war and destruction may be avoided.

(d) *Learning to be:* The holistic development of human beings so that they may work with more autonomy, decision-making, competence and personal responsibility.

Delors Commission has clearly pointed out that informal education or alternative education for the poor children should *not* mean cheap, contingent and purely ad hoc education. Further, it talks of 'education bank' (education-and-work sandwich as in Germany), especially in alternative education, wherein for every child, education years are fixed and a child may study in a school for some time, then go to work and again join the school. Thus, the cycle of education and work would go on and on.

In the Indian context, A.N. Maheshwari mentions that several types of skills maybe developed among the students: computation skill, communication skill, technical skill, household skill, psychological skill, learning-to-learn skill, and healthful-living skill.[6] He further emphasizes that 'learning to learn with love' should be inculcated among the children.

II

We have selected Champaran (Bihar), from where Mahatma Gandhi launched his first *satyagraha* (peaceful resistance) at the initiative of a local farmer, Raj Kumar Shukla, against the mighty British empire's indigo planters, who compelled the peasantry to earmark one-third of their lands for indigo cultivation – this was called the 'Tinkathia' system. Moreover, in the eastern part of Champaran, the great imaginative novelist George Orwell (of *Animal Farm* and *1984* fame) was born at Motihari.

The origin of the Tharus is contested. While some of them claim to have migrated from Thar (Rajasthan) during the Mughal period (the Rajput women allegedly fled away with their servants in order to save their honour from the Muslim oppression and later got married to them because their husbands did not come), others claim to belong to Nepal's Rajput (Rana) caste. It is perceived that Tharu women have a better social status, are free to choose their life partners, do not allow their husbands to enter the kitchen, and celebrate social functions with songs and dances by freely mixing with men. The Tharu tribe has turbulently passed through several stages of 'community identity' for over a century – from a tribe to Rajput Kshatriyas to backwards to again a scheduled tribe. Thus, three major processes of *tribalization, detribalization* and *re-tribalization* have taken place at different moments of their history with structural and cultural tensions.[7]

We find the following facts, as perceived by the Tharus, which clearly disprove the myth of monolithic dalit–tribal unity:

(a) For a long period of five years, a dalit was the Minister of Secondary Education in Bihar but he too looked at the Tharu tribals as 'weaker rather than different' – the same discrimination which dalits have been alleging against the so-called upper castes.

(b) Dalit representatives did not invite the Tharus in any celebrations of election victory, marriage, birth and death ceremonies. Nor did they launch any united struggle against the exploiting landlords, bureaucrats, moneylenders, forest officials, contractors, etc.

(c) The Bagaha parliamentary constituency is reserved for the Scheduled Castes since long but the elected dalit representatives neglected the 22 Don settlements of Tharu tribals directly and indirectly. The Member of Parliament (Lok Sabha) neither visited the tribal belt of Don nor released money from the MP Local Area Development Fund at his discretion. Nor did he pursue with the Government of Bihar for connecting their villages with roads and bridges, buildings of schools or other development works.

Thus, the hiatus between the representative and the represented has widened as elsewhere because of no checks on the former by the latter.

Often, it is said that there exists an unquestioned binding unity within the tribal community and a general hostility towards outsiders (*bajis,* as Tharus call them). This is not true in the 22 Don villages of Tharus in Ramnagar Block in West Champaran. There is no undifferentiation, homogeneity and total unity among Tharus. During our visit (on 24 September 2004), it was found that all the eight teachers, one clerk and two peons have not been attending Rajendra Prasad Memorial High School (named after the first President of India), Gobaria Don (West Champaran) for 10 years (1994–2004). Similar has been the case of the middle school (1–8) there. Consequently, the children of the tribal settlements were and are deprived of school education but the tribal parents/guardians' views on this significant pathology are of three different types:

(a) 40 per cent of the local tribal guardians constantly complained against the unauthorized absence of school teachers and non-teaching staff;

(b) 40 per cent of the local tribal guardians surprisingly supported the teachers (saying that they do not shirk from school regularly);

(c) 20 per cent of the local tribal guardians blamed the prevailing adverse conditions rather than the teachers (viz., non-connectivity of the village with roads and bridges, activities of extremists, and no residential facility to teachers).

In fact, in 2003, due to the non-functioning of R.P. Memorial High School Gobaria Don, a large number of guardians/parents were agitated, and they complained against the eight teachers and three non-teaching staff to the Chief Minister, Minister (Secondary Education), Divisional Commissioner, Tirhut and District Magistrate, West Champaran. Consequently, the Divisional Commissioner, Tirhut (who himself hailed from the Meena tribe of Rajasthan) viewed it seriously and organized some sort of a public hearing at a 'Janata Durbar' (people's court) in the premises of the high school itself in March 2004. However, when those school teachers and non-teaching staff were informed about this by some local tribal 'informers', they visited the village and cogently managed many tribal guardians through money, sweets, gifts, etc. in their favour. So, when the Divisional Commissioner inquired about the school being non-operational, most of those present there denied the complaint. This made him presume that the complaint was not true. The teachers celebrated their victory over non-performance, inaction, treachery and falsehood! Unfortunately, the Divisional Commissioner did not scratch beneath the skin by cross-questioning those involved intensively or by ensuring a subsequent sudden inspection by a sincere official. Rather, the 'dominant discourse' of the powerful teachers and their lobby overshadowed the 'whispering protest' of the local Tharu tribals, resulting into the 'unheard voice of the voiceless'.

As to why a large number of village guardians/parents supported the irresponsible teachers, four cogent reasons seem to be operative. First, there exists a *false consciousness* among many local guardians who are not critically conscious of their children's interests/future. Thus, a 'culture of silence' prevails there because of lack of mobilization of the masses (unlike Maharashtra and Tamil Nadu).

Second, the government teachers did not attend the school but had provided three 'contract teachers' (two from the same village and third from a neighbouring village) at the rate of ₹ 1,200 per month (that was even less than the wages of a daily worker, and one-tenth of a regular teacher's pay). This rate has been effective since 2001, before which only ₹ 400 was paid to them monthly. These 'contract teachers' had managed the community leaders and local vocal elements in favour of those government teachers and non-teaching staff. And this was seen in tune with the 'dysfunctional' tradition of *sab chalta hai* (anything goes on).

Third, the better-off Tharu tribals got a better alternative (private) school for their children. Hence, they did not remain aggrieved and consequently did not complain about the government school teachers.

Fourth, those who were involved in the running of private schools – the management, teachers and non-teaching staff – wanted the chaos to continue in that government school so that they might flourish at their cost. Thus, there has emerged an 'early selection' for ascent through 'sponsored mobility' (not 'contest mobility') through private school (like in urban areas), as Turner rightly observes,[8] though in a context different from Britain, by preparing for new skills, behavioural norms and values of elite status in their later life.

Further, it is usually believed by some scholars and leaders that the political leadership from backward castes (rather than upper castes) is more concerned for the tribals' development in general and their school education in particular. This assumption is not true in letter and spirit if we look at the state regime of backward castes' leadership in Bihar. During 1991–2005, Rashtriya Janata Dal was the ruling party in Bihar on the declared manifesto of 'social justice'. But there was no adequate policy for the development of the 'marginalized' in general and their education in particular. Most of the officers of the backward castes, minorities, scheduled castes and scheduled tribes were usually given prime (regulatory and development) postings during 1991–2005 (like District Magistrate, Superintendent of Police, Home Secretary, SDM, DSP, Block Development Officers and even *Darogas* or sub-inspectors of police), while most of the upright and tough officers of the so-called upper castes were shunted to some insignificant posts.

When the Rashtriya Janata Dal lost power, Lalu Yadav, ex-Chief Minister of Bihar, openly declared: 'I just used to see the names and titles of officers of backward castes, minorities, scheduled castes and scheduled tribes in the lists and used to give them prime postings.' That is, there were no objective criteria for transfer and posting (in terms of experience, performance and integrity), which flourished more as an 'industry' and led to the malfunctioning of the development and regulatory administration as pointed out by several experts and organizations. Often, the Central funds meant for the welfare of the poor, backwards, minorities, dalits and tribals were surrendered in Bihar. As Ramesh Thakur perceptively observes: 'Even if Lalu had worked to raise the life opportunities and prospects of his Yadav and Muslim vote banks, the average standards of living of Biharis would have risen considerably instead of steadily falling over 15 years. Ineffectual anti-forwards slogans could not compensate for the lack of effective pro-backwards policies.'[9] Consequently, the annualized growth rate of per capita income (2000–01 to 2005–06) was at the lowest ebb at 2.7 per cent against the national average of 5.3 per cent (at constant prices). Bihar's per capita state income (dividing gross state domestic product by its population) at current prices was only ₹ 5,157 against the national average of ₹ 16,555 in 2000–01, and in 2005–06, only ₹ 6,776 against the national average of ₹ 25,825. Thus, its proportion decreased from about one-third to one-fourth of the national average.[10]

Further, it is interesting to note that the government of Bihar did not provide adequate incentives like stipend, free books and stationery, free uniforms, free cycles, *Kanya Vidya Dhan* (lumpsum amount of ₹ 20,000 for girls passing 10+2), etc. to the marginalized children, though these were being distributed in many states like MP (during the regime of Digvijay Singh, hailing from an upper caste), Rajasthan (during the regime of Vasundhara Raje, hailing from an upper caste), and UP (during the regime of Mulayam Singh, hailing from a backward caste). Actually, these facilities are to be provided under SSA. Needless to say that the state government of Bihar (1991–2005), with a 'social justice' plank, did not practise the substance and essence of pluralism, inclusion, diversity and multiple identities, though the political leadership of the backward (middle) castes has been constantly accusing the upper castes on this very ground. Thus, the parochialism of the backward castes has been as detrimental to the marginalized like the Tharus, especially their *'first generation learners'*, as was that of the upper castes. Thus, the 'social justice' plank remained in Bihar during 1991–2005 more as a rhetoric than as a substantial tool for the empowerment of the marginalized.

Usually, it is talked about that the teachers would improve their punctuality and performance if their pay and perks were improved. In Bihar, on 2 October 1980, a large number of high schools run by the private managing committees were taken over by the government of Bihar – that is, a shift from the private sector to the public sector – because many political leaders with a say in the government had their own private schools. After the government takeover, a huge number of teachers and non-teaching staff were appointed, even from back date. Earlier, the Managing Committee was a hard taskmaster – giving less pay to teachers but taking optimum work from them ('less pay, more work' model). But after 2 October 1980, the situation of the school teachers reversed: 'more pay, less work' model as most of the teachers have unionized since then. Most of them belong to the teachers' wing of the Communist Party of India (CPI) and act as an appendage to the political party in letter and spirit. In Bihar schools, a maxim has been prevailing since 1980: *'Barah baje late nahin, tin baje bhent nahin'* (It's not late to come to school even at 12 o'clock; no teacher found in school at 3 o'clock). Further, the secondary school teachers' new basic pay (since 1 January 1996) was fixed at ₹ 5,500 and that of the headmaster at ₹ 6,500, which is comparable to private and public sectors in any region of India. Thus, a teacher of the R.P. High School was getting about ₹ 15,000–20,000 per month, but spending less than ₹ 500 each on the three contract teachers in 2001. In fact, these teachers and non-teaching staff have cornered about ₹ 20 million without any teaching/non-teaching work. The example cited above belies the presumption that a better pay and perk would automatically mean better performance and punctuality of the teachers.

However, it was found in Bihar in general that teachers are often engaged in non-teaching tasks like census, elections, polio drive, agricultural/cattle censuses, ration cards' preparation and so on. But the teachers of the R.P. High School, Gobaria Don (East Champaran) were not deputed for such tasks either. They have just remained 'absentee teachers', like the absentee landlords who command power as a strong pressure group. This is confirmed from the following:

First, for 10 years they manipulated the local education officers and the local civil society for not complaining against their inaction.

Second, when the school was inspected in September 2004 and an activist Chairperson of Bihar School Examination Board (BSEB), Patna really found absenteeism and reported that all the eight teachers and three non-teaching staff were found absent, without any prior sanction of leave, during the sudden inspection and that they had been absenting themselves for about 10 years, these absentees managed to delay the file for two months through their association. Later, when the Chairperson, BSEB, pursued it vigorously with the Secretary of the Secondary Education Department, these teachers and non-teaching staff were suspended and disciplinary proceedings were ordered against them.

Third, the teachers' association later successfully got appointed an inquiry officer of its choice who was of doubtful integrity (Under Secretary). He pointed out several loopholes in the proceedings and recommended only a minor penalty.

Finally, the teachers' association was successful in indulging in manipulations in the Department of Secondary Education and, lo and behold, these teachers and non-teaching staff were given a simple 'warning' with an order of payment of full pay for the suspension period and their suspensions were revoked in February 2006. It is to be noted that by now Janata Dal (U) had come into power on the 'development with social justice' plank (since November 2005).

The worst thing that happened was that they were posted in the same high school again! Thus, history repeated itself but, of course, as a tragedy! Had this school been situated in a relatively prosperous village of either upper castes or backward (middle) castes, perhaps a suitable action against these absentee teachers would have been taken without any loss of time, as Tharus perceive. Thus, the education of the marginalized was not the priority of the government, even of the 'social justice' leadership in Bihar.

This incident clearly proves that whether teachers go to school or not, whether they teach or not, it is at their discretion if the school is situated in a village of the marginal tribals. Second, the teachers' association has indulged in the dirty politics of supporting its members at any cost at every stage and to any extent, even with devilish acts and bad records. This incident establishes that social networks and networking do not always generate 'social capital' in a positive sense (as Robert Putnam had assumed). Rather, it results into a negative consequence from which a large section of the marginalized in the civil society suffer in a big way. Third, the politico-administrative system shields the wrongdoers and non-performers for *'paisa, pairvi aur prabhav'* (money, connection and influence). Finally, the leadership of the backward castes is as much unconcerned with the genuine interests of the tribals (Tharus) as was that of the upper castes. Thus, in practice, there was simply a 'circulation of ruling elites' (as Pareto and Mosca had observed) in Bihar. That is, the 'identity politics' of the middle (backward) castes often centres on their own interests and priorities rather than on the genuine interests of the poorest marginal tribals. Thus, it is established that 'identity politics' *per se* may be neither inclusive nor visionary.

Often, the teachers take the stand that in remote areas the extremist groups, especially the Maoists, disturb and disrupt the school system, especially the teachers. This makes the latter unable to perform their duties regularly and sincerely. This is more of a myth than a reality because the Maoists usually did not and do not harm teachers; rather, they have been launching movements since long for the vacating of the government school campuses in Bihar which are occupied by the police/paramilitary forces so the schools may run regularly and the children of the marginalized may be able to study. In the R.P. Memorial High School, Gobaria Don, though, some of their slogans were written on the walls of the school buildings, but those were directed against the state government and police, not against the school itself. Second, the villagers also told that they were ready to give free accommodation at their homes to the teachers and non-teaching staff and were willing to provide them security (through Gram Raksha Dal) during their arrival and departure. Third, there have been no incidents of teachers' abduction by extremists or traditional criminals in that area in the recent past. Finally, the local Tharu tribals have not supported the cause of the Maoists despite their villages bordering on Nepal (that were seething with Maoist agitation) and surrounded by rivers, forests and hills.

However, it also transpires that had that village (Gobaria Don) been well-connected with roads and bridges, the situation would probably not have been that bad because well-connected schools are relatively better managed and inspected than the R.P. Memorial High School, Gobaria Don. Thus, physical–geographical isolation is accompanied by social and economic isolation, and a locational periphery often remains a socio-economic periphery in the real sense. This fact also proves that the state of Bihar may not be considered as a homogeneous unit (geographically and socially) for development in general and education in particular. Second, the education administration has been slack in the inspection, monitoring and evaluation of performance of that school. In fact, a lack of vision and guidance from the government also led to the dereliction of duty among the bureaucracy at the lower, middle and higher levels in terms of no effective inspection, supervision and control. Hence, these teachers have crossed the *Lakshman Rekha* of propriety. They have indulged in a massive corruption in showing better 'performance' (on paper) in terms of both a high figure of regular students' enrolment in various standards and sections and allowing a large number of private candidates to fill up the Class X Board examination forms from that school. Table 1 gives a picture of the standardwise enrolment and attendance in the R.P. Memorial High School, Gobaria Don.

From Table 1, it transpires that for about three months no attendance was marked – June, being a summer vacation month, was, of course, understandable. Second, no student was marked absent; only a dot was shown against them so that this may be manipulated later. Third, the figures of the students present are not reliable because the contract teachers verbally admitted that the total actual number of students in 7th, 8th, 9th and 10th standards is not more than 80, whereas many more students have been shown present. Fourth, the headmaster keeps the attendance register of the tenth standard and the teachers' attendance register at his native home (30 km away) so the number of students appearing for the Class X Board examination is not known to others. Fifth, though many non-tribal students are shown as enroled, no fee was ever charged from them. This fact confirms that such outsider non-tribal students' enrolment is fake and has an ulterior motive of earning extra income from private candidates by showing them as regular ones. Finally, the contract teachers revealed that for the forthcoming Class X Board examination, the headmaster had got 287 students registered (including more than 200 private students). The large number of private students from such a remote place indicates the corrupt practices (charging higher fee than prescribed, manipulating examination centres, helping in copying, etc.) of the headmaster, other teachers and staff (clerk). Thus, these teachers are involved in a practice of 'putting profit before (the marginal) people'.

It is also notable that earlier, the government high schools were allowed to restrict the number of private students for Class X Board examination to half the actual number of regular students in the schools concerned. But some time back, the teachers' lobby, with an ulterior motive, filed a writ petition in Patna High Court and got this restriction removed. Most of the students enroled there as regular students do not belong to the local tribal villages. Rather, they hail from distant villages and towns (some of them even from a distance of 100 km from the district headquarters!). Second, they belong to

Table 1

Enrolment and Attendance in the R.P. Memorial High School (January–September 2004)

S. No.	*Standard*	*No. of Enrolled Students*	*Attendance*			
			Marked present	*Marked absent*	*Not marked at all*	*Remarks*
(i)	7th	35	19 (25 March) 23 (31 March) 17 (26 April) 35 (30 April) 32 (25 May) 28 (27 July) 29 (16 September)	None; only dot shown	January–February–June & August	(a) No fee charged and entered in any month.
(ii)	8th	74	41 (28 February) 15 (31 March) 21 (30 April) 14 (27 May) 16 (6 September)	None; only dot shown	January–June & August	(a) By Feb only 41 enrolled but increased to 74 later. (b) No fee charged and entered in any month.

Cont'd ...

... Cont'd

(iii) 9th	67	1 (Feb) 26 (31 March) 15 (30 April) 8 (31 May) 11 (6 September)	None; only dot shown	January–June–July & August	(a) By Feb only 5 enrolled but increased to 67 in March. (b) No fee charged and entered in any month
(iv) 10th	70	Not available	Not available	Not available	Contract teachers informed that the register of 10th is kept by the headmaster.

upper and middle (backward) castes (having titles like Sharma, Pandey, Mishra, Singh and Yadav being common among the so-called regular students). This was also done with an ulterior motive (from students' view) of filling forms from a remote school so that during the Board examination, the centre is fixed at suitable and favourable places! That is why the result of the Class X Board examination of the R.P. Memorial High School had been quite high consistently for three years (2001–03), but in 2004, when the Bihar School Examination Board changed its policy of examination centres (students of schools in one subdivision would appear from some school in another subdivision in order to avoid favour), the result of the school fell down from 81 per cent to 38 per cent. During 2001–04, the number of appearing candidates increased 10 times, which is abnormal on all counts. This is vividly shown in Table 2.

Table 2

Profile of the Results of 10th Board Examination in the R.P.M. High School

Year	*Total Number of Students Appeared*	*Total Passed*
2001	33	26 (78%)
2002	141	110 (78%)
2003	235	189 (81%)
2004	334	131 (38%)

Analysis of Table 2 reveals that in 2001 there was no manipulation in number of students enrolled as regular in class X. But in 2002 the number increased more than four-fold and in 2003 seven-fold and in 2004 ten-fold! The pass percentage was very high during 2001–3 but declined in 2004 (from 81% to 38%) because BSEB changed the centre to other sub-division and tightened the conduct of examination.

Though D.S. Kothari had fervently appealed in his Education Commission Report (1968) for a 'Common School System' in India for the sake of equity and justice, neither the Union Government of India nor the state government of Bihar could implement it. Hence, private schools have been flourishing at the cost of Government schools in the entire country and the R.P. Memorial High School, Gobaria Don, is the best example of its decay and collapse. These eight teachers and three non-teaching staff do not go to school, except on the Independence Day (15 August), Republic Day (26 January), and Saraswati Puja (Vasant Panchami), deceiving the people as 'patriots' (they have kept some old clothes and utensils in a school room and pretend to stay there). So, with this prevailing situation in the Gobaria Don village, an English-medium private school has been established and many children of the relatively better-off Tharu tribal families have got themselves enrolled in it and are paying fees (let us not forget that fees not charged from tribals in government schools). Though that private school is neither recognized by any Board/Government nor has trained teachers, its 'outer shining' and punctuality of teachers, both of which stand in stark contrast to the government school, have attracted a large number of students (more than 100). Thus, the flourishing of the private school in remote Gobaria Don is a 'push-out' and 'demand-driven' syndrome, while in cities it may be more of a 'supply-driven' affair. Amongst the children of school-going age in the village, 30 per cent have joined the new private school, 20 per cent are still enrolled in the government school, and 50 per cent have become dropouts and are working somewhere in Bihar or outside.

If we analyse the social background of the teachers of the R.P. Memorial High School, Gobaria Don, we find that two are Brahmins and two are Rajputs (four from the upper castes), while two are from backward (middle) castes and two belong to a minority community (Muslim). That is to say, the teachers of the upper castes, backward castes and minority community have all been equally responsible for such a sordid state of affairs there. None of them was sincere to, sympathetic to or concerned for the marginalized. It may sound surprising for some leaders/scholars, but it is absolutely correct that, as per local Tharu parents/guardians, during 1978–81 Mr Shrikant Tiwari was the headmaster in that school, stayed in that village, taught regularly with dedication and ensured that other teachers be punctual and dedicated. As a headmaster, he also advised his colleagues in academic matters. His upper-caste background did not come in the way at all in imparting good education to the poor children of the marginal Tharu tribals. Hence, it emerges that the attitude and commitment of individual teachers is more important than their social background in a school situated in a village of the marginalized.

Here one more point is notable. Not only was the formal elementary and secondary education found in doldrums in Gobaria Don but also the so-called 'alternative innovative education' (AIE).

For instance, in the local office of the Bihar Education Project or BEP (for SSA), two carpenters were working to make new doors and windows privately and there were four big pots full of paddy kept by the landlord of the rented room. There was no trace of aid materials of teaching, sports and cultural activities, not even posters. Thus, the BEP centre was not functioning at all, though its *saheli* (Staff) from the Tharu community itself admitted to get ₹ 700 per month as honorarium. Similarly, the Anganwadi Kendra (meant for the care of early childhood) was also non-functional. The school children of the middle school never got mid-day meals: all the foodgrains were siphoned off jointly by the teachers and the public distribution system dealer.

Thus, the following diversified strategies of Education Guarantee Scheme (EGS) and AIE (of Government of India)[11] for 'out of school' children have remained only on paper in East Champaran and in most of Bihar:

(a) Coverage of children in remote, school-less habitations

(b) For children migrating with or without parents

(c) Support to *maktabs/madarsas to adopt a formal curriculum*

(d) Bridge courses/back-to-school camps

(e) Long-duration residential camps for older out-of-school children

(f) Remedial teaching

(g) Short-duration summer camps or schools

Thus, from the above, it may be deduced that the concept of education at different levels and agencies varies so much that by the time it reaches the ground at the local level, it gets reduced to mere rhetoric or even to the reverse of the original concept at the international level. This is shown in Table 3.

Just the previous night, George Orwell appeared in my dream and remarked perceptively with a laugh: 'The Animal Farm exists even in the education field at different levels: the racehorse at the top, the load-carrying pony at the middle, and the sheep at the bottom.' Who can dare to disagree with his view? He also reminded me of the 'double speak' by different stakeholders, and finally remarked: 'In the R.P. Memorial High School, Gobaria Don, the teachers have developed four pillars of education: (a) learning to know nothing; (b) learning to do nothing; (c) learning to live separately; and (d) learning not to be.' Then he suddenly disappeared like 'absentee teachers'.

Table 3

Concept of Education at Different Levels and Agencies

No.	*Level*	*Agency*	*Concept of Education*
1.	International	United Nations (Delors Commission)	Inclusive, quality, employability, contextual, flexible, attractive, pluralistic, trained teachers, child-centred learning.
2.	National	Government of India (Ministry of HRD)	In policy, more focus on quality, flexibility, pluralism, inclusion, employability, trained teachers and child-centred learning, but in practice, more ad hoc, temporary, quantity rather than quality, target-filling, cheap, contingent, distractive, para-teachers rather than trained regular teachers, partly exclusive.
3.	Regional/Local	Government of Bihar/Panchayati Raj system at village level	Neither quantity nor quality, ad hocism, neglect of pluralism, absentee teachers like absentee landlords, high unionization of teachers, absence of pressure groups to resist, culture of silence of the oppressed marginalized, school on paper only, highly distractive, exclusion of the poor and marginalized.

Policy Implications

The following points deserve consideration of policy here.

First, the Tharu tribals have usually been a peaceful community and have adopted the language (Bhojpuri) of the majority Hindus ('great tradition') and some rituals of the latter, though they also practise their own specific 'little tradition' in terms of gods and goddesses as well as rites and rituals. There is a need for their social and economic development with a distinct tribal identity and, for this, a model of 'development with identity' seems to be appropriate where the complementing of 'great tradition' and 'little tradition' will enrich each other in a fruitful way through inter-cultural sharing and understanding, but not 'identify with development' model (where the former relegates the latter). So, the approach of 'mainstreaming' the marginalized should be disbanded and the state should become a facilitator and enabler for the 'development with identity' of the marginalized.

Second, the political leadership of the backward (middle) castes with a 'social justice' plank *per se* is not inclusive, plural and diversified in spirit. In fact, this leadership got opportunities time and again to develop and empower the marginalized masses but it failed to carry out its responsibility sincerely as per the people's mandate to raise them – *'charwaha'* (grazers') schools did not take off despite much fanfare in Bihar during 1991–2005. It unfortunately sees the Tharu tribals as 'weaker rather than different'. But the need of the hour is that it should see them as 'different rather than weak' and practise 'good governance' with the culture of diversity and pluralism in word and deed by going beyond 'identity politics'.

Third, since education is as much a 'process of change' as it is a process of socialization of the prevailing norms and values, the government's role should go beyond providing the necessary infrastructure to providing trained and dedicated teachers, quality teaching–learning and an environment conducive to learning to the extent that the delinquent teachers should be duly punished with a deterrent effect. In fact, both reward and punishment should be adopted for school teachers lest too much freedom results into anarchy and the ruining of the marginalized children's future.

Fourth, 'Alternative Innovative Education' (AIE) has unfortunately become an 'artificial interim education' due to ad hocism, lack of quality and commitment, contingency and superficiality in both perception and performance. Since 2004, a two per cent education cess has been levied on all major Central taxes to finance for 'quality basic education' but, in reality, there is no quality education in government schools in rural areas. In fact, when there is no 'education at all', expecting of quality education is either an imagination of luxury or an insult to the injury of the Tharu tribals of Gobaria Don. Hence, it is imperative that the existing government schools should be strengthened and innovated as 'smart schools' under a common school system in all respects in order to ensure a child-friendly education. In 2006, the new Government of Bihar appointed a Commission on Common School System whose recommendations are yet to be implemented due to paucity of fund or other reason. Only after its implementation there would be a broad-based 'creative and diversified mobility' of the marginalized masses as against the 'sponsored mobility' of the upper and middle classes (through private schools).

Fifth, it is experienced that neither total state dependence nor total privatization works in school education, especially in Bihar, because the takeover of the private schools by the state government in October 1980 has resulted into too much unionization of teachers, due to which the education of all the children in general and that of the marginalized, in particular, in rural areas, has suffered both in terms of quantity and quality. Hence, the state has to play a critical role of 'relative intervention' by balancing the two extremes keeping in view primarily the future of school children belonging to the marginalized in rural areas who are treated by 'others' as 'less equal than others' in almost all respects.

Sixth, a genuine education ensures looking critically at the social situations, events and processes in which the learner lives, especially the 'culture of silence' of the dispossessed, as Paulo Freire correctly terms it.[12] He is of the view that an oppressed person is capable of looking critically at the world in a dialogical encounter with others: 'people educate each other through the mediation of the world' – a local farmer may do so more effectively than a teacher brought in from outside. Freire points out that the role of liberating education is 'conscientization', i.e. 'learning to perceive social, political and economic contradictions, and to take action against the oppressive elements of reality.'[13] He further explains that subjectivity and objectivity join in a 'dialectical unity' producing knowledge in solidarity with action, and vice versa. Since the oppressed people internalize the image of the oppressive, they are 'fearful of freedom'. While the oppressed are afraid to embrace freedom, the oppressors are afraid of losing the 'freedom' to oppress. The pedagogy of the oppressed is an instrument for their 'critical discovery that both they and their oppressors are manifestations of dehumanization.'[14] The oppressed Tharus have to realize that they are not only fighting for freedom from hunger but also for 'freedom to create and to construct, to wonder and to venture' (to use Eric Fromm's words). Freire terms the existing education of filling the minds of students as a 'banking' concept where the students receive and store the deposits given by the teachers. The teachers think themselves as 'knowledgeable' and the students as absolutely ignorant – a feature of ideology of oppression – and, on the other hand, the students accept their ignorance as justifying the teacher's existence. In this regard, in the context of the R.P. Memorial High School, Gobaria Don, the following findings are noteworthy:

1. The teachers are absent, so students are either absent or dropouts.
2. The teachers are kept on contract, so students have also given their learning on contract to their brothers and sisters in private schools.
3. The teachers are masters; the students are slaves.
4. The teachers decide the fate of the students; the students allow this obediently.
5. The teachers ignore the local tribal students totally but are active in bringing outside students for appearing in the examination in lieu of a handsome amount.
6. The teachers see and know everything; the students need not see from their eyes and know anything.
7. The teachers manipulate the local and state educational administration through their association that engages in rigorous trade union politics as an oppressor of students.

Finally, the oppressed Tharus have not understood their problem critically so far because they fear from freedom and the oppressive mentality is ingrained in them. This can be broken only through a critical pedagogy of the oppressed through a dialectical unity of subjectivity and objectivity, word and action, i.e. through dialogical action for freedom: cooperation, unity, organization and cultural synthesis. B.R. Ambedkar had rightly given a call long back to 'educate, organise and struggle'. But his concept of dalits (depressed castes) was not as broad as Paulo Freire's concept of the oppressed, in which even the victim students are included. Thus, we find how the 'culture of silence' prevails among the oppressed Tharus in West Champaran (Bihar) and how the teachers have become 'oppressors' in the worst forms by perpetuating their dominance and playing with the future of tribal children.

This is the sordid story of the Rajendra Prasad Memorial High School, Gobaria Don, West Champaran (Bihar). The brilliance of Dr Rajendra Prasad is well known. A genuine teacher–examiner had once perceptively remarked about him: 'Examinee knows more than the examiner.' But, for the students of the school named after him, it may be observed: 'Examinees know nothing as their teachers allowed them to learn nothing. Nothing begets nothing.'

Thus, structural tensions (absenteeism of teachers, collapse of the formal public school system, and geographical isolation accompanied by social isolation) are more prominent than cultural tensions (segregation from others, shrinking of space due to hegemony of non-tribals, and denial of diversity and pluralism) in Gobaria Don. Consequently, there is an *'accentuation of marginalization'* of the Tharu children in Bihar.

Notes

1. See Subhash Sharma (2007) *Bharat Mein Bal Majdoor* (Child Labour in India), Prakashan Sansthan, New Delhi.
2. Government of India (2007) *Annual Report 2006–07*, Ministry of Human Resource Development, New Delhi, p. 2.
3. Government of India (2007a) *Selected Educational Statistics 2004–05*, Ministry of Human Resource Development, New Delhi.
4. Government of India (2006) *Towards Faster and More Inclusive Growth: An Approach to the 11th Five Year Plan*, Planning Commission of India, New Delhi, p. 48.
5. See Subhash Sharma (2007) *Shiksha Aur Samaj* (Education and Society), Prakashan Sansthan, New Delhi, pp. 109–10.
6. Ibid., pp. 111–12.
7. For details, see Subhash Sharma (2006) 'Dialectics of Identity and Development of Tharus in Bihar: A Sociological Analysis', *Prajna Bharati*, XII, pp. 140–57.
8. R.H. Turner (1961) 'Modes of Social Ascent Through Education: Sponsored and Contest Mobility', in A.H. Halsey, J. Floud and C.A. Anderson (eds), *Education, Economy and Society*, The Free Press, Glencoe, III.
9. Ramesh Thakur (2007) 'Good News from Bihar', *The Times of India*, 5 January.
10. L. Bhandari and Sunita Kale (eds) (2007) *Bihar: Performance, Facts and Figures*, Pearson, Delhi, pp. 19–20.
11. Government of India (2007a), op. cit., p. 16.
12. Paulo Freire (1996) *Pedagogy of the Oppressed*, Penguin Books, London.
13. Ibid., p. 17.
14. Ibid., p. 30.

8

Why the Marginalized Protest

Environmental Movements as a Critique of Dominant Development Discourse

In this chapter, our objective is to provide an overview of globalization and its discontents at a macro level in terms of weakening of the sovereign nation-state, deregulation, liberalization, privatization and marketization. Second, we would present the grand narrative of 'Dominant Development Discourse' (DDD) with its perceptions and priorities, vision and model, especially in the context of India. Third, we would analyse as to why the marginalized people protest in their everyday life. Finally, we would try to explore as to whether there emerges an 'Alternative Development Paradigm' (ADP) in a manifest or latent form. We divide our essay into four sections for the sake of convenience.

Globalization and its Discontents

Historically speaking, the long span from 1600 to 1950 was a period of colonialism and imperialism, wherein economic interests were accompanied by grabbing direct political rule. The 1950s and 1960s were described by the West as *'development decades'* and the 1970s as *'the lost decade'* but in fact there emerged neo-liberal globalization (strategic-economic interests at the centre). Globalization is actually a grand narrative with a packaged process of inter-connectedness going beyond the borders of nation-states. But its essence is not compatible with real internationalization as it does not question the multi-dimensional unequal relations of the contemporary world order. Hence, one has to take an inter-disciplinary holistic approach to understand globalization and its discontents.

Global economic inequality (as the world was never flat and even now is not flat though Thomas Friedman wrongly presumed so) perpetuated by the dominant trans-national corporations (TNCs), technological advancement, escalating militarization (going beyond 'balance of power' and 'balance of terror'), cultural fusion (remixing), and the decline of sovereignty of nation-states are its salient features. Undoubtedly, globalization is America-centric in letter and spirit. As Jan N. Pieterse (2004) correctly remarks: 'The most recent globalization project, neo-liberal globalization, is the deluxe model of Pax Americana that combined economic unilateralism with political multilateralism.' In fact, neo-liberal policies add to the globalization package (of informatization, flexibilization, regionalization and reconfiguration of states), 'to deregulation (liberalization, privatization), marketization (unleashing of market forces), financialization and securitization (conversion of assets into tradable financial instruments), and the ideology of lean government', to use Pieterse's words. In fact, neo-liberalism was reflected in the policies of Ronald Reagan (US) and Margaret Thatcher (UK), especially in their 'low wage, low tax model' in the 1970s and 1980s as much as in the Chicago School's (Frederich Von Hayek, Milton Friedman). The Chicago School provided an economic rationale and justification to the prevailing 'backward, conservative and impoverished economic condition'. Hayek actually claimed that market forces give better circulation of information while Friedman's monetarism, attacking Fordism, stated that the Laffer Curve (fewer taxes stimulate the economy and yield more tax revenue) justified rolling back government – cheap government and weak public sector.

In the US and other western countries, the free market model assumes that all individuals are free, fully rational, and have free choices, hence they are just rational buyers and sellers in all circumstances (though it is not true in the context of developing countries). Thus, it emerged that deregulation and tax cuts were necessary for more 'competitiveness' and 'flexibility'. 'Washington Consensus', a manifesto (for Latin America) published by the Business Roundtable in 1979, prescribed balanced budgets, tax cuts, tight money, deregulation and anti-labour union laws. Such changes led to 'low-wages, high-exploitation regime'. In Pieterse's view, 'the postwar period of 'proto-neoliberalism' coincides with the cold war era' and the anti-communist critique in Hayek's 'From Serfdom to Slavery' and W.W. Rostow's 'Take-off to Economic Growth' became 'free world' policy. He points out several continuities and discontinuities between the Cold War and Neo-Liberal Globalization (Table 1):

Table 1

Continuities and Discontinuities between the Cold War and Neo-Liberal Globalization

Dimensions	*Cold War*	*Neo-liberalism*
Ideology	Free world, open door, anti-communism	Free market, free trade, pro-American capitalism
Key state agencies	Pentagon, CIA	Treasury, commerce
Economic Centre	Military-industrial complex, MNCs	MNCs, banks, Silicon Valley, telecommunications, media
Pressure on developing countries	Join the free world	Structural adjustment
Means of pressure	National security and economic incentives	Financial discipline and economic incentives
Agents of pressure	US government, Pentagon	IMF, World Bank, WTO
Investments	Sunbelt	Third World made safe
Security	Strong US military	Strong US military
Politics of containment	Military intervention, covert operations	Humanitarian intervention, nation-building
Allies	NATO, Israel, etc. religious movements (*Mujahideen*, Hamas)	NATO, Israel, etc. 'clash of civilisations': Islam as opponent

Source: Pieterse (2004: 10)

The US applied the following strategies for neo-liberal globalization, rather empire-building (Pieterse, 2004):

(a) Free trade

(b) Export-oriented growth

(c) Trade as a foreign policy instrument (imposing/lifting tariffs, most favoured nation status – if given to one – to be given to all members of WTO); making Iraq the new strategic oil reserve of the US

(d) Influencing other countries' exchange rate (appreciation of yen)

(e) Prying open markets

(f) Legalism into world trade rules via WTO (which is a 'tariff-trading bourse')

A major ingredient of globalization is privatization, wherein the role of government and public sector is so much weakened that it ultimately results into the disappearance of accountability. Though the leadership of US globalization talked of transparency, accountability and good governance, yet, as Pieterse (2004: 48–49) correctly observes, 'the Bush II administration shows decreasing transparency (empire requires secrecy), accountability (empire requires broad executive privilege), and good governance (civil liberties and due process impede the concentration of power).' Beneath the so-called 'free trade' lies the US hegemony (it has not implemented many decisions passed against it in dispute settlement measures in WTO regime) as US Trade representative Robert Zoellick once remarked: 'Trade is more than economic efficiency. It is about America's role in the world' (Pieterse, 2004: 50). Interestingly, while the western developed nations pressurize the developing countries for relaxing import laws, charging user fees for irrigation, health and education, and for reducing agricultural subsidies (on irrigation, water, electricity, fertilizers, insecticides/pesticides, seeds, and so on), they tighten their own import laws in the name of sanitation and phyto-sanitation (SPS) and increase agricultural subsidies in one form or the other under the Blue Box (as provided in the WTO Agreement on Agriculture). For instance, agricultural subsidies in Europe and the US are to the tune of one billion dollars per day, which amounts to six times the annual aid given to developing countries. The developed nations, particularly the US, practise free trade selectively – often preventing developing countries to take advantage in the world market. Further, in neo-liberal trade, there is more focus on marketing than on the product, as the *business of business is business*. Interestingly, in May 2003, the UN Security Council authorized the creation of a Development Fund for Iraq but was controlled by the US with advice from the World Bank and IMF. America claims to be a future-looking nation in strategic matters and, hence, after the 9/11 incident (2001), US Secretary of Defence Donald Rumsfeld remarked: '... the nation must be prepared to defend itself "against the unknown, the uncertain, the unseen, and the unexpected"' (in Pieterse, 2004: 57). Therefore, it justifies the spending of a huge amount on its military.

If we look at the world, we find that though the ratio of the poor in the total world population has been reducing, yet the gap between the richest 20 per cent and the poorest 20 per cent has been increasing over a long period (Table 2).

Second, as per the UNDP's Human Development Report (1990), the net worth of 358 richest people is equal to the combined income of the poorest 45 per cent of the world's population – 2.3 billion people. Third, L. Eliott and C. Denny (Pieterse, 2004) estimated that the richest 1 per cent of the world have income equivalent to the poorest 57 per cent. But, unfortunately, instead of adequately helping the poor of the developing countries, the US prefers to attack them in order to preserve its hegemony. Thus, globalization does not come to the rescue of the poor people and poor nations.

Table 2

Global Poverty Scenario(1820–1997)

Year	*Gap between the richest 20 per cent and the poorest 20 per cent*
1820	3:1
1870	7:1
1913	11:1
1960	30:1
1970	60:1
1997	74:1

Source: UNDP, HDR, 1998

Further, globalization brings in borderlessness but only for capital, communication, travel and consumption. Labour, in fact, faces border restriction policies not allowing free migration of labour. For example, US visa (H1B) is restricted to only 60,000 persons in a year and within three hours of its opening this meagre quota is exhausted like an eagerly awaited IPO! Further there has emerged an army of labour agents or 'dalals' to facilitate labour migration but more often their passports are snatched by private contractors, less wages than agreed is paid, working conditions are unhygienic and they are not allowed to go back to their homes. Again, globalization has weakened the power of the nation-states, hence the latter are unable to control crimes and conflicts.

Thus, globalization has many positive outcomes for the rich and for the capitalists but more negative outcomes for the poor and the labour class. The global inequality, in terms of technology, geopolitics and economy, has led to several kinds of conflicts – manifest or latent. Geoff Mulgan (1998), linking technology and politics, argues that the heavy technologies of industrialism in the mass production phase were paralleled by heavy command and control politics; standardized production was matched by standardized administration and regulation, standardized politics and coalitions. These involved top-down hierarchical relations between the government and the governed, and within bureaucracies, parties and trade unions. Usually the technologies of work, war and politics are 'intertwined but their interrelations are uneven within and across countries' (Pieterse, 2004). The western dominant view is to prefer 'high tech' with 'flexible production' and 'smart war'. No doubt, technology matters but technological determinism is not acceptable as it is only an enabler – a necessary but not a sufficient condition for action. For technology, human capability, political will and contextuality are equally significant. In practice, it is seen that propaganda about profitability, speed, less risk, economy of scale, less drudgery, more output, etc. is spread. Second, often the politics of representation becomes decisive in matters of purchase, use, maintenance, sale, etc. of technology. Third, the politics of violence involves a play of technology or capability differentials across terrains and social contexts (during the colonial period, 'we have got the Maxim gun/and they have not' was the motto). Fourth, a western nation-state wants a level of technology that enables it 'to effectively monopolize the means of coercion' (Pieterse, 2004). That is why most of the developed nations focus more on providing training for better capacity-building of human resources in developing countries but ultimately do not share the nitty-gritty of the latest technology. But a Chinese saying correctly explains the problem: instead of giving fish to the poor, tell them how to catch the fish.

II
Dominant Development Discourse

Development means different things to different scholars, groups, organizations and establishments. Neoclassical economists equate development with economic growth measured in terms of Gross Domestic Product and per capita income. Hence, they desire an increase in per capita income to ensure better purchasing power. But it is only one aspect of development as the UNDP talks of 'human development' with three aspects: income, school enrolment and adult literacy, and longevity. Amartya Sen expands it to include 'development as freedom'. However, the concept of social development is very comprehensive and takes a holistic view of the real progress of a society in the economic, social, demographic and political arena.

Mainstream social scientists in the North (especially America) like Talcott Parsons, W.W. Rostow, Lerner, Eisenstadt, and others formulated a modernization theory (with difference in their emphasis and focus on cultural, psychological or economic factor) for the 'catching-up development' following the path adopted by the West. They differentiated between 'traditional' and 'modern' societies in terms of their social value system, psychological motivation, attitudes and aptitudes, and economic capital accumulation. For instance, Parsons, focusing on behavioural orientation, made dichotomies of pattern variables like ascription–achievement, role-diffusedness–specificity, etc. where the former in each pair represents the traditional societies and the latter the modern ones (Webster, 1990). Parsons' dichotomization is actually based on that of earlier sociologists like Tonnies' *gemeinschaft–gesselschaft* (community–association) and Durkheim's 'mechanical solidarity' and 'organic solidarity'.

In 1960, W.W. Rostow wrote a book *Stages of Economic Growth: A Non-Communist Manifesto*, wherein he declared: 'It is possible to identify all societies, in their economic dimensions, as lying within one of five categories: the traditional society, the preconditions for take-off, the take-off, the drive to maturity, and age of high mass-consumption' (Webster, 1990). There are five key elements of modernization theory: *evolutionism* (change through a fixed set of stages), *unilinearity* (all societies are to pass through the same route and in the same order), *internalism* (crucial changes are internally generated), *exposure and diffusion* (of Western ideas, values and technology), and *recapitulation* (to follow the path of developed countries). Rostow went beyond the dichotomy syndrome of Parsons by stating five stages. His key concept is the 'take-off' stage of economic growth when barriers to economic growth are removed, especially by the onset of an adequate rate of capital investment so that growth becomes a normal condition. World Trade Organisation (WTO), since its inception in 1995, prescribes to remove trade barriers on the borders. Under the rubric of traditional society, Rostow put many diverse societies ranging from the Stone Age cultures to pre-Revolution France, emphasizing their so-called features like 'pre-Newtonian' science and technology, a basically agricultural economy, and a basically rigid ascriptive social structure based on kinship. In the second stage, triggered off by some impulse from outside, agriculture is augmented by an increase in trade, service and extractive industries like mining. Now, the economy becomes less self-sufficient and localized due to growth in trade and communications. Consequently, an elite class emerges to reinvest the surplus. Further, due to the emergence of new scientific ideas, the natural world is no more seen as a given. In the third stage, investment rises to a minimum of 10 per cent of the national income, and one or more sub-sectors of manufacturing take a leading role. Now, social and political structures are reshaped to suit the take-off stage, which takes about 20 years: 1783–1803 for Britain, 1843–60 for US, 1878–1900 for Japan, 1890–1914 for Russia, 1950s and onwards for China and India. The fourth stage of 'drive to maturity' is one of consolidation where modern science and technology are extended to almost all spheres of the economy. Now the rate of investment is 10 per cent to 20 per cent of the national income. With political reforms continuing, the economy stands on its own feet in the international context. Finally, in the 'age of high mass consumption', the productive power of a society has three strategic choices of orientation, according to Rostow: first, wealth may be concentrated in individual consumption, as in the US; second, it may be channelled into a welfare state as in western Europe; third, it may be used to build up global power and influence, as in the erstwhile USSR (Foster-Carter, 1985).

But the modernization theory does not stand the test of ground reality in most of the developing countries. It may be criticized on the following main grounds:

First, all societies cannot be dichotomized as 'traditional' and 'modern' because (a) all societies with pre-Newtonian science had a wide range of differences in their economy, technology, values, policies and political order; (b) a developing society may be having one modern sector (say, manufacturing) with another traditional sector (say, agriculture) at the same point of time; (c) even the so-called modern societies themselves are not in the same stage, say, the age of high mass consumption – only the US may be put in that stage in the real sense; (d) some developing societies had indigenous industrialization, though non-western, before the onset of Newtonian science and technology; e.g. India in the seventeenth and eighteenth centuries; (e) even a modern society like Japan practises ascriptive criteria (family background, age and sex) in promotion of employees who were appointed on the basis of achievement criteria of skills and education (A.G. Frank in Sharma, 1998). In addition, as Yogendra Singh (1973) rightly says, Indian value system consists of collective behaviour and transcendence (spirituality due to belief in life after death) whereas western civilization focuses on individualism and materialism, hence path of Indian modernization would be different from the west. He talks of four models of modernization: structural – universalistic, structural – particularistic cultural – universalistic, and cultural – particularistic. Further, gender discrimination is very much evident in many developed countries of the North.

Second, this theory ignores the historical fact of imperialism and colonialism, which were, to a large extent, responsible for the underdevelopment of Third World countries; e.g. the process of 'de-industrialization' in India by the British Empire in the nineteenth and early twentieth century.

Third, it confuses pre-industrial and non-industrial paths of development, and wrongly puts the two together.

Fourth, even the modern technologies and facilities may contribute to reinforcement/resurgence of old traditional religions/ethnic values and attitudes; for instance, *purdah* by women during the Islamic Revolution in Iran, or Sikh separatist activities in Punjab (north India) associated with the Green Revolution. Further, modern means of transport facilitate visits to religious places like Mecca by foreign Muslim devotees or to Mathura and Ayodhya by Hindu non-resident Indians. So is the case of extended families, caste and ethnicity.

Fifth, the modernization theory makes a grand generalization at a theoretical plane at the cost of concrete reality in a specific country.

Sixth, it ignores the contribution of religious values in the growth of capitalism. For instance, Max Weber did a pioneering work to show the relationship between the 'Protestant ethic' of salvation and the growth of the spirit of capitalism in the post-16th-century Western Europe.

Seventh, this theory suffers from the 'tragedy of psychologism' blaming all the peoples of the Third World as fatalist, passive, other-worldly, superstitious, backward-looking against the modern western peoples as forward-looking, creative, scientific, innovative, and entrepreneurial. In fact, the attempts of the West to diffuse their ideas through aid have resulted in debt crisis, political oppression, militarization, trans-boundary wars and war psychology, and racial discrimination against the developing countries, which have become the 'victim of development'.

Finally, and most significantly, the modernization theory has created a mad race for over-use and exploitation of natural resources in the name of development. Its *productionist* view sees problems like poverty, illiteracy, hunger, malnutrition and famine as those of production or lack of development. However, as Amartya Sen has correctly shown, the crux of the problem lies in people's entitlement or being able to command food supplies rather than in its production or supply. Thus, the modernization thesis emphasizes neither on entitlement nor on ecological sustainability; rather, nature is wrongly seen as of only instrumental/use value, not intrinsic value.

However, Dipankar Gupta (2000) talks of 'mistaken modernity' in India wherein middle class is severely wanting in modern attitude. To him, modernity means: dignity of the individual, adherence to universalistic norms, elevation of individual achievement over privileges or disprivileges of birth, and accountability in public life. But Indian elites are 'westoxicated' (superficial consumer display of fads and commodities in the west).

Subsequently, the anti-communist critique expressed in the modernization theory became a 'Free World' policy, and the Cold War geopolitics became the 'global financial regime'. For safe investment of Western capital (especially American), national governments and trade unions in developing countries were weakened in different ways – reforming/liberalizing of labour laws, providing land for industrial units at cheaper rates, giving tax holidays, providing regular electricity at lower rates, providing special economic zones (SEZs), and so on. Further, multilateral agencies like the World Bank and IMF pressurized developing nation–states, through loans, with conditionalities for structural adjustment. The globalization process has no world government (whereas nationalization has a national government) accountable to people – resulting into 'global governance without global government' (Joseph Stiglitz) – where the World Bank, IMF and WTO dominate the scene but the affected developing countries have no voice. The colonial mindset prevails in such institutions with the 'White man's burden' – to know what is the best for developing countries. Stiglitz (2002) has accused the IMF of taking a 'one size fits all' approach, 'maintaining global stability' and its programmes of being 'typically dictated from Washington' while he praises the World Bank's concern with eradicating world poverty. But, in fact, all the three multilateral institutions wrongly see market as a panacea for all the ills of developing countries. Stiglitz (2002) observes that lack of development in developing countries exists because 'markets are often absent, and when present, often work imperfectly. Information problems abound and cultural moves may significantly affect economic behaviour.' One cannot agree with Stiglitz fully because often market creates problems like unequal exchange.

Some neo-liberal social scientists have reformulated the modernization thesis in terms of 'Transfer of Technology' (TOT) that has five cardinal principles, as Robert Chambers (1996) rightly points out:

(a) Its main objective is the transfer of new technology from developed to developing countries.

(b) The needs and priorities of the local people (of developing countries) are analysed by outsider experts.

(c) It is based on experiment station, laboratory and greenhouse.

(d) Experts transfer precepts, messages and packages of new scientific practices to the local farmers.

(e) The menu is fixed from above and from outside.

It, thus, transpires that in TOT, development is seen as a modernizing force – a blueprint intervention – from research station to extension services to farmers. Second, the superiority of 'rational science' is assumed. Third, farmers are seen merely as 'adopters' or 'rejectors of science', not originators of technical knowledge/improved practice, which is discredited and undervalued. Fourth, this thesis does not empower the farmers; it rather sees them as a part of the problem of backwardness. Finally, its 'menu' is fixed, not open with alternative choices. It may be depicted in Table 3:

Table 3

Comparison of TOT Thesis and Alternative Paradigm

Dimension	*TOT thesis*	*Alternative Paradigm*
Primary goal	Transfer of new technology	Empower the people critically – recognizing power relations
Needs/priorities	By outsider experts	Critical interaction between farmers and experts
R&D location	Experiment station, lab, greenhouse	Farmers' fields and conditions
Contents' transfer	Precepts, messages and package of practices by experts	Contents' conflict-resolution mutually
Menu	Fixed blueprint	Open-ended
Science vs traditional knowledge	Superiority of science	Respect and value to traditional knowledge in addition to adapting of suitable science

Source: Chambers (1996).

Table 4

Views of Three Experts' Categories on Large Dams

S. No.	*Categories*	*Scholars/Activists*	*Views*
I.	Development optimists	Neoclassical economists (World Bank)	Catch-up development with West, modernization, cost-effective, multipurpose, to increase per capita water storage easily – the larger the size of the population, the more need for big reservoirs
II.	Conditionalists	R. Blackwelder, Philip Williams, Barbara Bramble, Bruce M. Rich, Shekhar Singh, et al.	EIA, to benefit large population, labour-intensive work and for food production, not to compromise public health, not to affect national parks/heritage, scientific and educational systems, rainforests and endangered animal species, not to silt for 100 years, no salinity, long-term sustainable resource enhancement, to ensure PAP's life better than earlier, not to build dam in seismic/landslide zone, not to damage estuarine/ocean fisheries, not to harm environment of a neighbouring country – these conditions to be met
III.	Negativists	E. Goldsmith and N. Hildyard, S. Sanghavi, A. Kothari and R. Bhartari, Smitu Kothari and P. Parajuli	No objective EIA, no social impact assessment, land-losers not beneficiaries, not labour-intensive, dams encourage growing of cash crops, create diseases/epidemics, damage more plant/animal species, water-logging and salinity, large displacement, associated with earthquake – not to be constructed.

As far as the major question of the development projects of large dams is concerned, scholars are divided. A large dam or 'major project' is defined as one with a cultivable command area of more than 10,000 ha, a 'medium' one between 2,000 and 10,000 ha, and a 'minor' one below 2,000 ha (as per Government of India). There are three major opinions regarding construction of large dams: development optimists, conditionalists, and negativists. Table 4 gives a comparative picture of three categories:

(a) *Development Optimists:* Neo-classical economists, policy makers and mainstream developmentalists argue for the construction of large dams because, in their opinion, it is the most cost-effective (in short term and narrow economic sense) and multi-purpose work (electricity generation, irrigation, drinking water supply and flood control). The World Bank, especially during the 1950s to the early 1990s, has been the main proponent of this view. Just like we store water in households, a reservoir (dam) is perceived to do so at a macro level, in view of the uncertainty, variability and seasonality of rainfall so that water may be transferred from wet season to dry season, from good years to bad, and from water-abundant areas to water-deficit ones. The World Bank, in its report, 'India's Water Economy: Bracing for Turbulence,' observes that water storage per capita is much lower in India than in the US, and that India must add substantially to its storage capacity – 'water infrastructure'! The logic behind this is that the extent of storage of water to be built by a country must be determined by the size of its population – the larger its population, the more the storage. But Ramaswamy R. Iyer (2008) criticizes this view as large dams/reservoirs are location-specific – they can be built only on certain kinds of terrain; similar reservoirs cannot be built in two countries having hilly and flat terrains respectively, though they may have the same size of population. Second, even with similar terrains, topography and river features, similar reservoirs cannot be built in a too densely populated country and a sparsely populated country. Third, there cannot be similar reservoirs in two different countries – one with rich biodiversity and rare species of flora and fauna, and the other not so rich in terms of bio-diversity.

(b) *Conditionalists:* In their view, large dams may be constructed but only at geologically and ecologically appropriate sites and sufficient precautions are to be taken in advance. For instance,

B. Blackwelder (Environmental Policy Institute), Philip Williams (Principal, Philip Williams and Associates, San Francisco), Barbara Bramble (National Wildlife Federation, Washington) and Bruce M. Rich (Natural Resource Defence Council, Washington) are of this view. They put forward 13 conditional recommendations for construction of large dams (Goldsmith and Hildyard, 1992):

(a) No dam should be built until an adequate environmental impact assessment (EIA) has been done and made available to the public concerned (Blackwelder and Rich).
(b) Water development projects should be taken only if they benefit large sections of the population rather than only the urban elite (Williams).
(c) The scheme should favour labour-intensive economic activities (Williams).
(d) It should allow the production of food crops for feeding the local population rather than growing cash crops for exports (Williams).
(e) Not to construct such dams as these would compromise public health and safety in such a way that would be unacceptable to the people affected (Blackwelder).
(f) Not to build dams if they adversely affect national parks, heritage sites, areas of scientific and educational significance, tropical rainforests or areas of endangered animal species (Bramble, Rich and Blackwelder).
(g) Dams should be built only when they would not silt up within 100 years (Blackwelder).
(h) Dams should not be built if the irrigation schemes associated with them tend to lead to the salinization of agricultural land (Blackwelder and Rich).
(i) The orientation of funding should be 'towards sustainable long-term resources' enhancement rather than 'short-term resource exploitation' (Williams).
(j) Dams are not to be built 'if they displace indigenous peoples from their homes and destroy their cultures' or 'unless compensation is provided to ensure that the affected people are made no worse off, and preferably better off, than before' (Rich).
(k) Dams having significant engineering and/or safety problems (e.g. in seismic zone or landslide areas) should not be built (Blackwelder).

(l) Dams should not be built at a place where they are likely to cause significant damage on estuarine or ocean fisheries (Blackwelder).

(m) Dams should not be built if they tend to harm significantly the environment of a neighbouring country without its full consent (Rich).

(C) *Negativists:* According to the negativists like Goldsmith and Hildyard (1984), Sanghavi (1995), Kothari and Bhartari (1984), Kothari and Parajuli (1993) and Kothari (1995), large dams necessarily bring serious problems and, hence, are not desirable at all. In practice, if all the above 13 conditions are met with, dams can hardly be built.

Following points learnt from the Indian experience are relevant to note here:

First, a genuine objective environmental impact assessment (EIA) of large dams is not made, and if made at all, the team has neither the courage nor the morality to advise the government concerned not to build such dams. Moreover, 'the main motivation for commissioning environmental assessments is to rationalise decisions which have already been made' (Goldsmith and Hildyard, 1984). In the Sardar Sarovar Project (SSP) dam, no prior environmental impact assessment was made, and the SSP was started even before the approval came from the Planning Commission of India. In fact, in this case, the state government of Gujarat commissioned an ecological impact study by Maharaja Sayaji Rao University after the project had been sanctioned; it could not do adequate fieldwork and, therefore, mostly relied on the data from government sources rather than on empirical data (Kalpavriksha, 1985). Further, a conditional approval was given by the Ministry of Environment and Forests (Government of India) but those conditions were not fulfilled before the actual work started.

Second, in SSP, for instance, the electric power is to be used mainly by the industries, rich farmers and urban consumers (Gujarat and Maharashtra) while the land losers are generally the small peasants (Madhya Pradesh) in rural areas whose production mode (food crop for subsistence) and consumption pattern are different from those of the former. So, the question arises: Can the government acquire the lands of the people without their consent? In India, for instance, since the 1950s, 1600 major dams and thousands of medium and minor dams have replaced 10–12 million persons

(Kothari, 1996). Under the Land Acquisition Act 1894 (a colonial legacy serving the interests of the ruling class), anybody's land may be acquired for the so-called 'public purpose' that in reality is nothing but the government's purpose or the industrialists' and urban elite's purpose – thus, private or state purposes far exceed public purposes. Unfortunately, even the Supreme Court of India has declared such purpose and right of the state as the ultimate power of sovereignty on the principle of *'eminent domain'*. Thus, common property resources belonging to the people are not recognized at all. So is the case in most of the developing countries.

Third, large dams are incompatible with labour-intensive activities like agriculture, handicraft or small-scale industries. They have not been economically successful in the developing countries – maintenance and operational costs far exceeding the revenue earned from water taxes and electricity charges. For instance, in India, in 1979–80, the total national loss on irrigation projects was about ₹ 3,480 million, which was ultimately met by the Government of India (Bandyopadhyay, 1986).

Fourth, most of the dams encourage growing of cash crops to earn foreign exchange for the loans taken as well as to finance other projects; e.g. in the case of SSP, it is the rich farmers of Gujarat who are planning to grow sugarcane, and licences for sugar factories have already been issued. Even the productivity need not increase after irrigation from the dam. In the case of Tawa dam in MP, the yield of wheat and maize declined in the post-dam period in 1978–79 (Mishra, 1986).

Fifth, big dams create diseases and epidemics like malaria, bilharzia or schistosomiasis etc. as has been found in many large dams.

Sixth, big dams affect the rare rainforests along with rare medicinal plants (e.g. in the case of SSP) and the endangered species of animals.

Seventh, since rivers in tropical areas in the developing countries carry high quantities of silt, it cannot be guaranteed that dams like SSP will not silt up within 100 years.

Eighth, canal irrigation during the British rule in India resulted into both water logging and salinity. As a study noted, 'increasing salinity in irrigated solids on arid lands is practically universal' (V. Kovda, cited in Goldsmith and Hildyard, 1984), hence it is not sustainable in the long run. In Madhya Pradesh itself, the earlier

Tawa dam scheme caused water-logging of 800 ha of fertile land. There is all likelihood of the same happening in the case of SSP. In India as a whole, irrigation water has caused water-logging of 10 million ha and another 25 million ha is threatened with salinity (Bandyopadhyay, 1986).

Ninth, almost all big dams displace a large number of local people. SSP has displaced 1,50,000 persons, mostly the marginalized people. Unfortunately, there is no 'social impact assessment' (SIA) of most of the proposed/planned dams to study how the critical life chances of local people will be affected – from livelihood to cultural heritage.

Tenth, dams are also associated with, if not cause, earthquakes. Many areas of the developing countries like India are in the seismic zone, thus being more prone to earthquakes. A former Environment Commissioner of Madhya Pradesh warned about the SSP that 'a chain of reservoirs on Narmada could create seismic aftereffects' (Kalpavriksha et al., 1986).

Finally, large dams cause inequality, indebtedness and corruption (in inflated estimates, payment of compensation and rehabilitation). In Africa, too, this experience is common: 'Africa's history of large dams is filled with tragedy. Many have caused indebtedness, political inequalities, widespread environmental degradation, and have sapped resources from more appropriate, smaller scale development projects' (Horta and Pottinger, 2008).

Thus, the perceptions and priorities of different quarters differ. For instance, the Save Narmada Movement's 'perception from below' differed from the 'perception from above' of the policy-makers, financing agencies, contractors, political representatives and industrialists. This may be shown clearly in Table 5.

Table 5

Contrasting Perceptions on SSP

Perception from above (Dominant Development)	*Perception from below (at whose cost and for whom?)*
(a) To provide irrigation – 5 million ha	(a) power for use of rich farmers, industrial and urban dwellers, not the local people
(b) To check floods	(b) irrigation mostly by farmers in Gujarat but peasants mostly from MP to lose lands along others in Maharashtra and Gujarat – 37,000 ha of lands in 3 states to be submerged; loss of biodiversity

Cont'd ...

... Cont'd

(c) Employment generation to increase	(c) The dam will cause floods and earthquakes, submerge forests (a source of people's livelihood) and cause silting.
(d) Water for domestic and industrial use	(d) temporary employment at the cost of losing permanent and secure livelihood – displacing 1,50,000 persons, plus 140,000 others to be affected by canal and irrigation system
(e) To promote tourism	(e) wrong data produced without specifying villages, and urban centres to be provided drinking water
	(f) tourism for the rich at the cost of the submergence of temples/graves
	(g) no faith in government regarding compensation and rehabilitation, as land to be given for the land lost is not available – 90 per cent of land survey numbers given by Gujarat for rehabilitation are non-existent
	(h) an ecological impact study commissioned by the Gujarat government after the initiation of the project to justify it; over-estimation of benefits and under-estimation of environmental and social costs
	(i) loss of the tribals' cultural identity

Despite such contrasting perceptions of the people on the one hand, and those of the state, industrialists, rich farmers and contractors on the other, large dam construction has been in practice in developing countries for long. For instance, in India, by 1979, 154 large dams had been constructed and planned by the states, of which the largest three were Maharashtra (631), Gujarat (276), and Madhya Pradesh (131) – these three states are also jointly involved in SSP. Why is there so much of gap between the perceptions of the rulers and the ruled, between the prosperous and the marginalized? The first reason is 'damming the river and damning the people'; i.e. the 'promise a dam and win an election' syndrome. In India, there are more than 300 unfinished irrigation projects initiated under the illogical and undue pressure of some political representatives of the people decades back. Jawaharlal Nehru talked of dams as 'temples of modern India', but they are now 'unholy monuments of waste and greed', a 'grand political statement', a great scandal 'sucking money faster than a tubewell depletes groundwater' (Halarnkar, 1998). To complete new irrigation projects and renovate the old ones, a huge sum of ₹ 4,12,720 million was required, against which only ₹ 26,000 million was available in 1998–99, and of 119 incomplete major dams and canals, 24 have dragged on for more than 25 years! But politicians do not see this as a crisis. As a former Chief Minister of MP said: 'In our culture we first fix the marriage and then give the money' (Halarnkar, 1998).

The second reason is an opportunity for making money by many technocrats, bureaucrats, contractors, politicians, suppliers and traders. There is a massive corruption involved in different ways: inflated estimates of the projects, expenditure on unnecessary items, cut in purchase of construction materials, nepotism in awarding contracts, revision of estimates, payment for materials not supplied and used, etc.

The third reason is the role of financing agencies as 'big brothers' usually seeing large dam as a symbol of 'grand narrative of achievement', 'big is beautiful', 'visible is successful' and 'only concrete is real'.

Finally, many aspects of dams become standardized, uniform and universal – rather than specific, diverse and local – so that no extra efforts in terms of time and labour may be required for the officials and technocrats concerned in conducting specific field surveys, preparing estimates as per local conditions, and checking these. Such standardized formats are also claimed to be easier for supervision, monitoring and evaluation. Thus, they duly fit in their 'book view of reality' as per 'dominant development discourse' (DDD) – a 'perspective from above', – though, of course, at the cost of 'field view of reality' – a 'perspective from below'. This may be depicted in Table 6.

III
Why Do the Marginalized Protest?

Here we take up four case studies:

(a) Damming of Narmada River (MP)

(b) Sale of Neera river with Deogarh dam (Maharashtra)

(c) Drying of Kosi river (Uttarakhand)

(d) Closure of Muhane–Nonai river (Bihar)

Table 6

Contrasting Perceptions of Large Dams

Dimensions	*Dominant Development Discourse (North, financing agencies, national governments in south)*	*Alternative Development Paradigm (Environmental movements in south)*
I. Negative outcomes		
(a) Number of persons displaced	Less (than beneficiaries)	More (than beneficiaries)
(b) Forests and bio-diversity submerged	Less area (than stated by movements)	More area (than formally notified)
(c) Agricultural areas submerged	Less area	More area
(d) Socio-cultural monuments submerged (religious places, graves, schools, health centres, festival/fair places)	Less area	More area
(e) Submerging of houses	Less number	More number
II. Positive outcomes		
(a) Water supply for domestic use in urban areas	More area	Less area (at the cost of land losers)
(b) Irrigation of agricultural lands	More area	Less area (land losers not benefited)
(c) Flood control	More area	Less area

Cont'd ...

... Cont'd

(d) Generating electricity	More consumers' demand to be fulfilled	Electricity supply to other areas at environmental, social and economic costs and at the cost of people displaced
(e) Tourism promotion	More visitors, more trade, more money	Graveyards don't inspire for life
(f) Employment generation	More employment	Anti-livelihood
III. Vision of development	Grand narrative, big is beautiful, only concrete is real, river water as a saleable commodity, macro level	Small is beautiful, social harmony and peace, river water as life, is real, micro level
IV. Model of development	Standardized, uniform, reductionist, quantitative and universal – techno-centric model from above	Local, diverse, specific, qualitative, holistic, eco-friendly people's model from below

Damming of Narmada River (MP)

About 20 million people live in Narmada (1,300 km length) basin, depending on the river for survival. Out of its 41 sub-rivers, 39 meet in MP; out of its flow area of 98,796 sq km, 89,850 sq km falls in MP. More than 80 per cent of these people live in villages and amongst them a large number are tribals (Bhils, Gonds, Baiga and others). But the basin is backward with low agriculture yield, low literacy, low life expectancy, and lack of medical, educational and banking facilities. The Narmada Valley Development Project has planned to 'develop' it with 30 major, 135 medium and 3,000-plus minor dams, of which 10 major, 20 medium and 893 minor dam projects have been completed. This may be seen in Table 7.

Table 7

Profile of Dams on Narmada River

	No. of Proposed and Planned Dams	*No. of Completed Dams*	*No. of Dams to be Constructed*
(a) Large	30	10	20
(b) Medium	135	20	115
(c) Minor	3,000+	893	2107

Claude Alavares has called the Narmada Valley Development Project the 'world's greatest planned disaster'. The World Bank agreed in 1985 to lend $450 millions for the Sardar Sarovar Project (SSP) dam and its canals but later, due to the pressure from international NGOs, gave signal to the Government of India to withdraw. Hence, the Government of India terminated the contract in March 1993, by when the World Bank had disbursed 280 million dollars. Since then, the S. Kumar Group has been constructing the dam. The local marginalized people, under the banner of Narmada Bachao Andolan (led by Medha Patkar), have been protesting against it for decades because it has displaced about 1.50 lakh people, of whom 60 per cent are tribals in 243 villages, of which 193 villages fall in MP. Similarly, the Indira Sagar Project dam on the Narmada river has submerged 249 villages in MP. An old town of 700 years old – Harsud – with 5,600 families was also submerged; rather, it was 'destroyed' by the state apparatus, says Ravindra Shah (Tiwari, 2005). Unfortunately, both the Congress and the BJP state governments, observes Ravindra Shah, while raising fingers at each other, 'did not give priority to the issue of rehabilitation'. The state government of MP submerged Harsud on paper on 30 June 2004 by creating an artificial flood, thereby releasing water from the Bargi dam in order to terrorize the people in Harsud. It was announced on loudspeakers: 'The compensation of ₹ 25,000 would be given only to those who will destroy their homes in the same night' (Arundhati Roy in Tiwari, 2005). Therefore, Arundhati Roy observes: 'Yes, both Baghdad and Harsud have similarity. Both are the instances of globalization where, keeping the humanity and right to life aside, the state power and armed protection are ensuring the profit of companies. The construction of Indira Sagar (on Narmada) and displacement of the people of Harsud dam was essential in order to assure the world capital that any law, policy, people's democratic rights or even humanism will not come in its way' (Tiwari, 2005). But at Harsud, a mass rally by various people's movements resolved to firmly fight for people's rights over forests, lands, rivers, etc. The resettlement and rehabilitation of the Project-affected persons (PAPs) in SSP is not satisfactory (as found by the Tata Institute of Social Sciences) in five localities Somaval, Dekati, Amoni, Roswa and Amlibari (Singh and Banerji, 2002):

(a) Land allotted to PAPs is not agricultural – rather forest land allotted – again environmental damage in the name of rehabilitation.

(b) Many PAPs have not got actual possession of land; allotted land encroached by others.

(c) Housing materials like roofing tiles and bamboos have not been supplied to PAPs.

(d) Many PAPs have not got compensation for trees and houses in submerged areas.

(e) For giving employment to educated PAPs, the 5 per cent reservation for oustees has not been followed.

(f) No streetlights have been provided in their colonies

(g) Non-parity of rehabilitation package across MP, Gujarat and Maharashtra.

(h) In Gujarat, land is bought for rehabilitation from the open market, but in small bits/pieces – even 30 families cannot resettle on one location. Thus, families from 19 villages have resettled in over 175 locations, thereby causing disharmony.

(i) Displaced persons from MP and Maharashtra not willing to settle in Gujarat due to different cultural and language backgrounds.

(j) It has caused deprivation to a group of people who lived beyond the 'development' strategies for centuries.

Sale of the Neera River with Deogarh Dam (Maharashtra)

One major aspect of globalization is privatization, hence we would show how the impact of globalization has resulted into the privatization of the Shivnath river in Chhattisgarh (2002) and Neera river in Maharashtra. Earlier, at Haridwar, the Ganga water was sold to a French company for its supply to the Sonia Vihar colony plant in Delhi. The Neera river flows in Pune and Satara districts of Maharashtra with a flow area of 208 km. The Neera–Deogarh project was planned in 1984. The Maharashtra Krishna Valley Development Corporation or MKVDC (a corporate development under the Government of Maharashtra's Water Resources Ministry, floated in November 2007 an expression of interest 'with a minimum reserve of ₹ 1,000 crore' (10,000 million rupees), to which five private tenders responded. The Neera–Deogarh project has a capacity to irrigate 43,000 hectares of land. In fact, 95 per cent of the Deogarh dam has been completed, hence the highest bidder will have to complete only the remaining 5 per cent – canal work of 164 km and water distribution structure.

Interestingly, against the original estimate of ₹ 62 crores, the Government of Maharashtra spent ₹ 450 crores – ₹ 196 crores on dam, ₹ 93.6 crores on canals, ₹ 87 crores on land acquisition, ₹ 21 crores in rehabilitation of PAPs and ₹ 50 crores as 'other' expenditure. In 2001–02, MKVDC assessed that ₹ 910 crores was further required. In November 2007, the latest requirement was ₹ 1,000 crores (Dutta, 2007).

The local farmers have been protesting against the privatization of Neera river with the Deogarh dam on the following grounds:

(a) The private company will impose high water tax on the use of river water.

(b) The irrigation water may be used by the company for industrial purpose also.

(c) Only rich farmers can afford to buy the river water.

(d) The facilities for tourism and water sports would reduce the availability of water for irrigation.

(e) Water is a fundamental right of the people and it is the social responsibility of the state. 'How can the state permit a private company to earn profit from it?' asks Shripad Dharmadhikari. Ramaswamy R. Iyer, ex-Secretary, Ministry of Water Resources, Government of India, rightly observes: 'Economic rights of some people should not be permitted to endanger the fundamental rights of others' (Dutta, 2007). However, the Minister of Water Resources, Government of Maharashtra, Mr Nayak–Nimbalkar has a different perception: 'I hail from that region, so I know the needs of people from there. They want water' (Dutta, 2007). But at what cost? Then he responds that he is simply implementing the Maharashtra Govt. Notification (GR No. BOT/702, 425/2002 MP-l)!

It transpires that the World Bank has been behind the curtain in the name of 'economic reforms' – Government of Maharashtra received a loan of 325 million dollars from the World Bank. Thus it is clear that the World Bank, the Government of Maharashtra and the private firms are in favour of the privatization of the Neera river along with the Deogarh dam, while the local people have been protesting against it as their critical life chances are at stake.

Drying of the Kosi River (Uttarakhand)

People of Kumaun and Garhwal regions of Uttarakhand undertook long footmarches from l January 2008 in order to save the rivers. They all met in Ramnagar (Nainital) on 16 January under the banner of 'Nadi Bachao Andolan' (Save Rivers Movement) or NBA. Thus, the spirit of Chipko Andolan (Hug the Tree Movement) of the early 1970s is being revisited in the region. NBA started with the drive for saving the Kosi river, which is not glacier-based. Rather, it originates at a height of 2340 metres at Panidhar in Kausmi from underground water and ends at Ramnagar (Nainital) by meeting with Ramganga.

In 1994, the flow of the Kosi river was 994 litres per second, which declined to 65 litres per second in 2003 and continues to decline, as per Jivan Singh Rawat, a hydrologist (Tiwari, 2008). If the trend continues, Kosi may dry up in 2020 – the deadline of 'India: Vision 2020' prescribed by the ex-President of India, A.P.J. Abdul Kalam. According to Rawat, the recharge level of the Kosi river is on an average 12 per cent whereas ideally it should be 31 per cent, and therefore it is continuously drying up. While in the Banj forests the recharge level is 23 per cent, in barren land it is only 5 per cent and in urban land only 2 per cent on an average. Rawat has further pointed out that about 40 years ago, the length of the perennial rivers (meeting the Kosi river) was 225.6 km but their network has shrunk to merely 40 km. Since afforestation helps the recharge level in 40 to 50 years, it is pertinent to construct more and more water reservoirs. Earlier, in the radius of 1 km of every small river, there used to be 3–4 indigenous water mills facilitated by check dams. But now, due to the prevalence of electric water mills, the reservoirs required for indigenous water mills (helping recharge) have become non-existent. In the Kosi range, the table of underground water has gone down more than that in other rivers. The movement activists are generating mass awareness with folk songs sung by the local people's poet Girda (who used to sing during Chipko Andolan also) – 'Heard from grandmothers and grandfathers/about flowing of healthy Kosi/But alas! it has become as tiny as a little finger/our Kosi is lost.' Another song also he sang:

Oh! What to talk of you
You are a water trader
Sucking all the water
Looting rivers and oceans
What will happen to you
When you will be deprived of a single drop?

What will happen to you then
Tell me, the trader of World Bank?

It is notable that in the Saryu Valley of Uttarakhand, four villages are being submerged and 78 families are being displaced due to two dam projects at Patali Bagar. People are protesting through a relay hunger strike demanding agricultural fields, not dams. An activist Radha Bahan remarked that agriculture in the region depends on the Kosi river and if this 'life line' dries up, where would local residents go? Further, Shamsher Singh Bisht of Uttarakhand Lok Vahini observed that the government was not coming up with projects to conserve water and increase the water table; instead, hand pumps had been installed but 60 per cent of them do not work due to further depletion of the water table.

Closure of Muhane–Nonai River (Bihar)

Muhane-Nonai river had been flowing in the length of about 165 km (mainly in the Nalanda district of Bihar) for centuries. The local people used to take water from it for the irrigation of one lakh ha of their agricultural fields in more than 1200 villages through 365 irrigation channels *(pynes)* in four districts of Bihar–Nalanda, Gaya,

Jahanabad and Patna. Its water was also used for drinking by humans and animals. But the Government of Bihar constructed a six-foot-high dam weir – water reservoir at Uderasthan – on this river (which originates from the Falgu river that spreads into various small rivers at different places) in 1967 at the cost of about 12 crores (120 millions) rupees and since then has not been allowing the passage of rain water into the Muhane-Nonai river – it should not be called a river now as it has no water and most of its long bed has been encroached upon. Here a sarcastic popular anecdote is notable about Gaya town: 'Hills without forest, men without brain/river without water, road without drain'! Consequently, 250,000 people were affected by this weir construction, which facilitated only the farmers in the Ghosi block in Jahanabad district through Nataur branch at the instance of the influential local MLA (Jagdish Sharma of the then Congress). Due to the closure of this river, water table has gone down and in some areas (Patna–Gaya road) there is often flood, while in 1200 villages in Nalanda, Gaya, Jahanabad and Patna, there is drought due to non-availability of water for irrigation. At the time of its construction, the local people were assured that a sluice gate will be constructed there through which water will pass to the Muhane–Nonai river but this remained a hollow promise.

The local people have protested against the closure of this river for long. In the beginning, the protest was unorganized, but from 11 October to 23 December 2002, it was well-organized by the local Muhane–Nonai Sangharsh Samiti (led by Sadhu Sharan Singh, the local *mukhia*) and Ekta Parishad (led by Ravindra Pratap and Pradip Priyadarshi), wherein about five thousand persons participated directly in *dharnas* (sit-ins) and rallies. Due to lobbying by the movement, some of the people's representatives raised the question about the movement in the Vidhan Sabha/Parishad in December 2002, where the Government of Bihar (of the Rashtriya Janata Dal) at first justified the construction of the dam and the closure of the Muhane-Nonai river. However, after a long debate in the Vidhan Parishad, a committee was constituted with the experts of the Water Resources Department and those nominated by the movement organizations (2 January 2003). Thus, the local people have been deprived of irrigation of their fields due to closure of this river. However, the new government in Bihar laid the foundation (January 2006) of a new barrage there to ensure the flow of water in that river, but nothing has come up there even after two years.

Thus, it transpires that due to financing by multilateral agencies as well as government's policy of liberalization and privatization, these interventions with four rivers have many negative consequences:

(a) displacement of local people due to the damming of river, by the government (Narmada);

(b) privatization of river water by the government depriving the masses of their fundamental right to water (Neera);

(c) financing by multilateral agencies like the World Bank leads to a neo-liberal techno-centric model of 'development from above' in favour of the rich and against the poor (Narmada, Neera);

(d) there is a wide gap between the marginalized people's view and their political representatives' – while the former see dam as anti-people, the latter see it as necessary and developmental (Narmada, Neera); and

(e) dominant development discourse, in the name of so-called development, takes steps resulting into the permanent closure of a river (Muhane–Nonai).

This may vividly be seen in Table 8:

Thus, it transpires that the causes of the marginalized people's protest are various kinds of their disempowerment:

(a) *Economic Disempowerment:* As the main sources of livelihood of the marginalized people (agricultural lands, forests, common property resources) are lost, they become economically disempowered, unable to meet their basic needs of food, shelter, clothing, health and education.

(b) *Social Disempowerment:* Due to displacement, the PAPs are resettled in new locations, thus their old neighbourhood and community life is lost and, therefore, problems are created. Further, often new locations provide the challenge of new language (displaced persons from MP not willing to be resettled in Gujarat), thereby leading to incapacities. On the other hand, due to dislocation, their mother tongues/dialects often go into disuse, leading to their slow death. Losing old homes and social ties leads to homelessness in the real sense.

(c) *Environmental Disempowerment:* This is due to physical isolation in terms of remoteness, pollution at new places, lack of access to natural resources like forests, water reservoirs, pasture, etc. and new climatic conditions.

Table 8

Profile of Dominant Development Imposed on Four Rivers in India

Dimension	*Narmada River (MP)*	*Neera River (Maharashtra)*	*Kosi River (Uttarakhand)*	*Muhane-Nonai River (Bihar)*
Traditional use	Irrigation, socio-cultural functions, drinking by humans/animals	Irrigation, socio-cultural functions, drinking by humans/animals	Irrigation, socio-cultural functions, drinking by humans/animals	Irrigation, socio-cultural functions, drinking by humans/animals
Perception of technological intervention	Dam for more irrigation, electricity, flood control, water supply for urban-industrial purposes	Dam for more irrigation	Dam for more irrigation, hand pumps for drinking water, electric water mills	Dam for more irrigation
Financing agency	World Bank, corporate group, govt.	World Bank, state govt. and corporate group	World Bank, state government	State government
Negative outcome	huge displacement, submergence of biodiversity, houses/heritage	Displacement, privatization of river water depriving people	Displacement, drying of river, lowering of water table	Full closure of river – leading to non-irrigation of fields, lowering of water table
Political representatives' view	Necessity of dam	Necessity of dam and privatization (due to lack of govt. fund)	Necessity of dam, hand pumps and electronic water mills	Necessity of dam weir
Marginalized people's view	Dam as anti-people	Dam and river's privatization as anti-people	Dam, large number of hand pumps/electric water mills as anti-people	Dam as anti-people

(d) *Political Disempowerment:* If the state apparatuses are unfavourable to the marginalized, they become powerless. Often, there is no proper political process, channel or opportunity structure to address their political claims. Further, due to displacement, their political constituencies also change from equal participants to *'less than equals'*.

(e) *Cultural Disempowerment:* Since the PAPs lose their religious places of worship (temples, mosques, etc.), their ancestors' graves or funeral places, places of fair and weekly markets, they feel rootless at the new places of resettlement. Further, due to dislocation, the ill-effects of globalization, liberalization and privatization are more pervasive among the new generations of PAPs because of age, new contacts with outsiders (especially traders), new patterns of consumerism and casualization of jobs. Thus, physical dislocation also leads to cultural dislocation.

IV
Alternative Development Paradigm

Various environmental movements are not limited to the questioning of the dominant development discourse. Rather, in manifest or latent forms, they provide a vision of an alternative development paradigm which may be analysed in terms of economy, polity, science and technology, culture and consumption pattern as well as linkage to world economy.

(a) *Economy:* Environmental movements usually question the ethos of industrialism (for green green) and sometimes question even the very capitalist mode of production (red green). For instance, the Narmada Bachao Andolan (NBA) has an alternative development paradigm of the economy with a decentralized planning where the community would be the lowest unit of planning, as asserted by Medha Patkar (Roy and Sen, 1992). Further, NBA aims to achieve Jyotiba Phule's model of *indigenous development* in the form of making nullah, bunding on the hills, small check dams to harness rain water and recharge groundwater, constructing tanks and small reservoirs, soil conservation, using indigenous knowledge for exploring sources of water (with the help of 'pandiyas'), use of forests only for fuel and fodder, employment and improving agriculture, literacy and health care (Sanghavi, 1994).

(b) *Polity:* Environmental movements like NBA want a democratic and environmental socialism – 'a combination of green and red ecological values and ideas' (Medha Patkar) – and participatory decision-making system. NBA considers the state apparatus as illegitimate and repressive. Their 'three levels of politics – local, *sangath and andolan* – together show the possibilities as well as limitations,' observes Amita Baviskar (1997). It seems that NBA focuses more on political mobilization and sensitization of the masses for their entitlement.

(c) *Science and Technology:* Environmental movements like NBA have openly criticized the western science and technology based on reductionism. Rather, they focus on public-interest science and technology to be used cautiously and critically for the 'real progress' of rural tribals and peasants on a smaller scale. They rate, with due respect and dignity, the local people's indigenous knowledge, which is more useful in local conditions.

(d) *Culture and Consumption Pattern:* Most of the environmental movements like NBA have a broader outlook on limited consumption on the grounds of equity, morality and ecological sustainability. Conspicuous consumption by the rich is held to be more responsible for ecological damage than the consumption pattern of the poor (though in large numbers). NBA, for instance, stands for a change of the entire lifestyle based on greed, consumerism and capitalistic values of mass production that unnecessarily creates new demands. It puts forward a new cultural theme of 'manaviyata" (humaneness) in lieu of caste–religious discrimination.

(e) *Linkage to World Economy:* Environmental movements like NBA focus more on local and national economy (and at the most South–South cooperation), and recognize only a weak linkage to the world economy because of the adverse terms of trade, the dominance of developed countries' products and inequitable international laws. They provide a critique of globalization, liberalization and privatization. Not everything is to be left to the market; rather, the state has to play a critical role of intervention to protect the interests of the marginalized in terms of providing subsidy in agriculture, food, health and education.

An alternative development paradigm (by the environmental movements) may be seen in Table 9.

Table 9

Alternative Development Paradigm of Environmental Movements

Theme	*Alternative Development Paradigm*
Economy	Mixed economy, or even eco-socialism, decentralized planning, development with people
Polity	Democratic socialism, full participation of the excluded
Science and technology	Small scale, labour-intensive, mix of indigenous and public-interest scientific knowledge, appropriate technology, moderate rate of change
Culture and consumption pattern	Limited consumption, rejection of superstitions and irrational practices, equitable and just culture
Linkage to world economy	Critique of globalization, liberalization and privatization, focus at local level–think globally, act locally, weak linkage to world economy

Conclusion

From the above, we find that most of the environmental movements emphasize on 'collective empowerment' – i.e. some kind of development *with people*, not for the people. In fact, environmental movements, more or less, believe in the credo of Y.C. Yen of the Rural Reconstruction Movement in China in the 1920s (Sharma, 2010):

(a) 'learn from people, plan *with* the people and work *with* the people';

(b) 'not to conform but to transform';

(c) 'not relief but release'.

They aspire for genuine participation of the marginalized people in the decision-making process at all stages at all levels from village to nation with a flexible and dynamic process approach, not a 'blue print' approach. The ultimate goal of real social development is 'collective self-reliance' and critical empowerment with the critical adaptation of *'think globally, act locally'* praxis. This may be done in three ways, as was rightly pointed out by D.R. Gadgil long back and appreciated by Schumacher (Schumacher, 1973):

(a) improvement of traditional technology

(b) adjustment and adaptation (not adoption)

(c) innovative experiential research – going beyond (b)

Further, unlike the credo of '*expansion in consumption and enhancement of welfare*' (Cohen, 1985), as in DDD, we have to limit our consumption to the extent of necessity only and go beyond welfare (under industrialization and urbanization) to social development (well-being in harmony with nature, culture and equity) in letter and spirit; otherwise our ecological epoch of Holocene would be renamed as 'anthropocene epoch' (due to increasing human population and economic activities), to use the term coined by the Nobel laureate Paul Crutzen. Karl Marx emphasized on sustainability by ensuring earth's maintenance for the sake of 'chain of human generations' and insisted that the 'excrement produced by man's natural metabolism' along with waste of industrial production and consumption should be returned to the soil (*Capital*, vol. 3). For achieving this goal there should be a genuine effort for capability-building of the local people. And the ultimate goal should be 'development of all', not just for one community or creed. We should also learn from our best indigenous ecological practices of various groups and communities like Bishnois (who gave their lives for saving Khejari trees in Rajasthan) and tribals, who have learnt well to live in harmony with nature for centuries. In our ancient tradition, there is a concept of *Panch Mahabhutas* (five basic elements) that constitute our being and the universe: *kshiti* (earth), *jal* (water), *pavak* (fire), *gagan* (space) and *sameer* (air). Thus, the river and its water (*Gangajal*) are considered as sacred and essential in India as air for humans. But there is contradiction in our words and deed because, on the one hand, we worship Ganga as goddess but, on the other hand, we pollute and destroy Ganga in different ways like throwing domestic, municipal and industrial wastes (without treating) as well as flowers, dead bodies, urns and idols (not biodegradable).

Thinking globally and acting locally as well as sustainability in outcome (rather than big size that does not matter) should be a guiding ethos in all kinds of development. Small is beautiful – micro irrigation and hydro-plants at local level to suit the needs of people without displacement and disaster of ecology should be given the top priority. But it does not mean that one should ignore 'global' because at present both local and global are becoming inter-dependent because we are members of a village/urban settlement and the humanity at the same time. Only then would there be social, economic, political, cultural intra- and inter-generational equity and ecological sustainability through a dialogical relationship between nature, labour and culture. The environmental movements share with M.K. Gandhi's firm belief: 'Earth has everything to fulfil everybody's need but not anybody's greed.' With this credo, they provide a 'paradigm shift' in development and technology for liberating the marginalized people rather than enslaving them. Unfortunately, the dominant development discourse (DDD), based on large dams and the culture of consumerism, is more enslaving than liberating – as it takes a myopic view with immediacy ('here and now', as the phenomenologists term it) at the cost of *ecological sustainability*. Hence, an alternative development paradigm with specificity, locality, diversity, equity, quality (not merely quantity), collective self-reliance, critical empowerment and sustainability, as propounded and practised by the environmental movements, is the need of the hour. And this is possible through a new 'science of quality' or 'science of relationships', as F. Capara (2008) correctly terms it: 'The planet is a collection of ecosystems that regulates and organizes itself. Life evolved according to certain principles, such as forming networks, sharing resources, cycling matter, developing diversity, and so on. Endeavours to create sustainable societies should be led by an understanding of how nature has done it for billions of years.' Further there is an urgent need of fusion of towns and villages on the one hand, and creation of micro community based organizations or civil society organizations like neighbourhood committees, women's swawlamban samitis (self-reliance committees) etc. Further at local level good governance should be practised by actively participating in the decision-making of Panchayati Raj institutions, government programmes as well as local self-initiatives like 'shramdam,' 'swachchhata abhiyan' etc. Moreover, local people have to be conscious enough to ensure transparency and accountability in all works and decisions of government and panchayats so that participatory democracy is deepened and people are really empowered. But unfortunately today the market-led globalization is fanning the unhealthy cut-throat competition in bidding process between different countries and also between different states within a developing country.

The marginalized people have, thus, protested in developing countries like India against the dominant development paradigm (DDD), imposed from above with a grand narrative that size matters, big is beautiful and only concrete is development. Environmental movements have shown that their needs are different from the greed of the elite consumers and the industrialists. Further, these movements have an alternative vision and paradigm of development that takes care of local needs, social equity, sustainability and economic development. That is, an ecologically sustainable and egalitarian (inter-generational, inter-class, inter-locational) social development is called for by according due weightage to the marginalized people as well as to the ecology. And for this there is a need to structurally change the capitalist mode of production by conceintising the ruling class and the people at large. Hence public sector should not be privatized or disinvested for meeting the expenditure because it ensures India's economic sovereignty by reducing dependence on foreign capital. However, leakage and extravagance should be removed drastically, and transparency and accountability must be ensured at any cost. We tend to agree with Aseem Shrivastava and Ashish Kothari (2012: 330): 'The way to the economic future for the vast majority of people is ecological, is rooted in the local and the regional, and is built on the past. It depends crucially on the recovery of the best traditions of Indian cultures, even while rejecting the worst, and combining these with the best of modernity … . This is not a "back to nature" approach so much as one of "return to nature" in the best sense of the expression – something we are compelled to embrace in the face of the ecological crisis.'

References

Agarwal, P. (2009) *Indian Higher Education: Envisioning the Future*, Sage Publications, New Delhi.

Altbach, Philip G. (2010) 'The Giants Awake: Higher Education Systems in China and India', *Economic and Political Weekly*, XLIV (23), 6 June, pp. 39–51.

Asian Development Bank (2008) *Irrigation Management Transfer*, Sage Publications, New Delhi.

Balakrishna, R. and C. Ravi (2004) 'Malnutrition in India', *Economic and Political Weekly*, 39 (7), pp. 671–76.

Balakrishnan, Rajiv (ed.) (2011) *Demographic Transition: An Asian Perspective*, Konark Publishers Pvt Ltd, New Delhi.

Bandhyopadhyay, D. (2008) 'Does Land Still Matter?', *Economic and Political Weekly*, XLIII (10), 8 March.

Bandyopadhyay, J. (1986) 'The Economics of Large Dams in India', in E. Goldsmith and N. Hildyard (eds), *The Social and Environmental Effects of Large Dams*, Vol. II, Wadebridge Ecological Centre, Cornwall.

Banfield, Edward C. (1973) *The Unheavenly City*, Little Brown, Boston.

Baran, P.A. and P.M. Sweezy (1966) *Monopoly Capital*, Monthly Review Press, New York.

Baviskar, Amita (1997) *In the Belly of the River*, Oxford University Press, New Delhi.

Beskhamp, G. and Claudia W. Sadoff (2008) 'Water in a Sustainable Economy', in Worldwatch Institute, *State of the World 2008*, Earthscan, London.

Bhaduri, Amit (2005) *Development with Dignity*, National Book Trust, New Delhi.

Bhandari, L. and Sunita Kale (eds) (2007) *Bihar: Performance, Facts and Figures*, Pearson, Delhi, pp. 19–20.

Bhardwaj, Krishna (1974) *Production Conditions in Indian Agriculture*, Cambridge University Press, Cambridge.

Capara, F. (2008) 'Consciousness is an Aspect of Life', *The Times of India*, 5 March.

Chambers, Robert (1996) *Whose Reality Counts?*, Intermediate Technology Publications, London.

Cohen, J.L. (1985) 'Strategy or Identity: New Theoretical Paradigms and Contemporary Social Movements', *Social Research*, 52 (4), Winter.

Dutta, S. (2007) 'Hajar Crore Rupaye Mein Kharido Nadi', *Outlook Saptahik*, 24 December.

Foster-Carter, A. (1985) *Sociology of Development*, Causeway Books, Lancashire.

Goldsmith, E. and N. Hildyard (eds) (1984) *The Social and Environmental Effects of Large Dams*, Vol. I, Wadebridge Ecological Centre, Cornwall.

— (1992) *The Social and Environmental Effects of Large Dams*, Vol. III, Wadebridge Ecological Centre, Cornwall.

Gupta, Dipankar (2000) *Mistaken Identity*, HarperCollins, New Delhi.

Halarnkar, S. (1998) 'The Dam Scam', *India Today*, 25, 16–22 June.

Horta, K. and L. Pottinger (2008) 'Africa's Dams Not Helping Poor Communities', *The Hindu*, 24 January.

Iyer, Ramaswamy R. (2008) 'Water: A Critique of Three Concepts', *Economic and Political Weekly*, 5–11 January.

Kalpavriksha (1985) 'Narmada Valley Project: Development or Destruction', *The Ecologist*, pp. 1595–96.

Kalpavriksha et al. (1986) 'Narmada Valley Project: Development or Destruction', in E. Goldsmith and N. Hildyard (eds), *The Social and Environmental Effects of Large Dams*, Vol. II, Wadebrdige Ecological Centre, Cornwall.

Kothari, S. (1996) 'Whose Nation? The Displaced as Victims of Development', *Economic and Political Weekly*, XXXI (24), 15 June.

Mishra, A. (1986) 'The Rawa Dam: An Irrigation Project That Has Reduced Farm Production', in E. Goldsmith and N. Hildyard (eds), *The Social and Environmental Effects of Large Dams*, Vol. II, Wadebridge Ecological Centre, Cornwall.

Mulgan, G. (1998) *Connexity*, Vintage, London.

Pieterse, J.N. (2004) *Globalization or Empire*, Routledge, New York.

Roy, D. and G. Sen (1992) 'The Strength of People's Movement', in G. Sen (ed.), *Indigenous Vision*, Sage Publications, New Delhi.

Sanghavi, S. (1994) 'Nation, Nationalism and Mega Projects', *Economic and Political Weekly*, XXIX (10), 5 March.

Schumacher, E.F. (1973) *Small is Beautiful*, Abacus, London.

Sharma, Subhash (2010) *Why People Protest: An Analysis of Ecological Movements*, Publications Division, New Delhi.

Shrivastava, Aseem and Ashish Kothari (2012) *Churning the Earth: The Making of Global India*, Penguin Books, New Delhi.

Singh, Shekhar and Pranab Banerji (eds) (2002) *Large Dams in India*, IIPA, New Delhi.

Singh, Yogendra (1973) *Modernization of Indian Tradition*, Thomson Press, Faridabad.

Stiglitz, J. (2002) *Globalization and Its Discontents*, Penguin, Allen Lane, London.

Tiwari, Rakesh (2008) 'Panidhar Bane Sukhapani', *Jansatta*, 9 January.

Tiwari, Vijay Mohan (2005) 'Harsud, 30 June', Foreword, Rajkamal Prakashan, New Delhi.

UNDP (1990) *Human Development Report*, Oxford University Press, New Delhi.

— (1998) *Human Development Report 1998*, Oxford University Press, New York.

Webster, A. (1990) *Introduction to Sociology of Development*, Macmillan, London.

Bibliography

Basant, Rakesh (2008) 'Decoding Access', *Seminar*, 587, July, pp. 19–22.

Bhaduri, Amit (2014) 'Paradoxes of Economic Growth and Inequality', in K.B. Saxena and G. Haragopal (eds) *Marginisation, Development and Resistance*, Vol. 1, Aakar Books, New Delhi.

Birdsall, Nancy (2001) 'Comments', in B. Plescovic and N. Stern (eds), *Annual Conference on Development Economics*, World Bank, Washington, D.C.

Bluestone, Barry (1969) 'Lower-Income Works and Marginal Industries', in Louis A. Ferman et al. (eds), *Poverty in America*, University of Michigan Press, Ann Arbor.

Bosch, C. et al. (2000) 'Water, Sanitation and Poverty', in World Bank, *Poverty Reduction Strategy Source Book* (Draft), World Bank, Washington, D.C.

Bose, N.K. (1982) *Some Indian Tribes*, National Book Trust, New Delhi.

Brown, Lester R. (2008) 'Business as Usual is No Longer a Viable Option', *The Indian Express*, 13 June.

Capara, F. (2008) 'Consciousness is an Aspect of Life', *The Times of India*, 5 March.

Chakrabarti, M. and S.K. Datta (2000) 'Agriculture', in Alternative Survey Group, *Alternative Economic Survey 1998–2000*, Rainbow Publishers Ltd, Delhi.

Chambers, Robert (1997) *Whose Reality Counts?*, Intermediate Technology Publications, London.

Chen, S. and Martin Ravallion (2008) 'The Developing World is Poorer Than We Thought, But No Less Successful in the Fight Against Poverty', Policy Research Working Paper 4703, Development Research Group, World Bank, August.

Cohen, J.L. (1985) 'Strategy or Identity: New Theoretical Paradigms and Contemporary Social Movements', *Social Research*, 52 (4), Winter.

CSD (2006) *India: Social Development Report*, Oxford University Press, New Delhi.

Dasgupta, Partha (2003) 'Economic Growth Often Accompanies a Decline in a Poor Country's Wealth', *New Statesman*, 3 November.

Desai, A.R. (ed.) (1978) *Rural Sociology in India*, Popular Prakashan, Bombay.

DuBois, W.E.B. (1985) *Black Reconstruction in America 1860–1880*, Atheneun, New York (1st ed. 1935).

Dutta, S. (2007) 'Hajar Crore Rupaye Mein Kharido Nadi', *Outlook Saptahik*, 24 December.

Easterly, W. (2009) 'The Poorman's Burden', *Foreign Policy*, January–February.

— (2007) 'The Ideology of Development', *Foreign Policy*, July–August.

Evans, Peter (2000) 'Sustainability, Degradation, and Livelihood in Third World Cities: Possibilities for State-Society Synergy', in Pamela S. Chasek (ed.), *The Global Environment in the Twenty First Century*, United Nations University Press, Tokyo.

Firodia, Arun (2008) 'Rising Food Prices: The Blame Game', *The Economic Times*, 9 June.

Foster, A.S. (1998) 'Ground Water in Urban Development', World Bank Technical Paper No. 390, World Bank, Washington, D.C.

Foster-Carter, A. (1985) *Sociology of Development*, Causeway Books, Lancashire.

Frank, A.G. (1969) *Capitalism and Underdevelopment in Latin America*, Monthly Review Press, London.

Freire, Paulo (1996) *Pedagogy of the Oppressed*, Penguin Books, London.

George, Henry (1958) *Progress and Poverty*, Robert S. Foundation, New York (1st ed. 1879).

George, Susan (1981) *How the Other Half Dies*, Penguin Books, Harmondsworth, Middlesex.

Ghate, P. (2006) *Micro Finance in India: A State of the Sector Report 2006*, Care and Ford Foundation, New Delhi.

Gilder, George (1981) *Wealth and Poverty*, Basic Books, New York.

— (1989) 'The Nature of Poverty', in I.C. Colby (ed.), *Social Welfare Policy*, Dorsey Press, Chicago.

GOI (2004) *Serving Farmers and Saving Farming*, National Commission on Farmers, Ministry of Agriculture, New Delhi.

— (2006) *Towards Faster and More Inclusive Growth: An Approach to the 11th Five Year Plan*, Planning Commission of India, New Delhi.

— (2007) *Annual Report 2006–07*, Ministry of Human Resource Development, New Delhi.

— (2007a) *National Family Health Survey 3–2005–6*, Vol. I, International Institute for Population Sciences, Mumbai.

— (2007b) *Selected Educational Statistics 2004–05*, Ministry of Human Resource Development, New Delhi.

— (2010) *Annual Report 2009–10*, Ministry of Human Resource Development, New Delhi.

— (2011) *Economic Survey 2010–11*, Ministry of Finance, Department of Economic Affairs, New Delhi.

Golden, Daniel (2006) *The Price of Admission*, Three Rivers Press, New York.

Goldsmith, E. and N. Hildyard (eds) (1992) *The Social and Environmental Effects of Large Dams*, Vol. III, Wadebridge Ecological Centre, Cornwall.

— (1984) *The Social and Environmental Effects of Large Dams*, Vol. I, Wadebridge Ecological Centre, Cornwall.

Goldsmith, William W. and Edward J. Blakely (1992) *Separate Societies*, Temple University Press, Philadelphia.

Gordon, Marshall (1998) *Oxford Dictionary of Sociology*, Oxford University Press, Oxford.

Griffin, K. (1968) *Underdevelopment in Spanish America*, George Allen and Unwin, London.

Guha-Khasnobis, Basudeb, S.S. Acharya and B. Davis (eds) (2008) *Food Security*, Oxford University Press, Oxford.

Gupta, Asha (2008) 'Introduction', in Asha Gupta, D.C. Levy and K.B. Powar (eds), *Private Higher Education*, Shipra Publications, New Delhi.

Gupta, Dipankar (2000) *Mistaken Modernity*, HarperCollins, New Delhi.

Gupta, Shekhar (2007) 'Walk the Talk with Vikram Akula', *The Indian Express*, 4 June.

Halarnkar, S. (1998) 'The Dam Scam', *India Today*, 25, 16–22 June.

Haq, E. (2007) *Sociology of Population in India*, Macmillan India Ltd, New Delhi.

Horta, K. and L. Pottinger (2008) 'Africa's Dams Not Helping Poor Communities', *The Hindu*, 24 January.

Hoselitz, B.F. (1960) *Sociological Factors in Economic Development*, Free Press, Chicago.

Iyer, Ramaswamy R. (2008) 'Water: A Critique of Three Concepts', *Economic and Political Weekly*, 5–11 January.

Jana, M.M. (2005) 'Water Resource in India and its Sustainable Management', in A. Kumar (ed.), *Sustainable Water Management*, SPM Govt Degree College, Phaphamau, Allahabad.

Jha, A. (2009) 'Abysmal Global Ranking of India's Best University', *Education World*, February, pp. 64–72.

Jha, P.S. (2001) 'Political Economy of Crisis Management', *The Hindu*, 2 October.

Kalpavriksha (1985) 'Narmada Valley Project: Development or Destruction', *The Ecologist*, pp. 1595–96.

Kalpavriksha et al. (1986) 'Narmada Valley Project: Development or Destruction', in E. Goldsmith and N. Hildyard (eds), *The Social and Environmental Effects of Large Dams*, Vol. II, Wadebrdige Ecological Centre, Cornwall.

Kandula, Kalayani (2004) 'Environment and Development: The Links', in Kiran B. Chhokar et al. (eds), *Understanding Environment*, Sage Publications, New Delhi, pp. 263–78.

Kapur, Devesh (2008) 'The Supply Mix', *Seminar*, 587, July, pp. 14–18.

Karlsson, Mats (2001) 'Opening Address', in B. Plescovic and Nicholas Stern (eds), *Annual World Bank Conference on Development Economics*, World Bank, Washington, D.C.

Kewalramani, S. (2008) 'Green Revolution II Needed, and Not Export Curbs', *The Hindu, Business Line*, 7 June.

King, M.L. Jr. (1967) *Where Do We Go From Here: Chaos or Community?*, Beacon Press, Boston.

Korten, D.C. (1990) *Getting to 21st Century: Voluntary Action and the Global Agenda*, Kumarian Press, West Hartford.

Kothari, S. (1996) 'Whose Nation? The Displaced as Victims of Development', *Economic and Political Weekly*, XXXI (24), 15 June.

Kumar, Aravind (2005) 'Sustainable Water Management with Special Reference to Ganga and Allahabad: An Appraisal in Aravind Kumar (ed.), *Sustainable Water Management*, SPM Govt Degree College, Phaphamau, Allahabad.

Kundu, Amitabh (2006) 'Introduction', in Council for Social Development, *India: Social Development Report*, Oxford University Press, New Delhi.

Layard, Richards (2005) *Happiness: Lessons from a New Science*, Penguin, New York.

Lobina, E. and D. Hall (2001) *Potential for Public Sector Water Operations in Developing Countries*, Public Service International Research Unit, London.

Long, Norman (1982) *Introduction to the Sociology of Rural Development*, Tavistock Publications Ltd, London.

Mahajan, V. (2005) 'From Micro Credit to Livelihood Finance', *Economic and Political Weekly*, 8 October.

Majumdar, P.K. (2010) *Fundamentals of Demography*, Rawat Publications, Jaipur.

Mandel, Jay R. (1978) *The Roots of Black Poverty*, Duke University Press, Durham, NC.

Marable, Manning (1983) *How Capitalism Underdeveloped Black America?*, South End Press, Boston.

— (1987) 'The Contradictory Contours of Black Political Culture', in Mike Davis et al. (eds), *The Year Left 2*, Verso, London.

Martin, Linda R. and D. Giannaros (1990) 'Would a Higher Minimum Wage Help Poor Families Headed by Women', *Monthly Labour Review*, August.

Maxwell, S. (1999) 'The Measuring and Measurement of Poverty', ODI Poverty Briefing 3, Overseas Development Institute, London.

MCI (2011) 'Undergraduate Education Working Group Note', *The Times of India*, 7 March.

Mckibben, Bill (2007) *Deep Economy*, Holt Paperbacks, New York.

Mishra, A. (1986) 'The Rawa Dam: An Irrigation Project That Has Reduced Farm Production', in E. Goldsmith and N. Hildyard (eds), *The Social and Environmental Effects of Large Dams*, Vol. II, Wadebridge Ecological Centre, Cornwall.

Molekhi, Pankaj (2011) 'Population Explosion or Celebration?', *The Economic Times*, 30 January.

Mukhopadhyay, Partha (2008) 'Learning to Work', *Seminar*, 587, July, pp. 52–57.

Mulgan, G. (1998) *Connexity*, Vintage, London.

Munshi, K.M. and R.R. Diwakar (eds) (1969) *Radhakrishnan Reader: An Anthology*, Bhartiya Vidya Bhawan, Bombay.

Murray, Charles A. (1984) *Losing Ground: American Social Policy, 1950–1980*, Basic Books, New York.

NABARD (2006) *Annual Report*, Mumbai.

Narayan Murthi, P. and V.K. Shunglu (2000) *Audit Report of Ganga Action Plan 2000*, Publications Division, New Delhi, 13 December.

National Knowledge Commission (2009) *Report to the Nation 2006–09*, Government of India, New Delhi.

New Economics Foundation (2003) *Real World Economic Outlook*, World Bank, Washington, D.C.

Nilekani, Nandan (2008) *Imagining India: Ideas for the New Century*, Penguin, New Delhi.

Osborne, David (1990) *Laboratories of Democracy*, Harvard Business School Press, Cambridge, Mass.

Oxfam (2008) 'Bio-fuels Pushing Thirty Million into Poverty', *The Times of India*, 26 June.

Panagariya, Arvind (2008) *India: The Emerging Giant*, Oxford University Press, New York.

Pandey, B.N. (2005) 'Is Third World War Inevitable for Water Crisis in 21st Century?', in A. Kumar (ed.), *Sustainable Water Management*, SPM Govt Degree College, Phaphamau, Allahabad.

Pant, Ruchi (2003) 'From Communities' Hands to MNCs' BOOTS: A Case Study from India on Right to Water', Paper submitted to Rights and Humanity, UK.

Patnaik, Utsa (2008) 'Reconceptualising Poverty', *The Hindu*, 3 September.

Pieterse, J.N. (2004) *Globalization or Empire*, Routledge, New York.

Planning Commission of India (2008) *Eleventh Five Year Plan*, Vol. I, Oxford University Press, New Delhi.

Rao, Smriti (2005) 'Women's SHGs and Credit for the Poor: A Case Study from Andhra Pradesh', in V.K. Ramchandran and Madhura Swaminathan (eds), *Financial Liberalisation and Rural Credit in India*, Tulika Books, New Delhi.

RBI (1999) *Report on Micro Credit*, Micro Credit Special Cell, Reserve Bank of India, Mumbai.

— (2006 and 2007) *Quarterly Statistics on Deposits and Credit of Scheduled Commercial Banks*, Reserve Bank of India, Mumbai, March.

Reddy, Sanjay G. (2007) 'Poverty Estimates: How Great is the Debate?', *Economic and Political Weekly*, 10 February.

Reinert, Erik S. (2007) *How Rich Countries Got Rich ... and Why Poor Countries Stay Poor*, Carroll and Graf Publishers, New York.

Ritter, Peter (2008) 'No Grain, Big Pain', *Time*, 21 April.

Rodrik, Dani (2001) 'Development Strategies for the 21st Century', in B. Plescovic and N. Stern (eds), *Annual World Bank Conference on Development Economics*, World Bank, Washington, D.C.

Rose-Ackerman, S. (1996) 'The Political Economy of Corruption: Causes and Consequences', World Bank Public Policy for Private Sector, Note No. 74, World Bank, Washington, D.C.

Roy, D. and G. Sen (1992) 'The Strength of People's Movement', in G. Sen (ed.), *Indigenous Vision*, Sage Publications, New Delhi.

Sachs, J. (2001) 'A New Global Consensus on Helping the Poorest of the Poor', in B. Plescovic and N. Stern (eds), *Annual World Bank Conference on Development Economics*, World Bank, Washington, D.C.

— (2008) *Common Wealth*, Penguin, Allen Lane, New Delhi.

Sachs, Jeffrey D. (2005) *The End of Poverty*, Penguin Press, New York.

Sandel, Michael J. (2000) 'It's Immoral to Buy the Right to Pollute', in Robert N. Stavins (ed.), *Economics of the Environment*, W.W. Norton & Co., New York.

Sanghavi, S. (1994) 'Nation, Nationalism and Mega Projects', *Economic and Political Weekly*, XXIX (10), 5 March.

Sarkar, Anindita (2011) 'Socio-Economic Implications of Depleting Groundwater Resource in Punjab', *Economic and Political Weekly*, 12 February, pp. 59–66.

Saxena, N.C. (2004) 'Synergising Government Efforts for Food Security', in M.S. Swaminathan and Pedro Medrano (eds), *Towards Hunger Free India*, East West Books Pvt Ltd, Chennai.

Schiller, Barry R. (1976) *The Economics of Poverty and Discrimination*, Prentice Hall, Englewood Cliffs, NJ.

Schumacher, E.F. (1973) *Small is Beautiful*, Abacus, London.

Schumpeter, Joseph A. (2005) 'Development', *Journal of Economic Literature*, XLIII, March.

Sen, Amartya (2008) 'Democracy is More Than the Sum of Its Parts', *The Indian Express*.

Sengupta, Arjun et al. (2008) 'India's Common People', *Economic and Political Weekly*, 15 March.

Shah, Mihir (2008) 'Direct Cash Transfer No Panacea by Itself', *The Hindu*, 20 September.

Shah, Mihir, Raghu Rao and P.S. Vijay Kumar (2007) 'Rural Credit in 20th Century India', *Economic and Political Weekly*, XLII (15), 14–20 April.

Shankar, Kripa (2007) 'Poverty in India', *Mainstream*, 19–25 October.

— (2008) 'Siyasat Ke Raste Nilam Hota Pani', *Pratham Impact*, 5, 16–29 February.

Sharma, Subhash (2002) *Dialectics of Agrarian Development: A Sociological Study in North India*, Yash Publications, New Delhi.

— (2006) 'Dialectics of Identity and Development of Tharus in Bihar: A Sociological Analysis', *Prajna Bharati*, XII, pp. 140–57.

— (2007) *Bharat Mein Bal Majdoor* (Child Labour in India), Prakashan Sansthan, New Delhi.

— (2007a) 'Dynamics of Violence in Rural South Bihar', in B.K. Choudhary (ed.), *Readings in the History of Rural South Bihar*, K.P. Jayaswal Research Institute, Patna.

— (2007b) *Shiksha Aur Samaj* (Education and Society), Prakashan Sansthan, New Delhi.

— (2008) 'Dynamics of Use and Abuse of Water', *Management in Government*, 6, July–September.

— (2008a) 'Micro Finance for Rural Women's Empowerment', *Management in Government*, XXXIX (4), January–March.

— (2010) *Why People Protest: An Analysis of Ecological Movements*, Publications Division, New Delhi.

Shetty, S.L. (2005) 'Regional, Sectoral and Functional Distribution of Bank Credit', in V.K. Ramchandran and M.S. Swaminathan (eds), *Financial Liberalisation and Rural Credit in India*, Tulika Books, New Delhi.

Shrivastava, Aseem and Ashish Kothari (2012) *Churning the Earth: The Making of Global India*, Penguin Books, New Delhi.

Simon, Julian L. (1981) *The Ultimate Resource*, Princeton University Press, Princeton, NJ (2nd ed. 1996).

Singh, Vijay P. (1991) 'The Underclass in the US', *Sociological Inquiry*, 61 (4).

Singh, Pallavi (2011) 'More Population Means More Migration', *The Economic Times*, 30 January.

Singh, Shekhar and Pranab Banerji (eds) (2002) *Large Dams in India*, IIPA, New Delhi.

Singh, Yogendra (1973) *Modernization of Indian Tradition*, Thomson Press, Faridabad.

Sirothia, Rajesh (2008) 'Jal Bachane Par Hua Manthan', *Outlook Saptahik* (Hindi), 9, 4–10 March.

Smelser, N.S. (1963) 'Mechanism of Change and Adjustment to Change', in B.F. Hoselitz and W.E. Moore (eds), *Industrialization and Society*, Mouton, The Hague.

Smith, Mark et al. (eds) (2006) *Pay – Establishing Payments for Watershed Services*, IUCN, Glad, Switzerland.

Solow, Robert M. (2000) 'Sustainability: An Economist's Perspective', in Robert N. Stavins (ed.), *Economics of the Environment*, W.W. Norton & Co., New York.

Srinivasan, T.N. (2007) 'Poverty Lines in India', *Economic and Political Weekly*, 13 October.

Stiglitz, J. (1998) 'Towards a New Paradigm of Development', Paul Prebiseh Lecture at UNCTAD in Geneva, 19 October.

— (2002) *Globalization and Its Discontents*, Penguin, Allen Lane, London.

Stiglitz, Joseph, Amartya Sen and J.P. Fitoussi (2009) *Report by Commission on Measurement of Economic Performance and Social Progress*, Government of France (Internet).

Streeten, Paul et al. (1981) *First Things First*, Oxford University Press, Washington, D.C.

Streitfeld, D. and K. Bradshet (2008) 'Weather Adds to Challenge of Food Shortages', *The Hindu*, 11 June.

Subbarao, D. (2011) 'Rural Prosperity is Fuelling Food Inflation', *The Economic Times*, 28 February.

Swaminathan, M.S. (2004) 'Vision for a Hunger Free India', in M.S. Swaminathan and Pedro Medrano (eds), *Towards Hunger Free India: From Vision to Action*, East West Books Pvt Ltd, Chennai.

— (2008) 'Beyond the Green Revolution', *Seminar*, 589, September.

— (2008a) 'Food for Thought', *Yojana*, 52, June.

Takahasi, K. et al. (2002) 'Driving Forces and Incentives for Change: Towards Sustainable Water Development', *Water Science and Technology*, 45 (8), pp. 141–44.

Tema, Wazha (2001) 'Water Education in African Cities', in UNCHS, *Water Education in African Cities*, Nairobi.

Thakur, Ramesh (2007) 'Good News from Bihar', *The Times of India*, 5 January.

Thomas, Alan (2000) 'Poverty and the End of Development', in Tim Allen and Alan Thomas (eds), *Poverty and Development into 21st Century*, Open University/Oxford University Press, New York.

Tilak, J.B.G. (2010) 'The Foreign Educational Institutions Bill: A Critique', *Economic and Political Weekly*, XLV (19), 8 May, pp. 12–15.

Tiwari, Rakesh (2008) 'Panidhar Bane Sukhapani', *Jansatta*, 9 January.

Tiwari, Vijay Mohan (2005) 'Harsud, 30 June', Foreword, Rajkamal Prakashan, New Delhi.

Tobin, J. (1970) 'On limiting the Domain of Inequality', *Journal of Law and Economics*, 13 (2).

Turner, R.H. (1961) 'Modes of Social Ascent Through Education: Sponsored and Contest Mobility', in A.H. Halsey, J. Floud and C.A. Anderson (eds), *Education, Economy and Society*, The Free Press, Glencoe, Ill.

UNCTAD (2008) *Trade and Development Report*, Geneva.

UNDP (1990) *Human Development Report*, Oxford University Press, New Delhi.

— (1998) *Human Development Report 1998*, Oxford University Press, New York.

— (2001) *Human Development Report 2001*, Palgrave Macmillan, New York.

— (2005) *Human Development Report 2005*, Palgrave Macmillan, New York.

— (2006) *Human Development Report 2006*, Palgrave Macmillan, New York.

UNICEF (2011) *State of the World's Children*, Geneva.

Valentine, Charles A. (1968) *Culture and Poverty*, University of Chicago Press, Chicago.

Varma, Subodh (2008) 'As Food Crisis Worsens, Firms Push GM Seeds', *The Times of India*, 4 June.

Vickery Jr, R.E. (2010) 'Obama's India Opportunity in Higher Education', *The Guardian Weekly*, 16 July.

Virmani, Arvind (2007) 'The Sudoku of Growth, Poverty and Malnutrition: Policy Implications for Lagging States', Planning Commission of India Working Paper No. 2/2007, New Delhi.

Webster, A. (1990) *Introduction to Sociology of Development*, Macmillan, London.

West, Cornel (1987) 'Race and Social Theory', in Mike Davis et al. (eds), *The Year Left 2*, Verso, London.

WHO and UNICEF (2010) *Progress on Sanitation and Water – 2010 Update*, Geneva.

Wilson, William J. (1987) *The Truly Disadvantaged*, University of Chicago Press, Chicago.

Wolf, Martin (2008) 'The Food Crisis is a Chance to Reform Global Agriculture', *Financial Times* (London), 30 May.

World Bank (1991) *World Development Report 1991*, Oxford University Press, New York.

World Resource Institute (2007) 'Earth Trends' Environmental Information', online database.

Yugandhar, B.N. (2014) 'Poverty: Need to Address its Foundational Elements' in K.B. Saxena and G. Haragopal (eds) *Marginalisation, Development and Resistance*, Vol. 1, Aakar Books, New Delhi.

Yunus, M. (2008) 'Give the Man Credit', *Yojana*, 52, January.

Yusuf, Shahid (2009) *Development Economics through the Decades*, World Bank, Washington, D.C.

Zachariah, K.C. and S. Irudaya Rajan (2011) 'Demographic Transition in Kerala and Tamil Nadu', in Rajiv Balakrishnan (ed.), *Demographic Transition: An Asian Perspective*, Konark Publishers, New Delhi.

Index